Wrestling with time

Wrestling with time

Problems in economic theory

Martin Currie *and* Ian Steedman

Manchester University Press

Copyright © Martin Currie and Ian Steedman 1990

Published by Manchester University Press
Oxford Road, Manchester M13 9PL

British Library cataloguing in publication data
Currie, Martin
  Wrestling with time: problems in economic theory.
  1. Economics theories
  I. Title   II. Steedman, Ian
  330.1

ISBN 0 7190 2801 9 *hardback*

Typeset in Great Britain
by Williams Graphics

Printed in Great Britain
by Biddles Ltd, Guildford and King's Lynn

Contents

Preface

Arthur Schopenhauer's aphorism, 'Not the least of the torments which plague our existence is the constant pressure of *time*, which never lets us so much as draw breath but pursues us all like a taskmaster with a whip' (*On the Suffering of the World*, 1851), has often seemed vividly to the point during the writing of this book. It is our hope that the reading of it will encourage more economists to face with full seriousness the problems which that taskmaster poses.

While we have no intention, after so many hours of discussion and revision, of indicating which author took primary responsibility for any particular part of the text, it is only just to point out that the first author wrote considerably more than half of the work. We must also remark that earlier drafts of some of the following chapters were presented to seminars at Manchester University or read by colleagues and friends either in Manchester or elsewhere; most of the material was also scrutinised by Manchester University Press and the University of Michigan Press readers. To all those who have produced helpful criticisms, suggestions or encouragement we offer our grateful thanks. We also wish to thank Charmaine Arnold-Reed and, in particular, Sue Massey for their quite excellent word processing.

1

Introduction

It is impossible to meditate on time and the mystery of the creative passage of nature without an overwhelming emotion of the limitations of human intelligence (A. N. Whitehead).

Lindahl once tried to specify the conditions under which time would be of no importance for economic analysis. He found this extremely difficult to do. It is easy to understand why this should be so. Most activities – whether involving production, consumption, communication, learning, *etc* – take time. Even the planning of activities takes time. Furthermore, planning activities are necessarily forward-looking and involve speculating about the unknown, if not unknowable, future. As Aldous Huxley observed: 'But the one thing we all know about the future is that we are profoundly ignorant of what is going to happen, and that what in fact does happen is generally very different from what we anticipated.'

Alfred Marshall was not exaggerating when, in 1890, he asserted that 'the element of Time ... is the centre of the chief difficulty of almost every economic problem'. How could one avoid the centrality of time when seeking to understand the behaviour of economies in which, for example, innovations in productive methods, the competitive introduction of new commodities and speculation are important phenomena? Economic theorists are thus *still* wrestling with the perplexing question of how best to analyse economies which are 'moving through time'. This book is about that struggle.

Conceptualisations of time

What then is time? Notoriously, Saint Augustine of Hippo asked himself this question and answered: 'If no one asks me, I know what it is. If I wish to explain it to him who asks me, I do not know.'

The 'mystery' of time has, of course, been a perennial source of perplexity for philosophers – from the pre-Socratic philosophers, Heraclitus, Parmenides and Zeno, to the recent philosophers, McTaggart, Bergson and Alexander. We cannot, of course, become embroiled in the fundamental disagreements between philosophers over the nature of time. For our purposes, it is appropriate to consider Elliot Jaques, who, though not an economist, has discussed the nature of time in a way which should be meaningful to most economists. Specifically, Jaques differentiated between two conceptualisations of time, namely, the 'time of succession' and the 'time of intention'. The time of *succession* relates to the sense of passing time expressed in successive readings of a clock:

Our ideas of earlier and later, before and after, temporal discontinuity and atomism, constancy and permanence are ... exclusively associated with the temporal axis of succession. They are expressions of our experience of a cross-sectional or spatial abstraction from events, expressions of our capacity mentally to make time for the moment stand still, while we record as in a photograph the happening of that moment. We can then date this frozen moment on a calendar or clock, as having occurred on such and such a day at such and such a time. (1982, p. xii)

The time of succession – or what we might call 'clock time' – is often thought of as the time of classical mechanics. The distinctly different notion of the time of *intention* relates time to the experience of purposive, intentional, goal-directed behaviour:

Our ideas of past, present, and future, passage and direction, flux and change, durée and continuity, are exclusively associated with the temporal axis of intention. They are expressions of our field of experience in the flowing present. The past is the experience of the flow of memory, the present of perception and the future of expectation and desire. Durée, flux, and passage are the experience of the interaction of memory, perception, and desire, and direction is the experience of the goal-directedness of intention (1982, p. xii).

Leaving aside his particular terminology, this distinction is neither arbitrary nor peculiar to Jaques. In broad terms, it can be found throughout the perennial discussions about the nature of time.

In invoking these two conceptions of time, we do not suggest – nor does Jaques – that one is obliged to choose between them; on the contrary, both conceptions appear to be necessary in economic analysis. There is therefore no occasion for surprise if both conceptions can be found, albeit often implicitly, in the writings of a given economist. Mainstream economic theorists generally place more emphasis on the time of succession rather than on the time of intention. In contrast, radical subjectivists stress the time of intention. Nevertheless, rigid dichotomies are misleading. On the one hand, mainstream micro-economic theorising often builds up from an individual agent who, located somewhere on the 'axis of succession', is making forward-looking decisions in the light of personal expectations influenced by perceptions of past events. On the other hand, a radical subjectivist such as Shackle gives clear recognition to 'the endless extension of time which thought can be about' (1961, p. 14). Even if it be true that, for understandable reasons, the less orthodox writers are more inclined to provide explicit discussion of our two alternative human conceptions of time, the fact remains that most writers make some appeal to *both* conceptions.

Lest it be thought that, in warning against the formulation of an over-rigid dichotomy, we are reducing the two conceptions to a drab homogeneity, we must note that these two conceptions of time are often associated with fundamentally different notions about the nature of the 'future'. It is certainly the case that those who emphasise the time of intention typically reject any notion that the future 'already exists'; for them, the future is always to be *created*, with the implication that it does not exist out there waiting to be revealed. Whereas Laplace, of course, conceded that we cannot know the future *in practice*, the radical subjectivists maintain that we cannot do so even *in principle*. It is harder to be sure what views more orthodox writers have on this matter. However, one certainly does not find any insistence that the future cannot be known even in principle. Indeed, orthodox theorists often assume that economic agents possess perfect foresight of the future.

What follows

Given the mysterious nature of time itself, it is perhaps not surprising that discussions *about* time in economic theory can easily become somewhat nebulous. Our approach reflects the conviction that a careful study of how selected serious theorists have grappled with the element of time is far more illuminating than indulging in generalisations. Accordingly we examine a number of deservedly famous works by eminent economists, our attention being focused in each case on the original text, rather than on secondary sources. Even if we may hope, in the course of the following chapters, to correct some stereotyped characterisations of certain authors, the present work is not offered as a work in the history of economic thought. The following chapters are to be seen rather as case-studies in how different economists have sought to deal with what are still current (and pressing) problems in the treatment of time in economic theory. We are, so to speak, raiding the past for the purpose of a contemporary discussion.

Marshall's *Principles of Economics* provides a useful starting-point. Every economist is familiar with the 'textbook' Marshallian periods. But not every economist is familiar with the *Principles*. An intriguing question, considered in the next chapter, is whether the textbook periods correspond with Marshall's own temporal approach. We will also seek to set in context Marshall's frequently quoted assertion: 'The Mecca of the economist lies in economic biology rather than in economic dynamics.' But we may note here that many authors have found it extremely difficult to characterise Marshall's treatment of time and that, correspondingly, both mainstream writers and radical subjectivists have found inspiration in Marshall's *Principles*. This illustrates at once that rigid dichotomisation can be pernicious.

If few economists have studied Marshall's *Principles*, it is becoming increasingly difficult to find any economists who have studied Léon Walras' *Elements of Pure Economics*. Of course, most economists know the *Elements* by repute. The fact that they do not seem to have studied the work does not deter at least some of them from offering inept criticisms of Walras. In Chapter 3, we will see that, while Walras formulates his general equilibrium model primarily in terms of clock time, he is nevertheless acutely aware of the difficulties which arise from the time of intention.

It is entirely fitting that a work on time in economic theory consider a representative of the 'Swedish school'. We consider Erik Lindahl. Indeed, we devote two chapters to Lindahl. In Chapter 4, we examine his essay, 'The place of capital in the theory of price', first published in Swedish in 1929. Motivated by a desire 'to bring the theory of price into closer contact with reality', Lindahl sought to confront directly the complications posed by time. In presenting a sequence of models which increasingly approximate reality, Lindahl introduced not only the notion of inter-temporal equilibrium but also what may be described as a sequence of temporary equilibria. In Chapter 5, we examine Lindahl's 1939 essay, 'The dynamic approach to economic theory'. This essay, motivated by his dissatisfaction with his earlier essay, involved a fundamentally different approach: it offered a general theory which can then form the basis for more specific theories designed for particular purposes. The time of intention was much more the focus of attention in the 1939 essay than it had been in the 1929 essay. Lindahl's new emphasis was on individuals and, in particular, on their purposeful behaviour in the face of an uncertain future. Since the plans of individuals will typically be incompatible with one another, attempts to implement them will be frustrated. Accordingly, individuals will review their experiences, modify their prognoses of future conditions and revise their plans. The exploration of such a process provides, in particular, a disequilibrium analysis of price movements.

Sir John Hicks' *Value and Capital* has often – and rightly – been described as a landmark in the development of economic theory. As we will see in Chapter 6, this work reflected the influences of Marshall, Walras and Lindahl. Hicks sought to combine Walras' insights into the interdependence between markets with Marshall's insights into the importance of the time taken by production. Following a lead from Lindahl, Hicks presented the notion of a 'process in time', conceived of as a sequence of temporary equilibria, each temporary equilibrium on the Monday of any week being dependent on individuals' expectations of the future. It is instructive to examine the nature of this process and, in particular, the way in which Hicks exploited to the full the possibility of applying static analysis to the individual period.

For many years, 'serious' Walrasian general equilibrium analysis has been equated in the minds of many, not with Walras' own work, but with the Arrow-Debreu economy. In Chapter 7, we examine Gerard Debreu's *Theory of Value*. A close scrutiny of this work is instructive, partly because Debreu's treatment of time raises sharply such issues as the implications of entering an economy at an arbitrary point in time, the appropriate choice of the time horizon of the analysis and the appropriate durations of elementary time periods. We do, of course, consider the persistent complaint that the Arrow-Debreu model 'reduces' time to space.

If the Arrow-Debreu model is sometimes praised for its aesthetic appeal, George Shackle is sometimes regarded as a poet. In Chapter 8, we examine the writings of Shackle, not to assess his poetic ability but rather to understand the temporal themes which recur in his work, in particular, the theme that the 'moment-in-being' is solitary and self-contained and that 'decision' involves a cut between past and future. Like Shackle, Ludwig Lachmann is a subjectivist *par excellence*. Whereas Shackle concentrates primarily on the behaviour of individuals, Lachmann's emphasis is on the nature of the market process. In Chapter 9, we consider Lachmann's image of the market as 'a continuous process without beginning or end, propelled by the interaction between the forces of equilibrium and the forces of change'. It is, of course, in the works of Shackle and Lachmann that we find the greatest stress on what Jaques called the time of intention and on the belief that the future is yet to be created.

In examining the diverse approaches of our various authors, we inevitably encounter different conceptions of equilibrium. Mainstream economic theorists, of course, rely fundamentally on notions of equilibrium: indeed, such notions are the way in which they wrestle with time. But it should also be stressed from the outset − since this is not always understood − that Shackle, far from being dismissive of static general equilibrium analysis, describes it as 'brilliant'; and that Lachmann's conception of the market process as being 'propelled by the interaction between the forces of equilibrium and the forces of change' *must* involve some conception of equilibrium. It would be inappropriate for us to anticipate here the various conceptions of equilibrium which we will encounter. However, the reader may like to be reassured that, in Chapter 10, we contrast and evaluate these different notions of equilibrium. In addition to reflecting on equilibrium methods in general, we also consider the more specific question of the legitimacy of comparative statics. It will scarcely come as a surprise that we conclude that one cannot assess the legitimacy of comparative statics as a predictive device without confronting dynamic issues. In Chapter 11, we explore further such dynamic questions by examining some pertinent recent works, namely, Edwin Burmeister's *Capital Theory and Dynamics*, Franklin Fisher's *Disequilibrium Foundations of Equilibrium Economics* and Frank Hahn's *On The Notion Of Equilibrium in Economics*. We will see that serious economists are, indeed, still wrestling with time.

Readers may well wonder why we have not devoted chapters to the works of Adam Smith, Ricardo, Marx, Böhm-Bawerk, Wicksell, Schumpeter, Knight, Myrdal, Hayek, Keynes, von

Neumann, Georgescu-Roegen, ... That the list could be almost endless provides the answer to the question. If this work stimulates others to scrutinise the treatment of time by such eminent economists, it will have served one of its primary purposes.

2

Marshall

For the nature of the equilibrium itself, and that of the causes by which it is determined, depend on the length of the period over which the market is taken to extend. We shall find that if the period is short, the supply is limited to the stores which happen to be at hand; if the period is longer, the supply will be influenced, more or less, by the cost of producing the commodity in question; and if the period is very long, this cost will in its turn be influenced, more or less, by the cost of producing the labour and the material things required for producing the commodity. These three classes of course merge into one another by imperceptible degrees (p. 330).

The discussion of Alfred Marshall's treatment of time, which is presented in this chapter, will be confined to the version found in the eighth edition of his *Principles of Economics*, of 1920. Neither Marshall's other work, nor the changes which he made between successive editions of the *Principles*, will be considered here. Yet even subject to these restrictions, the task of interpretation is not straightforward, for at least two reasons. The first difficulty lies in our familiarity with the now conventional textbook microeconomics of the firm and the industry, which it is easy to think of as 'essentially Marshallian'. It can reasonably be argued, however, that that familiar apparatus is a post-Marshallian construction, due at least as much to Pigou (1927, 1928), Harrod (1930), Viner (1931) and others, as to Marshall himself (cf. Ridolfi, 1970-72). Peter Newman, indeed, prefaced his 1960 paper on the erosion of Marshall's theory of value with the claim that

in the course of time [Marshall's] analysis has been unwittingly perverted from its original intention, so that much analysis, even of purely competitive conditions, that is today presented as Marshallian is quite foreign to his thought. This would not matter if the new doctrines were superior in all important respects to the old; but that is not the case. Marshall's long-run analysis embodies, however imperfectly, a richness of vision which has been almost completely lost (Wood, III, p. 385).[1]

The second difficulty is that Marshall's *Principles* is a far from pellucid work. This has led to conflicting interpretations of some aspects of Marshall's analysis, *e.g.*, of the 'representative firm'; and, no doubt, played an important role in the rapid development of the post-Marshallian construction referred to above. In Hutchison's view, 'Marshall himself gave much higher priority to practical instrumental relevance ... than to the drawing up of the precise and logical demarcations and definitions, logically needed by his partial methods' (1953, p. 74) and Hutchison even concluded that it is not helpful to attribute 'precise logically self-consistent models' (p. 75) to Marshall if one is to understand his *Principles*. A perhaps more positive description of the difficulty of Marshall's writing, which connects it directly with our temporal concerns, is given by Loasby (1978), who considers that,

Marshall's endeavours to incorporate time as an essential component of his analysis is [*sic*] responsible for much of the careful imprecision so characteristic of the *Principles* ... and it is no accident that the modern striving for rigour has produced models which are strictly timeless. Even the recent extensions of equilibrium theory to include markets distinguished by date are devices for evading, rather than dealing with, the difficulties which Marshall had in mind (Wood, III, p. 587).

In seeking to understand Marshall's treatment of time, then, one must resist the temptation either to suppose that it is merely the treatment found in the modern textbook or to suppose that it is simple. A yet further obstacle lies in Marshall's interest in both biological and mechanical analogies in the study of economics.

Biology, evolution and organicism

In the light of Burrow's beautiful book *Evolution and Society. A Study in Victorian Social Theory* (1966), it is clear that Marshall was far from idiosyncratic in his attention to evolutionary styles of thought and to biological analogies. And indeed Marshall's own Appendix B, 'The Growth of Economic Science', presents the argument that,

At the beginning of [the] last century the mathematico-physical group of sciences were in the ascendant ... As the century wore on, the biological group

of sciences were slowly making way, and people were getting clearer ideas
as to the nature of organic growth ... At last the speculations of biology made
a great stride forwards: its discoveries fascinated the attention of the world
as those of physics had done in earlier years; and there was a marked change
in the tone of the moral and historical sciences. Economics has shared in the
general movement (*Principles*, p.764).

Thus, when Shove, in 1942, remarked of Marshall's famous assertion,
'The Mecca of the economist lies in economic biology rather than in
economic dynamics', that, 'The epigram carries its date on its face'
(Wood, II, p.146), his remark was well aimed.

The epigrammatic status of Marshall's statement has, however,
been partly – even largely – created by its frequent quotation as
an isolated sentence. In context, in the Preface to the eighth edition,
it simply provided an introduction, albeit a striking one, to four
paragraphs in which Marshall sought to explain how it is that the
Principles 'give a relatively large place to mechanical analogies; and
frequent use is made of the term "equilibrium"' (p. xiv), even though
'the central idea of economics ... must be that of living force and
movement' (p. xv). Biological conceptions are complex, Marshall
points out, and the forces to be dealt with are so numerous, that one
is obliged to proceed step by step, appealing to the phrase 'other things
being equal' and working out 'a number of partial solutions as
auxiliaries to our main study' (p. xiv). It is for these reasons that,
'Fragmentary statical hypotheses are used as temporary auxiliaries
to dynamical – or rather biological – conceptions' (p. xv).

The same theme is vividly restated in the opening paragraph of
Book V, 'General Relations of Demand, Supply and Value'. Marshall
first recalls his Book IV discussion of the importance of the life-cycle
of firms and then writes,

And as we reach to the higher stages of our work, we shall need ever more
and more to think of economic forces as resembling those which make a young
man grow in strength, till he reaches his prime; after which he gradually
becomes stiff and inactive, till at last he sinks to make room for other and
more vigorous life. But to prepare the way for this advanced study we want
first to look at a simpler balancing of forces which corresponds rather to the
mechanical equilibrium of a stone hanging by an elastic string, or of a number
of balls resting against one another in a basin (p. 323).

Marshall is not here belittling the use of mechanical analogies,
however, for he at once goes on to describe such reasoning as 'the

theoretical backbone of our knowledge of the causes which govern value' (p. 324). Rather, Marshall appears to write from within a constant (and indissoluble?) tension between the view that only biological conceptions provide 'depth', whilst only mechanical conceptions afford 'precision'. That tension is given forceful expression in the penultimate paragraph of Book V, chapter XII:

The theory of stable equilibrium of normal demand and supply helps indeed to give definiteness to our ideas; and in its elementary stages it does not diverge from the actual facts of life, so far as to prevent its giving a fairly trustworthy picture of the chief methods of action of the strongest and most persistent group of economic forces. But when pushed to its more remote and intricate logical consequences, it slips away from the conditions of real life. In fact we are here verging on the high theme of economic progress; and here therefore it is especially needful to remember that economic problems are imperfectly presented when they are treated as problems of statical equilibrium, and not of organic growth. For though the statical treatment alone can give us definiteness and precision of thought, and is therefore a necessary introduction to a more philosophic treatment of society as an organism, it is yet only an introduction (p. 461).

There is more than enough evidence in the *Principles* to justify Shove's assessment that,

Marshall's whole conception of the nature of economic change is coloured by what may be called the biological approach. For him, economic development ... is essentially a process of 'organic growth' and the methods of the science must be adapted accordingly .... In spite of the care lavished upon them, the long-period supply and demand curves were cast for a minor role only .... They cannot be used to forecast accurately and for any considerable distance into the future the direction in which outputs and values are likely to move, still less the position at which they may be expected to arrive (Wood, II, p. 146).

Irreversibilities in time and qualitative changes in both individuals and institutions indeed feature prominently in 'Marshall's conception of economic change as "organic growth" ' (*ibid.*). Yet, interesting and important as these concerns may be, two points must be kept firmly in mind. The first is that, within the *Principles*, Marshall did not come even within sight of the 'Mecca of the economist'. The *Principles* constitute 'a volume on Foundations' (p. xiv), and if there are ample warnings of the limitations to mechanical analogies and equilibrium reasoning, the brute fact remains that the *Principles* does not provide any general demonstration of the nature and of the results of an alternative reasoning; there are but hints. The 'higher stages of our work' and 'the high theme of economic progress' lie beyond the *Principles*. The second point which must not be lost from sight, even as one is attracted by Marshall's picture of irreversible, qualitative change over time, is that, as noted above, Marshall certainly did not disparage 'the statical treatment [which] is therefore a *necessary* introduction' (p. 461, emphasis added). Indeed he concluded the Appendix B, already cited above as emphasising the merits of biological conceptions, with an express warning of the concomitant dangers:

The growing prominence of what has been called the biological view of the science has tended to throw the notions of economic law and measurement into the background; as though such notions were too hard and rigid to be applied to the living and everchanging economic organism. But biology itself teaches us that the vertebrate organisms are the most highly developed. The modern economic organism is vertebrate; and the science which deals with it should not be invertebrate. It should have that delicacy and sensitiveness of touch which are required for enabling it to adapt itself closely to the real phenomena of the world; but none the less must it have a firm backbone of careful reasoning and analysis (p. 769).

Marshall's economy

Given Marshall's ambition to present a 'realistic' picture of an economy undergoing historical change, it is not to be expected that the vision of the economy found in the *Principles* will be readily amenable to simple, clear cut description. There are, of course, households and, indeed, emphasis is placed on the role of the family and of family affection in, for example, the forming of character and the motivation for hard work and accumulation. (It is taken for granted that preferences and ambitions are subject to significant social influence.) Book IV is devoted to 'The Agents of Production. Land, Labour, Capital and Organization', and it is to 'organization' that Marshall devotes the greatest attention. (We may note, though, that the heterogeneity of the 'grades of labour' is emphasised and that strikingly little attention is paid to 'capital'; the single chapter on capital takes up only one-tenth of Book IV.) Whilst the small private firm and its 'life-cycle' feature prominently in the *Principles*, of course, partnerships, joint-stock companies, profit-sharing enterprises, co-operative societies, public corporations, and trusts and cartels are discussed by Marshall (e.g. in Book IV, chapter XII). Correspondingly, businessmen, managers, directors, speculators, capitalists and the bureaucrats all appear; and, more analytically, Marshall distinguishes between supplying capital, bearing risk, ability in organising technical production, ability in leading people, and so on. He argues that 'business ability in command of capital' (p. 313) was highly mobile in the England of 1920 and regards its supply price as having three elements. 'The first is the supply price of capital [*interest*]; the second is the supply price of business ability and energy [*net earnings of management*]; and the third is the supply price of that organization by which the appropriate business ability and the requisite capital are brought together [which added to the second element gives *gross earnings of management*]' (p. 313).

In what form of market does Marshall take the various kinds of producing enterprise to be interacting? Unfortunately, it does not appear to be easy to give a simple, straightforward answer to this question. Book V opens with a chapter 'On Markets'. After quoting both Cournot and Jevons on the importance of free communication for the formation of a market, Marshall writes, 'Thus the more nearly perfect a market is, the stronger is the tendency for the same price to be paid for the same thing at the same time in all parts of the market' (p. 325). It will be noted that the adjective 'perfect' is applied to 'a market' and not to 'competition', Marshall's usual qualification of the latter being 'free competition'. Marshall then considers the spatial dimension of markets, taking stocks and shares, gold and silver as examples of commodities whose markets can even be worldwide, and fresh vegetables as examples of commodities with highly localised markets (even if there can be distant influences) (pp. 326–9). He concludes this discussion with the assertion that, 'about midway between these extremes lie the great majority of the markets which the economist and the business man have to study' (p. 329). While it is presumably this 'great majority' which provide the focus of Marshall's analysis, we have hardly been provided with an exact indication of the extent of competition in such markets. Marshall concludes this opening chapter by suggesting that the variation of time periods, as well as that of spatial areas, is important for markets and that 'this element of Time requires more careful attention just now than does that of Space' (p. 330). With this one is launched into the famous sequence of chapters on temporary, short-period and long-period equilibria.

In the second of those chapters (Book V, Chapter III, 'Equilibrium of Normal Demand and Supply'), Marshall writes,

we are investigating the equilibrium of normal demand and normal supply in their most general form ... Thus we assume that the forces of demand and supply have free play; that there is no close combination among dealers on either side, but each acts for himself, and there is much free competition; that is, buyers generally compete freely with buyers, and sellers compete freely with sellers ... we assume that there is only one price in the market at one and the same time [allowing for any transport and retailing expenses] (pp. 341-2).

Nothing is said here about the *number* of firms involved; it is the free flow of knowledge which is supposed to ensure the uniform price. Wolfe (1954) has argued that, 'Marshall's "free competition" was not perfect competition .... What it does imply is that "there is only one price in the market at one and the same time"' (Wood, III, p. 288).

Marshall, needless to say, recognises the existence both of approximately homogeneous commodities (raw produce, steel rails, calico) and of differentiated 'specialities' for which 'marketing is difficult' (pp. 286–7). Of these latter he writes,

manufactures, which are adapted to special tastes ... are the very industries in which each firm is likely to be [confined] more or less to its own particular market; and if it is so confined, any hasty increase in its production is likely to lower the demand price in that market out of all proportion to the increased economies that it will gain; even though its production is but small relatively to the broad market for which in a more general sense it may be said to produce (pp. 457–8).

In p. 458, n. 1, Marshall reiterates that, for an individual producer, 'the particular demand curve of his own special market ... will generally be very steep'. That the seeds of imperfect or monopolistic competition theory may be found here does not help one to decide just how Marshall interprets 'the market', the single price and the 'industry output' in any industry supply curve referring to a manufacturing industry. These questions are not made any less pressing by Marshall's well known references to fear of 'spoiling the market' (pp. 360, 374–5, 457–8, 498) and his argument that, if price should fall below average total cost, producers may well reduce output *more* than would be necessary to stay on their marginal cost curves. As Hague (1958) points out, this strongly suggests that 'Marshall's "large and open" market for manufactures does not contain enough firms to experience pure competition' (Wood, III, p. 352). Whether or not one takes the degree and type of interdependence involved here to constitute an oligopolistic position (*ibid.*, p. 353), it clearly complicates the concept of 'free competition'.

Is it possible to describe both briefly and accurately Marshall's assumptions about the nature of markets, industries and competition? Perhaps not; his concern for realism, and hence variety and complexity, may simply render it impossible.

The importance of time

Merely to say that Marshall considered time to be important would be to indulge in an unimportant waste of space. Yet it perhaps bears emphasis just how much importance Marshall attributes to the role of time in economic processes and in economic analysis. Newman had good reason to write that 'Marshall was *principally* concerned with ... the problem of time' (Wood, III, p. 392, emphasis added) and Shackle to suggest that 'the *Principles* is a relentless effort to bring into one fabric of argument the two incompatibles ... the mutually repellent strands of rationality and novelty ... the economist must study change. Yet he must be a seeker of principles ... the *Principles* is, in the main, an intense and unremitting struggle with this central theme' (1972, pp. 286–7). In the Preface to the first edition of the *Principles*, in 1890, Marshall suggested that 'the element of Time ... is the centre of the chief difficulty of almost every economic problem' (p. vii), which is an emphatic statement indeed by the cautious, ever-qualifying Marshall. Shortly into the main text (p. 36), Marshall writes that, 'the condition that time must be allowed for causes to produce their effects is a source of great difficulty in economics. For meanwhile the material on which they work, and perhaps even the causes themselves, may have changed; and the tendencies which are being described will not have a sufficiently "long run" in which to work themselves out fully. This difficulty will occupy our attention later on', this last sentence being a masterly understatement.

As Marshall wrote in Book V, Chapter V, 'The element of time is a chief cause of those difficulties in economic investigations which make it necessary for man with his limited powers to go step by step; breaking up a complex question, studying one bit at a time, and at last combining his partial solutions into a more or less complete solution of the whole riddle' (p. 366); it is the role of time which leads

Marshall to resort to 'a pound called *Coeteris Paribus*' (*ibid.*). But even the skilful use of this device naturally does nothing to alter the brute fact that

in the world in which we live ... every economic force is constantly changing its action, under the influence of other forces which are acting around it. Here changes in the volume of production, in its methods, and in its cost are ever mutually modifying one another; they are always affecting and being affected by the character and the extent of demand. Further all these mutual influences take time to work themselves out, and, as a rule, no two influences move at equal pace. In this world therefore every plain and simple doctrine as to the relations between cost of production, demand and value is necessarily false (p. 368).

A sufficient, albeit not unique reason for this 'necessary falsity' of any simple theory of value can be found in Marshall's persistent, if unemphatic reference to the role of expectations. (Given, that is, that no simple theory of expectations formation is acceptable.) It should suffice here to refer to Marshall's discussion in Book V, Chapter V, Section 5. Against the marginal note 'Restatement of the main result' (p. 372), Marshall begins by saying that, 'Market demands are governed by the relation of demand to stocks actually in the market; with more or less reference to "future" supplies.' He continues: 'But the current supply is in itself partly due to the action of producers in the past; and this action has been determined on as a result of a comparison of the prices which they *expect* to get for their goods with the expenses to which they will be put in producing them' (*ibid.*, emphasis added). The point is then made several times over in the next paragraph:

Whether the new production for which there appears to be a market be large or small, the general rule will be that unless the price is expected to be very low that portion of the supply which can be most easily produced, with but small prime costs, will be produced ... As the expectations of price improve ... the margin of production will be pushed outwards. Every increase in the price expected will, as a rule, induce some people who would not otherwise have produced anything, to produce a little; and those who would have produced something for the lower price will produce more for the higher price (p. 373).

Marshall then goes straight on to stress that whether the period involved be long or short, the normal supply price is that price 'the *expectation* of which is sufficient and only just sufficient to make it worth while for people to set themselves to produce' a certain aggregate amount (*ibid.*, emphasis added). Marshall's 'Restatement of the main result' (in V, v, 5) is replete with references to expectations, simply because expectations were central to Marshall's analysis, which took time seriously.

Marshall did not simply assent to the banal observation that time is important; he seized its importance in vivid fashion and kept it at the heart of his analysis. It was perhaps somewhat unfair of Opie (1931) to complain of 'Marshall's vague and loose general statements about the time analysis and the static method, which often give the reader the impression that unexplored mysteries are behind them' (Wood, I, p. 174), for it may be the reader who has attributed the mystery to Marshall's statements, but his conclusion, that 'If the time analysis is seen plainly as a simple part of the bit-at-a-time method of procedure ... it will not thereby lose any of its importance' (*ibid*), is acceptable − provided only that this 'simple part' is expected to be complex.

Equilibrium in statics, dynamics and stationary states

If Marshall took the importance of time with full seriousness, how did he attempt to encapsulate it, in practice, in the analysis of supply and demand? How did he formulate the 'theoretical backbone', as necessary to economic analysis as it was ultimately 'inferior' to a historical and organic theory? We begin here to consider these questions, leaving to subsequent sections more specific discussions of Marshall's various 'periods', his concept of the representative firm and his treatment of time-irreversibilities in demand and supply relations.

In Book V, Chapter III, Section 6, Marshall defines equilibrium-amount and equilibrium-price as the quantity (per unit of time) and the price involved, in a particular market, 'When the demand price is equal to the supply price' (p. 345). But it is noteworthy that Marshall leads up to this definition by emphasising what will happen when the quantity is not the equilibrium one. When 'the demand price is greater than the supply price ... there is at work an active force tending to increase the amount brought forward for sale. [But when] the demand price is less than the supply price ... there is an active force at work tending to diminish the amount brought forward for sale' (*ibid.*). Equilibrium is then defined, very briefly, and Marshall at once moves on to a discussion of the conditions for the stability of equilibrium-amount and equilibrium-price (pp. 345–6). While the concept of equilibrium is certainly central to Marshall's discussion here, it is firmly set within the context of constant change and the forces producing it: the emphasis is on *adjustment* whenever demand price and supply price are not equal. Nor is the pattern of change pictured as being a simple one: Marshall suggests that the 'movements of the scale of production about its position of equilibrium' may be as complex as those of 'a stone hanging freely from a string [which is] supposed to hang in the troubled waters of a mill-race, whose stream was at one time allowed to flow freely, and at another partially cut off, [when] the person holding the string swings his hand with movements partly rhythmical and partly arbitrary' (p. 346). Indeed, 'the demand and supply schedules do not in practice remain unchanged for a long time together, but are constantly being changed; and every change in them alters the equilibrium amount and the equilibrium price, and thus gives new positions to the centres about which the amount and the price tend to oscillate' (pp. 346–7). Thus actual quantity and price are for ever moving, in complex ways, around equilibrium quantity and price and, moreover, these latter are themselves constantly subject to change.

In seeking to get to grips with such complexity and turbulence Marshall, of course, had to resort to 'a pound called *Coeteris Paribus*', which he considered to be of sufficient importance even to be discussed in the Preface (pp. xiv-xv). In using this pound,

some group of tendencies is isolated by the assumption *other things being equal*: the existence of other tendencies is not denied, but their disturbing effect is neglected for a time. The more the issue is thus narrowed, the more exactly can it be handled: but also the less closely does it correspond to real life. Each exact and firm handling of a narrow issue, however, helps towards treating broader issues, in which that narrow issue is contained, more exactly than would otherwise have been possible. With each step more things can be let out of the pound; exact discussions can be made less abstract, realistic discussions can be made less inexact than was possible at an earlier stage (p. 366).

Before proceeding further with this argument, Marshall pauses to consider 'the famous fiction of the "Stationary state" in which [the] influences [exerted by the element of time] would be but little felt' (pp. 366–8) and a quasi-stationary state of proportional expansion (there being no scarcity of land) (pp. 368-9) but he does not exhibit great interest in these constructions. We may note one particular aspect of Marshall's discussion, however, namely that he does *not* take a stationary state to entail that every individual business is of constant size (p. 367). The various firms in an industry may each grow and then decline, in Marshall's stationary state, provided only that the aggregate volume of production in that industry is constant over time, as are the internal and external economies available to the 'representative firm'. 'Stationarity' is required only at the level of the industry and not at that of the firm; just as, presumably, individual consumers and households are allowed to change over time.

When Marshall does come to the method of analysis which he favours, he gives a curiously obscure definition of it. In using 'the *statical* method', he tells us, 'we fix our minds on some central point: we suppose it for the time [being?] to be reduced to a *stationary* state; and we then study in relation to it the forces that affect the things by which it is surrounded, and any tendency there may be to equilibrium of these forces' (p. 369). Fortunately, however, this 'definition' is followed immediately by the Book V, Chapter V, Section 4, examples of day to day, short-period and long-period changes in the fishing industries, from which it is clear, if only by implication, that 'the statical method' is merely another name for the use of the *Coeteris Paribus* device. And this identity is rendered almost explicit when Marshall writes that 'violence is required to keep broad forces in the pound of *Coeteris Paribus* during, say, a whole generation .... Thus the uses of the statical method in problems relating to very long periods are dangerous' (p. 379, n. 1).

The more forces are locked up in the pound, the more exact and the less realistic is the resulting analysis. Whilst insisting that an exact analysis is highly useful, Marshall is always desirous of moving towards realism, so that each impounding *should* only be provisional:

the problem of normal value belongs to economic Dynamics: partly because Statics is really but a branch of Dynamics, and partly because all suggestions as to economic rest, of which the hypothesis of a Stationary state is the chief, are merely provisional, used only to illustrate particular steps in the argument, and to be thrown aside when that is done (p. 366, n. 2).

Again, responding to the Catholic economist Charles Devas, Marshall writes, 'It is true that we do treat variables provisionally as constants. But it is also true that this is the only method by which science has ever made any great progress in dealing with complex and changeful

matter, whether in the physical or moral world' (p. 380, footnote).
These statements are perhaps difficult to fault as statements of *intent* but it is not merely captious to enquire when and how the
provisional assumptions of constancy will *in fact* 'be thrown aside'.
At one point, at least, Marshall may seem to suggest that it is not in
fact always necessary to dispense with them:

The theory of stable equilibrium of normal demand and supply helps indeed
to give definiteness to our ideas; and in its elementary stages it does not diverge
from the actual facts of life, so far as to prevent its giving a fairly trustworthy
picture of the chief methods of action of the strongest and most persistent
group of economic forces (p. 461).

But he goes on at once to say, 'But when pushed to its more remote
and intricate logical consequences, it slips away from the conditions
of real life. In fact we are here verging on the high theme of economic
progress' and hence problems 'of organic growth' and not 'of statical
equilibrium' (*ibid.*). One is thus left without clear criteria for what
to put in the pound, when to let it out, and what to do when the static
method is abandoned. This last statement is deliberately naive, for
the answer may well be given that 'one must use one's judgement,
applying it to a sound knowledge of the facts'. But that naivety may
not be unhelpful, since it is hardly self-evident that the putative answer
would actually be terribly instructive.

   Marshall certainly did not try to hide or to minimise the short-
comings of the static method; they are made far more evident in the
Principles than in many modern textbooks. On the same page, he
writes that,

The Statical theory of equilibrium is only an introduction to economic studies;
and it is barely even an introduction to the study of the progress and development of industries which show a tendency to increasing return. Its limitations
are so constantly overlooked, especially by those who approach it from an
abstract point of view, that there is a danger in throwing it into definite form
at all (p. 461, see also Appendix H).

The 'Short-comings of the Statical Method' (p. 501, marginal note)
are again stressed, in relation to the long period in increasing return
industries, in the Summary Chapter to Book V. And in the famous
Appendix H itself, Marshall considers multiple equilibria and the
time-irreversibility of quantity and price paths through time
(pp. 807–9) and suggests that one should think in terms, not of a two-
dimensional quantity-price curve, but of 'a *surface* of which the three

dimensions represented amount, price and time respectively' (p. 809, n. 2, running to p. 810). At this point Marshall appears to be breaking the bounds of the static method and entering the field of explicitly dynamic analysis. The fact remains, however, that conscious as he was of the limits to the static method, and eloquent as he was on 'organic' modes of thought, Marshall does not in fact overcome those limits or display those alternative modes at work.

It has already been noted that, even in the stationary state, Marshall did not take individual firms to be constant in size. It is all the more important to note that he did not take firm equilibrium to be entailed by industry long-period equilibrium. As Loasby put it in 1978, 'Marshall's theory of long-run equilibrium was an expedient for the analysis of growth and change. But, even in this role, it was an equilibrium of the industry only. The long-run equilibrium of the firm had no place in his analysis' (Wood, III, p. 596). Loasby does not refer here to Newman (1960), who provides a closely supportive assessment:

Industry output can be constant through time, even though some firms are growing and being 'born', and others are declining and 'dying', provided that the gains in output from the one cause are balanced by the losses in output from the other. Long-run equilibrium for Marshall meant the equality of long-run demand and supply; just that and no more. Nowhere can one find a statement that each firm has to be in full long-period equilibrium, while plenty of examples to the contrary can be found (Wood, III, p. 386).

The Newman-Loasby interpretation *must* indeed be correct, for it would be contradictory to require firm equilibrium in industry long-period equilibrium but not in the stationary state – since the latter is more restrictive than the former – and, as we have already seen, Marshall does not require it even in the latter. The modern textbook 'long-run equilibrium', then, is *not* Marshall's long-period equilibrium, which is far more flexible.

We now turn to a more detailed consideration of three special topics within Marshall's treatment of time.

The four periods and their nature

Marshall, of course, distinguished different periods of analysis and, as he put it, 'Four classes stand out' (p. 378). The first is the *market* period analysis of temporary equilibrium (as Marshall understood that term), the second is the *short* period analysis, then comes the *long* period analysis and, finally, one can engage in *secular* analysis (pp. 378–9). We shall focus here on the first three period analyses, considering their definitions, the determinateness of temporary equilibrium, the question whether Marshall's short period is self-contained and the question whether Marshall applied long period analysis to the firm.

It goes without saying that, in the modern textbook, it is insisted that the market period/short period/long period distinction is made in terms of 'operational time', such periods differing, by definition, with respect to possible degrees of adjustment.

To be sure, the short run normally does involve a shorter period of clock time than the long run but this is not necessarily and always true. It is conceivable, for example, that the time needed to increase output from existing facilities exceeds the time required to install new equipment. We would then have a long run preceding a short run. Since time is conceived operationally, Marshallian analysis does not preclude such oddities (Blaug, 1985, p. 371).

While this is certainly true of 'Marshallian' analysis, as that is commonly presented, it is not self-evidently true of Marshall's analysis, as we shall now see.

When Marshall introduces a temporary equilibrium in a local corn market (Book V, Chapter II, Section 2), the page heading is 'Market Day in a Local Corn-Exchange' (p. 333) and he introduces the following chapter by saying that, 'In the last chapter we looked at the affairs of only a single day' (p. 337); the summary chapter to Book V again refers to this 'market-day' (p. 496). There is no suggestion that the 'day' here is one of those artificial days, weeks, etc. to which economic theorists have become accustomed; it is a natural, everyday day. While Marshall does not say so explicitly, he is presumably thinking of a regular weekly or monthly 'market day in a local corn-exchange'. Presumably too, although Marshall is again silent on the matter, corn can be stored from one week (or month) to the next, both by producers of corn and by purchasers. It is not made clear, however, what role is played by price expectations concerning subsequent market days. Marshall certainly states that, 'The amount which each farmer or other seller offers for sale at any price is governed ... by his calculation of the present and future conditions of the market with which he is connected' (p. 332), yet he does not elaborate further on speculation as between market-days. Or, more exactly, he does not do so explicitly.

It is to be noted that Marshall nowhere states, within his short chapter on 'Temporary Equilibrium of Demand and Supply', that there is a predetermined, fixed supply, all of which will necessarily be sold. He several times refers to the sellers of corn as 'holders', which already suggests, perhaps, that they need not necessarily dispose of all their holdings within a given market-day. Moreover, in the course of discussing the market process during the day (to which we return below), Marshall refers to 'some of those who are really willing to take 36s. rather than leave the market without selling' (p. 333) and to 'those sellers who would rather take the price than leave the market with their corn unsold' (*ibid.*). It is difficult to reconcile these remarks of Marshall's with the idea that the market-day temporary equilibrium presupposes a rigidly fixed supply which *must* be sold — but it is easy enough to read them as meaning that Marshall is implicitly allowing for speculation as between market-days.

Certainly Marshall allows for speculative considerations to play a role *within* the market-day, for he is aware that the price of a quarter of corn may well vary in the course of the day's trading. (He does not, however, mention the possibility of there being positive trades at different prices at the same moment within the day.) This naturally raises the question whether the final price and the volume of corn traded by the close of the day will be independent of the course of the day's trading. Marshall's answer is clear but, as usual, multi-faceted and qualified. In principle, the answer is 'No' — and Marshall cites 'markets for labour' as possible examples in which this negative answer will hold good (pp. 335–6). In practice, he maintains, the answer will be 'Very nearly' in 'markets for commodities' for, with only 'rare and unimportant' exceptions (p. 335), the marginal utilities of money to the buyers and sellers in a given market 'would be practically the same' whether the early transactions had been carried out at a high or at a low price (*ibid.*).[2]

We turn now to the short period. When Marshall gives his summary statement of the 'Four classes [which] stand out', he refers to '*short* periods of a few months or a year. Supply [here] means broadly what can be produced for the price in question with the existing stock of plant, personal and impersonal, *in the given time*' (p. 379, emphasis added). The short period is a length of time, in which it *follows* that the plant involved is the existing one; the short period is not defined 'operationally'. Similarly, a few pages earlier, Marshall writes that, 'For short periods people take the stock of appliances for production as practically fixed' (p. 374); the virtually fixed character of the stock *results from* the shortness of the period − it *does not* define it. This point is perhaps made most graphically in the famous discussion of the fishing industries (Book V, Chapter V, Section 4), in which the phrase 'a year or two' occurs several times in connection with the short period (p. 370). In the short period analysis, Marshall writes,

We consider what old fishing boats, and even vessels that were not specially made for fishing, can be adapted and sent to fish for a year or two. The normal price for any given daily supply of fish, which we are now seeking, is the price which will *quickly* call into the fishing trade capital and labour enough to obtain that supply in a day's fishing of average good fortune (p. 370).

How could Marshall have made it more clear that neither the labour force nor the capital stock in a given industry need be fixed in his short period? Marshall's short period is a short period of calendar time, during which the inputs to a particular industry may or may not be adjustable.

Marshall's approach to the long-period, consequently, is also different from that of the post-Marshallian textbook. Defining the 'Four classes', Marshall writes that when we 'refer to *long* periods of several years, Supply means what can be produced by plant, which can itself be remuneratively produced and applied *within the given time*' (p. 379, emphasis added). Plant is variable because the given calendar time considered (several years) is sufficiently long; the variability of plant does *not* define the long period. Again, when Marshall states that 'In long periods [people] set themselves to adjust the flows of these appliances [for production] to their expectations of demand for the goods which the appliances help to produce' (p. 374), there is no reason whatever to interpret this statement in anything other than the 'commonsense' way; in a modern textbook, by contrast, the statement would be tautology. Returning now to the famous fishing trade, we recall that Marshall has already allowed 'capital and labour' in the industry to be variable within a short period. He then writes, 'But if we turn to consider the normal supply price with reference to a *long period* of time, we shall find that it is governed by a different set of causes, and with different results' (p. 370). 'Long period of time' here means what any non-economist would take it to mean and Marshall stresses that in long period analysis oscillations 'from day to day and from year to year' (*ibid.*) may be left on one side. The conclusion of Marshall's long period analysis of the fishing trade is that 'If ... the waters of the sea showed no signs of depletion of fish ... and the term Normal being taken to refer to a long period of time, the normal price of fish would decrease with an increase in demand' (p. 371). Yet again, there is no reason at all to give an 'operational' interpretation of 'a long period of time'. As Marshall writes, 'To sum up then as regards short periods. The supply of specialized skill and ability [etc.] has not time to be fully adapted to demand .... In long periods on the other hand all investments of capital and effort ... have time to be adjusted to the incomes which are expected to be earned by them' (pp. 376–7; see too the corresponding statements in Marshall's summary chapter to Book V, p. 501).

With respect to the fourth 'class' of time period, Marshall relates '*Secular* movements of normal price [to] the changing conditions of demand and supply from one generation to another' (p. 379); and in the footnote to this sentence he equates 'the course of a generation' with 'very long periods' (p. 379, n. 1). One would need to be obsessed with 'operational' definitions of periods in order to find one here.

Further evidence that Marshall's four kinds of period are not purely analytic ones is to be found in his statements about the continuity of time. (About which there is nothing particularly mysterious, *pace* Opie, 1931.) In the Preface to the first edition Marshall insists that

there is no sharp line of division ... between normal values and 'current' or 'market' or 'occasional' values ... they shade into one another by continuous gradations .... Nature knows no absolute partition of time into long periods and short; but the two shade into one another by imperceptible gradations, and what is a short period for one problem, is a long period for another (p. vii).

The values which are to be regarded as 'normal' – i.e. governed by laws (p. 34) – are relative to the length of real calendar time considered (*ibid.*). Similarly, Marshall ends the introductory chapter to Book V by saying that

the nature of the equilibrium itself, and that of the causes by which it is determined, depend on *the length of the period* over which the market is taken to extend. We shall find that if the period is short, the supply is limited to the stores which happen to be at hand: if the period is longer, the supply will be influenced ... by the cost of producing the commodity ... and if the period is very long, this cost will in its turn be influenced ... by the cost of producing the labour and the material things required for producing the commodity. These three classes of course merge into one another by imperceptible degrees (p. 330, emphasis added).

The influences on supply differ because the lengths of calendar time involved in the various periods themselves differ; the differences in influence do not define the periods. (In this passage Marshall uses 'short', 'longer' and 'very long' to refer to market, short and long periods, respectively; this very flexibility of terminology indicates that Marshall was not using the conceptually precise 'operational' distinctions of the modern textbook.) Moreover, and obviously, the three classes *could not* merge by imperceptible degrees if they were defined analytically; they do so just because they are conceived of, by Marshall, as real lengths of clock time.

A final consideration showing that Marshall's periods were lengths of calendar time turns on an issue not considered above and of interest in its own right. One of the most perceptive commentators on Marshall, Gerald Shove, insisted on

the fact that Marshall's theory of value is a theory of *general*, not particular, equilibrium. This is obvious enough in the Mathematical Appendix. It also comes out quite clearly in the text of the first edition, where it is not till we reach Book VII, dealing with the pricing of the agents of production, that 'Value' appears on a title-page. [In the seventh and eighth editions] Book VI (corresponding to the old VII) is headed 'The Distribution of the National Income', and we are no longer told, as we had been at the beginning of the old Book VII, that only now are we to 'deal with the problem of value as a whole' (1942; Wood, II, p. 161, n. 28; the reader is referred to this very interesting note for further details).

The whole cast of the eighth edition Book VI is indeed about the economy as a complete system. Chapters VII and VIII of that Book deal with 'Profits of Capital and Business Power' and in Chapter VIII, Section 5, Marshall writes, 'During all this inquiry we have had in view chiefly the ultimate, or long-period or true normal results of economic forces' (p. 618). He refers three times to the 'long run' on this page and on the following one he states that 'A long period of time is however needed in order to get the full operation of all these causes' influencing normal earnings and normal value (p. 619). Whilst it would be logically possible to apply the modern textbook definition of long period/long run to a complete economic system, the far more natural reading of the statements just cited is that here, as elsewhere in the *Principles*, Marshall is using long period, long run and long period of time as the non-economist would use them.

One must, of course, recognise that the *Principles* does contain statements encouraging the modern textbook conception of short and long periods. On p. 426, for example, we read of 'short periods, that is ... periods short relatively to the time required to make and bring into full bearing [agricultural] improvements'. And in the summary chapter to Book V, against the marginal note 'Short-period normal price or sub-normal price', Marshall writes of 'periods of time long enough to enable producers to adapt their production to changes in demand, in so far as that can be done with the existing provision of specialized skill, specialized capital, and industrial organization; but not long enough to enable them to make any important changes in the supplies of these factors of production' (pp. 497–8). Even these statements, however, can be read to refer to the obvious fact that short-periods of clock time will often be periods during which only limited adaptation is possible; while there are many statements in the *Principles* about short and long periods which cannot be interpreted in 'operational' terms. Our conclusion then is that, while length of calendar time and degree of flexibility will inevitably be well correlated, Marshall's periods really are periods of clock time and that he does not define them 'operationally' (cf., Ridolfi, 1970-72, pp. 145, 194).

According to Hicks (1965, Chapter V), Marshall's short period is characterised not only by the fixity of the fixed capital stock but also by 'the self-containedness' (p. 51) of that period. We have already seen that Marshall explicitly allows the number of fishing boats to vary within the fishing trade short period. And the 'fear of spoiling the market', which leads producers to respond to a fall in demand by reducing output by more than would be necessary in order for them to remain on their short period marginal cost curves, is based on longer term expectations. How can Hicks say that, in Marshall's short period, 'The fixed capital has become like land, "original" and "indestructible" *within the period*' (p. 51), in the face of Marshall's explicit remarks about the influence of supplementary costs on short period supply price (pp. 375–6)? It is not possible to attribute a fully 'self-contained' short period to Marshall, as Hicks does, (unless, of course, the adjective is interpreted so loosely as to lose its force).

We conclude this section with a point about the long period which connects with a previous section of the present chapter. This is that

Marshall's long run is intended to apply only to the industry as a whole, and not to each of the firms in it ... what Marshall was concerned with was, at one and the same time, the long-run equilibrium of the industry, and the movement towards, and away from, long-run equilibrium of the firm. Marshall's firm is never actually in equilibrium (Wolfe, 1954; Wood, III, p. 289).

It will be clear enough that this interpretation of long period equilibrium is completely different from that presented in the modern textbook.

The representative firm

Marshall's concept of the 'representative' firm, used in long period analysis, has given rise to much discussion; it is thus as well to begin by noting explicitly that it is an *inherently* imprecise notion, so that, beyond a certain point, fine disagreements about its definition and meaning are intrinsically pointless. Worthwhile questions about the representative firm in Marshall's *Principles* are: what was its broad meaning? for what purpose did Marshall think it useful? and is it in fact a useful concept which deserves to be retained?

Because particular firms may grow and then decline, 'the history of the individual firm cannot be made into the history of an industry .... And yet ... the aggregate production for a general market is the outcome of the motives which induce individual producers to expand or contract their production. It is just here that our device of a representative firm comes to our aid' (p. 459). This device allows Marshall to reason in a way which vividly calls to mind the expectations and calculations of an *individual producer*, even while he – Marshall – is writing about the *industry*. It is just because Marshall's focus is on the industry that the costs and supply prices of the representative firm are related, via the associated internal and external economies, to the aggregate volume of production in the industry (cf. pp. 317–18, 342–5). Thus Newman (1960) writes of the representative firm that 'its output remains constant if and only if the industry's output remains constant' (Wood, III, p. 387) and that 'If the representative firm's profits are above normal, then this is merely *another way of saying* that the industry's output is expanding .... Such a firm ... is simply a method of depicting *industrial* equilibrium in terms of the theory of the firm' (*ibid.*). It is, perhaps, not possible to present definitive arguments about the usefulness or otherwise of heuristic devices but if the representative firm was for Marshall 'only a useful piece of imagery' (Newman, p. 391), and if it opened the way to Pigou's 'equilibrium firm' and then to the 'typical firm' (or even 'each firm') of the textbook (*ibid.*), there is at least a strong case for saying that it would be better to expunge the representative firm from one's vocabulary and to refer only to the industry, while recalling that decisions are taken by individual producers.

Increasing returns, irreversibility and 'historical' supply curves

Even at the cost of some repetition, it may be useful here to draw together a number of issues relating to Marshall's treatment of cost and supply in the long period. We begin by quoting Newman (1960):

> Marshall's long-run supply curve ... does not give the amount forthcoming from the industry at any given price. It is a long-run cost curve which gives the 'average'(in some sense) cost per unit of the commodity after the industry has settled down to the equilibrium output for some time, so that all the appropriate economies have been obtained (Wood, III, p. 388).

It follows that the long-run supply curve is only an *ex post*, expository device which cannot be used to examine the path to equilibrium (*ibid.*).

Newman's interpretation is shared not only by Frisch (1950) but, for example, by Schumpeter and Shackle. Thus Schumpeter writes that Marshall's falling supply curves 'dealt with an irreversible process and are therefore not at all like the ordinary supply curves on which a firm can travel back and forth. They depict historical processes in a generalized form' (1954, p. 995, n. 9), while Shackle argues that Marshall's long period supply curve is only of use *ex post*, as a record (1972, p. 292). We see no reason to reject this interpretation. (Frisch (1950) seeks to emphasise the point that the long period unit cost curve of the 'representative firm' is not a conventional supply curve, by stressing the fact that while, for Marshall, the price-quantity combination will always lie on the demand curve, it need not lie on this unit cost curve (Wood, III, pp. 243−4). But while Frisch's conclusion is correct, when Marshall first introduces (non-temporary) equilibrium amount and price (*Principles*, p. 345), he immediately does so in a way which turns precisely on the assumption that 'amount-price' lie on the demand curve but not necessarily on the supply curve; and Marshall at this point is *not* restricting his discussion to long periods. The whole force of Marshall's discussion of how amount will tend to change when 'demand price' differs from 'supply price' presupposes the possibility that 'amount-price' need not be on the supply curve – whether the period be long or short. It is *only* when equilibrium is achieved that 'amount-price' will be on the supply curve.)

We turn now to Marshall's famous Appendix H, Section 3 discussion. He begins (pp. 807–8 and p. 808, n. 1) by noting that the demand price corresponding to a given amount may change, over time, 'if the normal production increases and afterwards again diminishes to its old amount' (p. 807). This is plausibly accounted for in terms of habit formation and 'wonted ways' (*ibid.*). Curiously, however, the marginal note on p. 807 reads, 'No great violence is involved in the assumption that the list of demand prices is rigid', a statement which receives no support whatever from the associated text! Having both explained the existence and denied the importance of time-irreversibilities in demand prices, Marshall turns to supply prices and it is worth noting that Marshall does not relate their time-irreversibility exclusively to increasing return industries. He writes:

The list of supply prices which had held for the forward movement [of supply over time] would not hold for the backward movement, but would have to be replaced by a lower schedule. This is true whether the production of the commodity obeys the law of diminishing or increasing return; but it is of special importance in the latter case, because the fact that the production does obey this law, proves that its increase leads to great improvements in organization (p. 808).

Even if we shall follow Marshall here in concentrating on the increasing return case, it should be clear enough that time-irreversibilities, in demand-price and in decreasing-return-industry supply-price, already suffice to raise sharp questions about just what role Marshall saw for long period demand and supply analysis. If, at each moment, amount is responding to the gap between current demand price and current supply price (not to mention expected prices), while each of those prices depends not only on current amount but also on the past time path of amount, the implied time paths of amount, demand price and supply price can be expected to be truly complex – and the existence, uniqueness and stability of equilibrium amount and price to be open to some question.

After some discussion of stability and uniqueness of equilibrium under increasing return, Marshall refers to 'The unsatisfactory nature of these results' (p. 809) and suggests that 'We should have made a great advance [in our scientific machinery] if we could represent the normal demand price and supply price as functions both of the amount normally produced and of the time at which that amount became normal' (*ibid.*). The associated footnote proposes a three-dimensional surface, with amount, price and time on the three axes. The time axis would represent the time allowed for the introduction of economies, while the amount-price cross section at a given time would represent the 'supply curve' achievable after that period of adjustment. It is to be noted that even this surface does not appear to allow the representation of time-irreversibilities, since the time axis cannot adequately represent the time-path of amount up to the time in question. Moreover, in this same footnote (pp. 809–10) Marshall traces out a curve on the surface by marking on each individual 'supply curve' the 'point corresponding to that amount which ... seems likely to be the normal amount for the year to which that curve is related' and says that this curve on the surface 'would be a fairly true long-period normal supply curve for a commodity obeying the law of increasing return'. We need not stay to quibble that 'fairly true' is vague or that this construction would seem to apply just as well – or badly – to a commodity obeying the law of decreasing return. More important is the fact that if, as Shackle interprets this footnote (1972, pp. 291–2), Marshall is using the assumed demand curves for various dates to pick out the points corresponding to normal amounts at those dates, then the resulting 'long-period normal supply curve', far from being defined independently of future demand curves, is in part defined *by* them. In this case, obviously enough, one could learn nothing whatever about the future evolution of amount and price by confronting such a 'supply curve' with the various demand curves. Such a 'supply curve' would be no more, and no less, than a putative historical record of the time paths of amount and price, with time itself recorded only implicitly. Unless one can interpret Marshall's 'picking out of normal amounts' in a manner which does not involve the demand curves – and we cannot see that one can – the conclusion that Marshall's long-period normal supply curve is simply a historical record would appear to be inescapable.

It may be of interest at this point to break our rule that only the eighth edition of the *Principles*, of 1920, is referred to. In his *Pure Theory of Foreign Trade* and *Pure Theory of Domestic Values*, written in the mid-1870s, Marshall was already discussing the analytical difficulties which can arise in the presence of economies of large-scale production and of the irreversibility of certain movements, especially in the case of increasing return. By 1904 Marshall was writing to Cunynghame, with reference to this work, that 'my case II, that of increasing returns, never seemed to me of much practical use; and in later years I warned people off it, on the ground that, if time was allowed for the development of economies of production on a large scale, time ought also to be allowed for the general increase of demand'. (See Whitaker, 1975, vol. 2, for reprints of Marshall's works referred to here; p. 112 for more on the letter in question; and the editorial apparatus generally for much helpful material.) Yet in 1920, some 45 years after the *Pure Theory* chapters were written, Marshall was still both grappling with increasing returns and with time-irreversibilities and expressing considerable dissatisfaction with the results obtained.

Whilst we are breaking our rule, we may also note that even Marshall's very early *Essay on Value*, probably written in 1870 or 1871 (Whitaker, vol. 1, pp. 119–22), contains many examples of falling supply curves, including one which – as Marshall is quite clearly aware – is a historical record of amount-price combinations and nothing more than that. (The example relates to the production of steel pens between 1820 and 1867; see *ibid.*, pp. 140-1.) Moreover, it is perfectly clear in this early *Essay* that when Marshall refers, as he does, to four 'different cases, the differences depending mainly on the length of the period of time to which the investigation applies' (p. 134), the periods of time he has in mind are periods of ordinary calendar time – and not 'artificial' periods of 'operational' time (see pp. 134 onwards). This naturally tends to support the interpretation of Marshall's periods, in the *Principles*, given above, Whitaker's apparent adherence to the 'operational' interpretation for the *Principles* (p. 123) notwithstanding. We must now return to our rule.

We conclude this section by considering how Marshall sought to reconcile the presence of increasing returns with the maintenance of competition; he did *not* seek to effect this reconciliation by resort to the later, Pigovian, emphasis on 'economies external to the firm but internal to the industry'. On the contrary, Marshall's own discussion involves a graphic account of economies internal to the individual enterprise. In Book IV, Chapter XI, Marshall follows a discussion of the advantages in production of a large firm by a discussion of the 'Limits to the Rapid Increase of a Business' (p. 285, page heading). After presenting a vivid account of the cumulative advantages experienced by an energetic businessman, and of the apparent conclusion that he may 'attain something like a limited monopoly; that is ... a monopoly limited by the consideration that a very high price would bring rival producers into the field' (p. 286), Marshall at once appeals to his concept of the 'life-cycle' of the firm to provide a check to any such conclusion. 'Long before' the limited monopoly is achieved, Marshall asserts, the business man's 'liking for energetic work' will decay (*ibid.*). And even if 'a successor almost as energetic as himself' is available, very rapid growth will be checked by the fact that, when there are strong 'internal' economies in production, there are usually also difficulties in marketing increased output (pp. 286–7).

In the summary chapter to Book IV, Marshall reiterates his graphic account of the cumulative advantages open to a business facing internal economies and of the consequent tendency to monopoly. He also repeats the 'life cycle' check to this process, now appealing to the analogy of 'the young trees of the forest' (p. 315). By contrast with the Chapter XI discussion, however, Marshall here pays careful attention to the possible role of joint-stock companies. 'And as with the growth of trees, so was it with the growth of businesses as a general rule before the great recent development of vast joint-stock companies, which often stagnate, but do not readily die. Now that rule is far from universal, but it still holds in many industries and trades' (p. 316). Marshall's (not entirely convincing) conclusion is that the great importance of internal economies need not much affect his conclusions concerning 'the broad results which the growth of wealth and population exert on the economies of production' (*ibid.*). Be that as it may, Marshall's reconciliation of increasing returns and competition certainly has little or nothing to do with the Pigovian device. Rather,

It is because the pace of growth, and the period of growth, for individual firms are both severely limited that a growing industry can yield the benefits of falling long-run costs without imposing the penalties of monopoly. In general, it is only when the whole industry is growing fast that the limits are significantly relaxed; and in these circumstances greater size need imply no increase in market share. That is Marshall's solution (Loasby, 1978; Wood, III, p. 595, cf. Ridolfi, 1970-72, pp. 134–7).

Concluding remarks

Marshall's attempt to wrestle with time in economic analysis was a serious and long-lasting one and if, in his efforts to promote both realism and rigour in economic theory, he did not always achieve their impossible reconciliation, we should perhaps respect his efforts more than we regret his incomplete achievement. (In part, that respect can take the form of recognising openly that Marshall's treatment of time is not fully captured in textbook 'Marshallian' theory.) Marshall's conception of industry equilibrium is inseparable from his account of the adjustment process and is not allowed to push the latter right into the background. Expectations are given due weight and Marshall's four periods − real time periods, not operationally defined constructs − provide a flexible framework for the organisation of one's thoughts. Marshall, of course, was anxious that his theoretical 'backbone' should not be *too* flexible, lest economics should become too 'invertebrate', merely an extended organicist metaphor. But he was perhaps over solicitous: a reasonably flexible, albeit 'half-rigorous' framework of thought, it could be argued, was a valuable bequest to economists wrestling with time. For that inheritance is easier to criticise than to improve upon.

Notes

1 Page references for articles will, in this chapter, often be given as here, to the reprinted version in Wood (ed.), 1982.
2 See Williams, 1986, Section IV, for a critical discussion of Marshall's claim for path-independence.

3

Walras

Such is the continuous market, which is perpetually tending towards equilibrium without ever actually attaining it, because the market has no other way of approaching equilibrium except by groping, and, before the goal is reached, it has to renew its efforts and start over again, all the basic data of the problem ... having changed in the meantime. Viewed in this way, the market is like a lake agitated by the wind, where the water is incessantly seeking its level without ever reaching it. But whereas there are days when the surface of a lake is almost smooth, there never is a day when the effective demand for products and services equals their effective supply and when the selling price of products equals the cost of the productive services used in making them (p. 380[1]).

It is universally acknowledged that Marshall was acutely aware of the complications posed by time. In contrast, economists are much less charitable to Léon Walras in this respect, often implying that he offered no more than an analysis of the 'timeless' allocation of a set of given resources. However, in his own way, he was as conscious as Marshall of the difficulties posed by time. A failure to appreciate this has frequently resulted in distorted portrayals of aspects of Walras' analysis.

The *Elements of Pure Economics or the Theory of Social Wealth* is a formidable work. The first edition was published in instalments from 1874 to 1877, the *édition définitive* being published in 1926. Stigler noted in 1941 the remarkable neglect of Walras' work by Anglo-Saxon economists. Despite William Jaffé's translation of the *Elements* into English in 1954, it is still true that Walras is often referred to but seldom read. This neglect is perhaps attributable to the fact that, as Jaffé has observed, the *Elements* is 'expressed in primitive mathematics and then paraphrased in crabbed prose' (p. 5). Certainly the obscurities in Walras' presentation explain why those economists who have made genuine efforts to understand the *Elements* often disagree over aspects of his analysis.

Walras does try to be systematic: 'Any order of phenomena, however complicated, may be studied scientifically provided the rule of proceeding from the simple to the complex is always observed' (p. 211). In accordance with this rule, he extends the scope of his analysis to develop successively a theory of exchange, a theory of production, a theory of capital formation and credit and a theory of circulation and money. Walras develops these theories from a *point de vue statique*. Thus, assuming that resources, techniques and tastes are invariant over a certain period of time, he examines the conditions under which prices would be stationary over that period. Walras seeks not only to characterise equilibrium but also to examine the 'spontaneous tendency' towards equilibrium under free competition. A difficulty which confronts him is that of reconciling his dynamic analysis of the process of *tâtonnement* with his *point de vue statique*. As Walras extends the scope of his analysis to incorporate production, capital formation and money, he is inevitably confronted by increasingly awkward temporal complications. He must at least be given credit for being aware of these complications. How compelling are his attempts to circumvent them is another matter.

Having completed his static analysis of general equilibrium under a hypothetical regime of perfect competition, Walras examines 'the conditions and consequences of economic progress'. The neglect of this part of the *Elements* is quite remarkable. From Lesson 35, in which Walras insists that actual economies are never in equilibrium, it is evident that his ultimate purpose is to illuminate the behaviour of an economy moving through time where 'the continuous market ... is perpetually tending towards equilibrium without ever attaining it, because the market has no other way of approaching equilibrium except by groping, and, before the goal is reached, it has to renew its efforts and start over again, all the basic data of the problem ... having changed in the meantime' (p. 380). An appreciation of Walras' vision of the continuous market is essential for seeing his static general equilibrium analysis in proper perspective. In Lesson 36, which involves an entirely different temporal perspective, Walras considers the systematic implications of 'economic progress'. As we will see, contrary to the impression recently conveyed by Jaffé, Walras regards this analysis as an integral part of his pure theory.

When examining the *Elements*, the easiest option for authors is to describe first the theory of exchange, then the theory of production, and so on. We resist the temptation to do so, because one of our principal objectives is to understand Walras' complete model of general equilibrium. Since we are interested in Walras' treatment of time, some important aspects of his analysis inevitably receive scant attention. We focus primarily on the *édition définitive* which, for the purposes of this chapter, is taken to constitute the definitive formulation of Walras' theory. We can make only parenthetical references to variations between editions and, in particular, to the recent claim by Walker that changes which Walras introduced into his analysis in 1900 constituted a regression which 'revealed the weakening of his creative powers' (1987, p. 769).

Walras' economy

In Lesson 18, Walras identifies the elements involved in the process of economic production by imagining that process to be 'momentarily arrested' (p. 218). He distinguishes landed capital, personal capital and capital goods proper yielding consumers' services, that is, services which are used in their original form for consumption; landed capital, personal capital and capital goods proper yielding productive services, that is, services which are transformed by agriculture, industry or commerce into products; new capital goods being held by producers for subsequent sale; stocks of consumers' goods being held by consumers for subsequent use; stocks of raw materials being held by producers for their own subsequent use; stocks of new consumers' goods and raw materials being held by producers for subsequent sale; and finally, with respect to money, the cash holdings of consumers, the cash holdings of producers and money savings.

Walras insists that 'the key to the whole of pure economics' (p. 40) is the distinction between capital and income:

I define *fixed capital*, i.e. *capital* in general, just as my father did in his *Theorie de la richesse sociale* (1849), as all durable goods, all forms of social wealth which are not used up at all or are used up only after a lapse of time, i.e. every utility limited in quantity which outlasts its first use, or which, in a word, can be used more than once, like a house or a piece of furniture. And I mean by *circulating capital* or *income* all non-durable goods, all forms of social wealth which are used up immediately, i.e. every scarce thing which does not outlast its first use, or which, in short, can be used only once, like bread or meat. Income comprises not only articles of private consumption but also the raw materials of agriculture and industry, like seeds, textile fibres, etc. The durability of which we speak in this context is not material durability, but durability in use or economic durability. Though textile fibres still continue to exist materially in the cloth, they cease to have existence as raw materials and cannot be used again as such once the cloth has been made. On the other hand, buildings and machines are items of capital, not of income (p. 212).

Fixed capital comprises landed capital and personal capital as well as capital goods proper. Walras emphasises the importance of differentiating between the capital goods themselves and the services which they yield. He insists that these services must be regarded as income, along with consumption goods and raw materials. He further argues that stocks of consumer goods and raw materials should be regarded not as 'capital' but as 'aggregates of income accumulated in advance for eventual consumption' (p. 213).

The essence of Walras' theory of circulation is to suppose that stocks of circulating capital goods, 'in the larders and cupboards of consumers and in the storerooms and salesrooms of producers', render *services d'approvisionnement,* translated by Jaffé as 'services of availability', these stocks rendering such services 'while being held for the eventual performance of their single act of *use service'* (p. 214). Money also provides its holder with a service of availability. Walras assigns money to a separate category, distinct from capital and income, because it plays a mixed role: 'From the social point of view, money is capital, since it is used in society more than once for making payments; from the individual point of view, money is income, for no individual can use it more than once, since he no longer has it after making a payment' (p. 219).

The economic agents, defined by their roles, comprise landowners, workers, capitalists and entrepreneurs. Although Walras acknowledges that, in reality, an individual often performs more than one role, he insists on the scientific importance of differentiating between roles, particularly between that of capitalist and that of entrepreneur. Landowners supply land services in return for rent; workers supply labour services in return for wages; and capitalists supply capital services and lend money in return for interest charges. Landowners, workers and capitalists demand products and services for consumption. They hold stocks of commodities and money for their services of availability, incurring the opportunity costs of doing so because of the lack of synchronisation inherent in the transactions habits of the economy. They provide the demands for new capital goods; using savings to acquire new capital goods enables individuals to receive the additional net incomes which will (in the future) derive from their ownership. Landowners, workers and capitalists base their effective offers and effective demands on utility maximisation. They always seek to sell for the maximum possible prices and to buy at the lowest possible prices.

Walras explains the role of the entrepreneur:

The entrepreneur is ... a person (natural or corporate) who buys raw materials from other entrepreneurs, then leases land from land-owners on payment of a rent, hires the personal faculties of workers on payment of wages, borrows capital from capitalists on payment of interest charges and, finally, having applied certain productive services to the raw materials, sells the resulting product on his own account .... Whenever entrepreneurs, of whatever category, sell their products or merchandise at a price higher than the cost of the raw materials, rent, wages and interest charges, they make a profit; and whenever they sell their products or merchandise at a lower price, they incur a loss. This is the alternative that the entrepreneur characteristically faces in the performance of his function (p. 227).

All productive services are freely mobile. Since technology is characterised by fixed input-output coefficients, an entrepreneur's output determines uniquely his needs for raw materials and for the services of fixed capital. Moreover, given transactions habits and prices, his output determines his need for the services of availability of circulating capital goods and money. For example, an entrepreneur may need to borrow money, that is, to acquire the services of availability of money, because he has to pay for productive services before he sells the products which those services produce. Entrepreneurs, motivated by the pursuit of profit and the avoidance of loss, seek to acquire productive services at the lowest possible prices and to sell their products at the highest possible prices. Furthermore, they expand the output of a commodity if its selling price exceeds its cost of production and contract output if its selling price is less than its cost of production.

Walras develops his analysis of general equilibrium for a hypothetical regime of perfect competition: 'we shall suppose that the market is perfectly competitive, just as in pure mechanics we suppose, to start with, that machines are perfectly frictionless' (p. 84). He asks: 'What physicist would deliberately pick cloudy weather for astronomical observations instead of taking advantage of a cloudless night?' (p. 86). His theory assumes *perfectly organised* competitive markets, the best organised markets being 'those in which purchases and sales are made by auction, through the instrumentality of stockbrokers, commercial brokers or criers acting as agents who centralise transactions in such a way that the terms of every exchange are openly announced and an opportunity is given to sellers to lower their prices and to buyers to raise their bids' (p. 84). Walras' conception of a perfectly organised market is not entirely pellucid. He seems to suppose sometimes that sellers, or agents acting on their behalf, announce prices at which they would be prepared to trade, buyers responding with quantities; sometimes that buyers, or agents acting on their behalf, announce prices at which they would be prepared to trade, sellers responding with quantities; and sometimes that some distinct third party announces prices to which both sellers and buyers respond. In any event, what is a characteristic of Walras' perfectly organised market is that no transactions are concluded until a price is located at which effective demand is equal to effective offer for the commodity concerned. Walras takes for granted that nobody – whether prospective trader or crier – has complete information on market schedules; there is no possibility of anyone 'calculating' equilibrium prices. The only way the market can establish equilibrium prices is by a process of trial and error, that is, by a process of *tâtonnement*. Competition involves prospective buyers outbidding each other and prospective sellers underbidding each other, so that price rises if there is excess demand and falls if there is excess supply. Walras assumes that prices are cried using some commodity as *numéraire*. We may assume that this *numéraire* is the commodity which is used as money, although, for Walras, this need not be so.

Temporal framework

Walras enters his economy at a particular point in time, the economy's resources, the pattern of their ownership, the agents' tastes and the known techniques of production being given. He insists repeatedly that the data may be any data whatsoever. On this basis, he seeks to analyse the behaviour of the economy over a certain period of time, which we will refer to as his 'unit time period'. Although he makes parenthetical allusions to calendar periods, he does not explicitly discuss the calendar duration of this time period. A failure to understand the time dimensions of Walras' variables has been the source of confusion, with, in particular, Friedman (1955) incorrectly accusing

Walras of incoherence. Effective demands and effective offers are amounts, that is, accumulated flows, and not average or instantaneous flow-rates. If the duration of the unit time period is, say, a week, the price of a service is the price paid for the use of the service for one week. The net income from one unit of a capital good equals the price of its service minus a depreciation charge and minus an insurance premium. The *rate* of net income from the ownership of a capital good, defined as the net income divided by the price of the capital good itself, is a pure number. If the unit time period is one week, it is a weekly rate; it would be unaffected if we were to refer to a week as seven days.[2]

Walras' approach is to analyse the economy over the unit time period from a *point de vue statique*. Accordingly he assumes explicitly not simply that resources, tastes and technology are exogenous at the beginning of the unit time period but also that they are invariant over that period. On this basis, he seeks to analyse the conditions under which prices would be stationary over that period.

Walras' economy is *not* stationary in a thorough-going sense. On the contrary, he explicitly confines his analysis to a progressive economy, that is, to an economy in which (loosely speaking) the production of new capital goods exceeds the production needed to replace those which are used up during the period. His analysis is 'static' in the sense that he is concerned with the conditions under which the economy would be stationary *over the unit time period:* 'Although the economy is becoming *progressive,* it remains *static* because of the fact that the new capital goods play no part in the economy until later in a period subsequent to the one under consideration' (p. 283). The assumption that both fixed and circulating capital goods produced during the period are not used until some subsequent period is required to maintain his *point de vue statique:* it is necessary to ensure that the services available for use during the period are strictly given.

Walras assumes that, at the outset of the period under consideration, all the circulating capital goods and money are owned by landowners, workers and capitalists. Entrepreneurs must borrow from capitalists the circulating capital goods and money they need. Although Walras is not explicit about this, this must apply to stocks of final products ready for sale to consumers. Although this appears artificial, it is consistent with his conception of roles. Indeed, the assumption is considerably less artificial if it is recognised that a producer, in his role of capitalist, may initially own stocks of final products which he would then loan to himself as entrepreneur. This may even explain why Walras, having seldom used the term 'producer' in the previous three hundred pages, does use it frequently in explaining his theory of circulation and money, since the term is consistent with an individual combining more than one role.[3]

It is of paramount importance to appreciate that Walras takes for granted that production takes time. As we will see, this explains why he conceives of a phase of preliminary *tâtonnement* involving 'tickets'. According to Walras:

Thanks to our hypothetical use of *tickets*, we are able to distinguish the following three phases quite clearly, particularly if we view them as successive: (1) the phase of *preliminary gropings* towards the establishment of equilibrium in principle; (2) the *static* phase in which equilibrium is effectively established *ab ovo* as regards the quantity of productive services and products made available during the period considered, under the stipulated conditions, and without any changes in the data of the problem; (3) a *dynamic* phase in which equilibrium is constantly being disturbed by changes in the data and is constantly being re-established. The *new capital goods,* both *fixed* and *circulating,* which are made available during the second phase ..., are not put to use until the third phase. This ... constitutes the first change in the data of our problem (p. 319).

Walras is perfectly explicit that, by differentiating between these phases, he is indulging in a 'fiction'. Nevertheless, for Walras, such a fiction is necessary to permit a formal analysis of the various processes of adjustment and of the conditions for equilibrium. The reality of the continuous market — which, we repeat, is perpetually tending towards equilibrium without ever achieving it — would otherwise be analytically intractable.

General equilibrium

For Walras, general equilibrium, involving 'stationary current prices', is *inseparable* from his conceptions of the various processes of adjustment: it is a state of rest for those processes. Whereas certain of Walras' equilibrium conditions are defined implicitly by our descriptions of the operation of markets and of the behaviour of entrepreneurs, certain other conditions will require rather more elucidation.

General equilibrium requires 'equilibrium in exchange'. Effective demand must equal effective offer for each of the services of fixed capital and for each of the services of availability of circulating capital and of money. Effective demand must equal effective supply for each product. Perfectly organised markets are such that actual transactions are not effected until such prices are located. But even for competitive markets which are not perfectly organised, these conditions would be required for equilibrium, since they are implied by his conception of competitive trading processes.

General equilibrium also requires 'equilibrium in production', that is, the selling price of each product – whether consumer good, raw material or new capital good – must be equal to its average cost of production: *les entrepreneurs ne font ni bénéfice ni perte*. That this is a requirement for equilibrium is implied by the behaviour of entrepreneurs, who expand the output of a commodity if its selling price exceeds its cost of production and contract output if its selling price is less than its cost of production. The equilibrium condition that entrepreneurs make neither profit nor loss has given rise to misgivings. How are entrepreneurs able to survive to undertake their role if they receive no reward for doing so? Anticipating this question, Walras states: 'They make their living not as entrepreneurs, but as landowners, labourers or capitalists in their own or other businesses.' Invoking the notion of opportunity costs, he continues:

In my opinion, rational bookkeeping requires that an entrepreneur who owns the land which he works or occupies, who participates in the management of his firm and who has his own funds invested in the business, ought to charge to business expense and credit to his own account rent, wages and interest charges calculated according to the going market prices of productive services. In this way he earns his living without necessarily making any profits or suffering any losses as an entrepreneur (pp. 225–6).[4]

General equilibrium also requires 'equilibrium in capital formation and in circulation'. We have already seen that the selling price of each new capital good must equal its cost of production. In addition, equilibrium requires that there be a *uniform* rate of net income on the ownership of *all* capital goods – landed capital, personal capital, old and new fixed capital goods proper and circulating capital – and on the ownership of money. For example, if p_x represents the price of a commodity and r_x represents the price of its service of availability then, in equilibrium,

$$r_x \,/\, p_x = i$$

where i is the uniform rate of net income. In particular, if money itself is the *numéraire*, so that its price is one, the price of its service of availability, that is, the rate of interest which entrepreneurs pay capitalists for borrowing money for the duration of the unit time period, is equal to the uniform rate of net income.

The notion of a uniform rate of net income is central to Walras' analysis of capital formation and of circulation. It is significant that this is the only equilibrium condition in the *Elements* which is not defined by some explicit adjustment process: in his analysis of the process of *tâtonnement*, Walras assumes *ab initio* that there is a uniform rate of net income. Although it is implicit that, if a particular capital good were yielding a lower rate of net income than some other capital good, owners of the former would profit by selling their holdings and using the proceeds to acquire titles to the latter, the explicit justification Walras offers for a uniform rate of net income is an appeal to the 'fact of experience' that, on the stock exchange, titles to property in capital goods are exchanged at prices proportional to their net incomes, at least under 'normal and ideal conditions' (see pp. 46 and 268). Invoking, *ab initio*, uniformity in the rates of net income simplifies the analysis considerably, since it enables Walras to conceive of an imaginary commodity (E) which consists of 'perpetual net income'. The holder of a unit of (E) is entitled to receive one unit of the *numéraire* per period, the price of (E) being equal to the reciprocal of the rate of perpetual net income. The introduction of this imaginary commodity, described by Schumpeter as 'a profound move on the analytical chessboard' (1954, p. 1018), enables Walras to reduce all the heterogeneous capital goods – including landed and personal capital – to a homogeneous income-yielding entity, so that the rate of perpetual net income represents the uniform rate of net income on capital goods. He then uses (E) to determine the total supply of gross saving as a function, *inter alia*, of the rate of net income.

The final requirement for equilibrium is that aggregate desired gross saving – or, equivalently, the aggregate value of the demands for new fixed and circulating capital goods – must equal the aggregate value of the outputs of new fixed and circulating capital goods. That this is a requirement for equilibrium is implied by Walras' conception of competition on the stock exchange, since, if there is excess demand for new capital goods, the price of (E) rises implying a fall in the rate of net income, and vice versa. The key to Walras' theory of capital formation is that the rate of net income, and thereby the rate of interest, is determined in the market for new capital goods. The prices of landed capital, personal capital and old physical capital goods proper adjust so that they yield the same rate of net income. Thus Walras claims: 'Once we have the rate of income, we can obtain not only the price of newly manufactured fixed capital goods, but also the price of old fixed capital goods (viz. land, personal faculties, and already existing capital goods proper) by dividing the prices of their services (i.e. rent, wages, and interest) by the rate of income' (p. 42). The prices of personal faculties are 'virtual' prices, since there are only markets for the services of workers, not for workers themselves.

We have seen that Walras explicitly confines his analysis to a progressive economy. A question which has caused controversy is whether or not his theory is applicable to an economy which is stationary in a thorough-going sense. Whereas initially Wicksell (1893) argued that it is not, Barone countered that it is. To understand the issues involved, first note that Walras insists that his theory depends on there being transactions in capital goods. Note, further, that, although Walras' presentation is somewhat convoluted on this, the assumption that the economy is progressive is sufficient but not necessary for there to be transactions in capital goods, since if the economy were to be stationary, production of, and transactions in, new capital goods would still be necessary to replace those capital goods used up in the process of production. Since gross saving would still be positive, the theory does accommodate a stationary economy. This is the substance of Barone's argument. Wicksell subsequently withdrew his objection.

Walras is emphatic that actual economies are never in equilibrium. Thus, having defined equilibrium for his production economy, he immediately states: 'It never happens in the real world that the selling price of any given product is absolutely equal to the cost of the productive services that enter into that product, or that the effective demand and supply of services or products are absolutely equal' (p. 224). Taken literally, this is a very strong statement, asserting not simply that it never happens that all the equilibrium conditions are satisfied simultaneously but also that it never happens that any one of the conditions is satisfied precisely.[5] Nevertheless Walras believes that the notion of general equilibrium is invaluable. He continues: 'Yet equilibrium is the normal state, in the sense that it is the state towards which things spontaneously tend under a regime of free competition in exchange and in production' (p. 224).

Tâtonnement

The spontaneous tendency towards equilibrium involves a process of *tâtonnement*. Whereas Walras regards the exposition of the equilibrium conditions as his 'static theory', he regards his analysis of the process of *tâtonnement* as his 'dynamic theory'. He consistently differentiates between, on the one hand, the 'mathematical or theoretical solution' provided by his system of equations and, on the other, the 'practical solution' provided in the market by the mechanism of free competition. He insists that these are solutions to the same problem. For example, for his exchange economy, having stated that prices are 'determined mathematically' by his system of equations, he continues: 'Now there remains only to show – and this is the essential point – that the problem of exchange for which we have just given a theoretical solution is the selfsame problem that is solved empirically on the market by the mechanism of free competition' (pp. 162–3). Similarly, at the final stage in the development of his complete general equilibrium model, he states: 'We shall describe equilibrium in principle, as before, first theoretically and mathematically, and then practically as it manifests itself in the market' (p. 318).

Although Walras' references to alternative solutions to the 'selfsame problem' do not, by themselves, establish conclusively that he is seeking to demonstrate that the process of *tâtonnement* converges on precisely those prices which solve his mathematical equations, rather than simply on an equilibrium set of prices, this *is* what Walras has in mind. He suggests (incorrectly) that, for an economy with more than two commodities, there cannot be multiple equilibria, that is, there cannot be more than one set of equilibrium prices for his mathematical equations. Moreover, as we will see, given his conception of perfectly organised markets, invoking a phase of preliminary *tâtonnement* involving 'tickets' eliminates the complication of path-dependence. Conceiving of such a phase is clearly artificial. Walras, himself, describes it as a 'fiction'. Nevertheless he evidently believes that his analysis does provide insights into *real* adjustment processes, namely, the price-adjustment process, whereby prices respond to excess demands and excess supplies, and the quantity-adjustment process, whereby producers expand or contract outputs in response to differences between product prices and their average costs of production.

As we will see, Walras imposes highly artificial sequences on his *tâtonnement* processes 'for purposes of demonstration'. However, there is a crucial temporal sequence implicit in his conception of the processes of adjustment, one which does have a counterpart in reality, namely, that entrepreneurs acquire productive services *before* they sell the products which those services produce. He appreciates that this gives rise to a complication: 'In production, productive services are transformed into products. After certain prices for services have been cried and certain quantities of products have been manufactured, if these prices and quantities are not the equilibrium prices and quantities, it will be necessary not only to cry new prices but also to manufacture revised quantities of products' (p. 242). To understand fully the complication, it is necessary to contrast carefully an exchange economy with a production economy. Suppose that, in an *exchange* economy, a set of disequilibrium prices is called out. With perfectly organised markets, it will become apparent more or less 'immediately' from the responses of prospective traders that this is not an equilibrium set of prices, the disequilibrium manifesting itself in excess demand or excess supply for some commodity. As we have seen, Walras' conception of perfectly organised markets rules out transactions at such prices. Suppose now that, in a *production* economy, a disequilibrium set of prices is called out. It will *not* necessarily be apparent 'immediately' that this is a disequilibrium set of prices – it is possible that, at these prices, effective demand and effective offer are equal for each productive service, that effective demand and effective supply are equal for each product but that, for some product, the selling price does not equal the cost of its production. Walras' conception of perfectly organised markets does not rule out transactions at those prices since the disequilibrium will not manifest itself in terms of excess demand or excess supply: given the quantities of products currently being offered for sale by producers, these prices will clear the markets. Transactions will thus take place and entrepreneurs will use the productive services they acquire to produce quantities which are not equilibrium ones.

It is in order to circumvent this complication that Walras explicitly conceives of a phase of preliminary *tâtonnement* during which equilibrium is established 'in principle', this phase involving the use of tickets:

In order to work out as rigorous a description of the process of groping in production as we did in exchange ... we have only to imagine, on the one hand, that entrepreneurs use *tickets* to represent the successive quantities of *products* which are first determined at random and then increased or decreased according as there is an excess of selling price over cost of production or vice versa, until selling price and cost are equal; and, on the other hand, that landowners, workers and capitalists also use *tickets* to represent the successive quantities of *services* at prices first cried at random and then raised or lowered according as there is an excess of demand over offer or vice versa, until the two become equal (p. 242).

Once the phase of preliminary *tâtonnement* has been concluded, the economy enters the stationary phase in which equilibrium 'will be established *effectively* through the reciprocal exchange between services employed and products manufactured *within a given period of time* during which *no change in the data is allowed*' (p. 242). The rationale for introducing tickets in the fourth edition of the *Elements* is that it enables Walras to conceive of such a stationary phase, one which corresponds to the 'theoretical solution' provided by his mathematical equations.

Walras' desire to conceive of such a stationary phase also explains why, in his introduction to the process of *tâtonnement* for an economy with production, he states that he is 'ignoring the time element at this point'. Specifically, having introduced the device of tickets to circumvent the complication of the production of disequilibrium quantities, he continues:

There is still another complication. Once the equilibrium has been established in principle, exchange can take place immediately. Production, however, requires a certain lapse of time. We shall resolve the second difficulty purely and simply by ignoring the time element at this point. And later on, in Part VI, we shall bring in *circulating capital* and *money* and thereby make it possible for productive services to be transformed into products instantaneously, provided that the consumers pay the interest charges on the capital required for this sort of transformation (p. 242).

The rationale for 'ignoring the time element at this point' is that, in the absence of circulating capital, his conception of a phase over which prices are stationary is undermined if production takes time. Thus, suppose that the period of time under consideration is one month and that, for prices to be stationary, the daily supply of each product to the market would have to be constant over that month. If the production period for some commodity is one week, it would not, in general, be possible to achieve the new equilibrium daily supply on, say, the first day of the month. It is this complication which he is ignoring – and only until he introduces circulating capital into his analysis.

Incorporating capital formation into the model entails the same two complications. The first complication – the problem of the production of disequilibrium quantities – is more acute in the case of capital goods. Whereas the production of disequilibrium quantities of many consumer goods could be 'reversed' – in that bread could be eaten – the production of an above-equilibrium quantity of some type of machine could not be reversed so easily. This complication is again circumvented by the fiction of tickets. As to the second complication, Walras states: 'We shall resolve the further difficulty apropos of the lapse of time required in the production of new capital goods in the same way that we resolved it in the case of final products, by assuming production to be instantaneous' (p. 282). This assumption is scarcely compatible with the assumption that newly-produced capital goods do not provide services until after the period under consideration. However, whereas the latter is a feature of his complete model, the assumption of 'instantaneous production' is provisional.

Walras' general equilibrium model is completed by the introduction of circulating capital goods and money. It is crucial to appreciate that, in the complete general equilibrium model, production *does* take time. Thus Walras is able to conceive of a stationary phase even though production takes time: given that there are stocks of circulating capital goods at the beginning of the period, the delivery of products can begin immediately. Landowners, capitalists and workers are thereby able to 'transform' their productive services into products immediately, provided that they are prepared to incur the interest costs involved (p. 242). Thus landowners, capitalists and workers, using borrowed funds, can purchase consumer goods and services *before* they receive payments for their productive services.

Whereas there is no doubt that, in the complete model, production does take time, we are certainly not prepared to be dogmatic on one matter. We have seen that Walras assumes that entrepreneurs borrow all the circulating capital goods which they need during the stationary phase; and that newly-produced circulating capital goods are not 'put to use' until after the stationary phase. We interpret these assumptions as meaning that the only goods actually sold to consumers during the stationary phase are from stocks which are inherited from previous periods and which entrepreneurs 'borrow' from capitalists in order to sell them; and that consumer goods produced during the stationary phase are 'sold' to capitalists but that they cannot render services of availability by being put on display – and, therefore, cannot be sold to consumers – until subsequent periods. This interpretation would seem to be consistent with Walras' claim that, if the economy were 'liquidated' at the end of the stationary phase, 'the *old capital goods, both fixed and circulating*, would be returned *in kind* by the entrepreneurs to the capitalists, and the circulating capital goods would be returned in the form of *similar* goods' (p. 319). If this interpretation is correct, this suggests that, with the incorporation of circulating capital and money, the time period needs to be thought of as 'short'. This is consistent with Walras' claim that the theory of circulation and money brings us 'as close as possible to the *dynamic* point of view' (p. 316) and with his reference to short-term loans. It is also consistent with the fact that the Lesson which immediately follows the presentation of this theory is concerned with the 'continuous market'. As we shall see, circulating capital plays a prominent role in his description of such a market.

That Walras' approach to demonstrating convergence is heuristic rather than rigorous is easily seen by considering his exchange economy. Starting from a random set of prices with commodity (A) as *numéraire*, Walras supposes that the price of (B) adjusts to equate effective demand and effective offer for (B); that the price of (C) is then adjusted to equate the effective demand and effective offer for (C); and so on. He claims:

It is quite true that in determining the price of (C), we may destroy the equilibrium with respect to (B), that in determining the price of (D), we may destroy the equilibrium both with respect to (B) and with respect to (C), and so forth. But since the determination of the prices of (C), (D) ... will, on the whole, entail certain compensating effects on the relationship between the demand and offer of (B), in all probability equilibrium will be approximated more and more closely at each successive step in the groping process (p. 470).

Thus the 'demonstration' amounts to an assertion that *in all probability* equilibrium will be approximated more and more closely at each step in the process. Note also how he imposes an artificial sequence on the process. The sequence which he invokes for his *tâtonnement* for a production economy is equally contrived. Thus, in his exposition in Appendix I, Walras *initially* assumes that the prices of services are fixed at random. On this basis, he works through the process whereby product prices and costs are brought into equality. Starting from random initial quantities of products, this is achieved through quantity adjustments by producers with product prices adjusting to market clearing levels. Walras *then* considers adjustments in the prices of services, each adjustment involving 'successive adaptations' in the quantities and prices of products. Granted that his analysis is obscure, there is no justification whatsoever for interpreting Walras as purporting to demonstrate *the* path towards equilibrium or as believing that markets come into equilibrium in some preassigned order. Indeed, Walras states explicitly that he is employing an expository device: 'We must remember that all these operations take place simultaneously, although, for purposes of demonstration, we had to imagine them as taking place successively' (p. 477).

Although it might seem that in various ways – e.g. by invoking tickets, by assuming constant returns to scale – Walras tries to make matters as easy as possible for himself, this is not always so. Thus he seeks to show convergence *ab ovo*, that is, he insists that the data of the problem may be any data whatsoever. Moreover, he always commences his *tâtonnement* by postulating completely random initial prices, the brokers or criers who centralise transactions having no prior information whatsoever regarding demand and supply schedules. Indeed, since the informational aspects of Walras' analysis have so often been ignored or distorted, it is worth noting parenthetically that, when he leaves his regime of perfect competition, he does not even assume that an entrepreneur with monopoly power 'knows' the demand curve for his product: the entrepreneur determines the profit maximising price by trial-and-error, by 'the simplest kind of groping' (p. 437). It is also worth noting that the assumption of constant returns to scale is a mixed blessing. Thus, whereas he can and does suppose that landowners, workers and capitalists maximise utility at any given set of prices, he cannot suppose that entrepreneurs maximise profits at any given set of prices: for an entrepreneur producing a single commodity, the optimal supply might be zero,

undefined or infinite. Arrow and Hurwicz suggest that Walras'
quantity-adjustment rule is 'an inevitable consequence of his assumption of constant returns to scale' (1977, p. 44). It may, of course, be
that Walras regards lagged adjustment as 'more realistic' than
instantaneous profit maximisation: he may not have postulated the
latter even if he had not assumed constant returns to scale. Be that
as it may, as Arrow and Hurwicz observe: 'Despite the necessary
character of lagged adjustment, Walras' successors were usually not
so careful' (1977, p. 44).

Walras' *tâtonnement* as others see it

Misrepresentations of Walras' theory of *tâtonnement* are legion and
range from the scarcely credible to the understandable. In the former
category is the claim that his *tâtonnement* is designed to determine
the path towards equilibrium. Thus according to Edgeworth:

What the author professes to demonstrate is the course which the higgling
of the market takes – the path, as it were, by which the economic system
works down to equilibrium. Now, as Jevons points out, the equations of
exchange are of a statical, not a dynamical, character. They define a position
of equilibrium, but they afford no information as to the path by which that
point is reached. Professor Walras's laboured lessons indicate *a* way, not *the*
way, of descent to equilibrium (1889, p. 435).

Although Edgeworth was responding to the second edition, the myth
has persisted. Thus, both Stigler (1941, p. 245) and Hutchison (1953,
p. 206) cite Edgeworth's criticism, apparently agreeing with it.
Hutchison is particularly dismissive, describing Walras' analysis of
tâtonnement as a 'brief dynamic fantasia' (brief, it certainly is not!).
However, as we have seen, Walras is quite explicit that the processes
of adjustment take place simultaneously and that he invokes an
artificial sequence purely 'for purposes of demonstration'.

   A common source of confusion has been the belief that Walras'
conception of markets admits transactions at disequilibrium prices.
Patinkin (1965) accused Walras of failing to recognise that such
transactions would, in general, create income effects and that these
would, in turn, imply path-dependence. In 1967, Jaffé advanced the
claim (which he retracted in 1981) that, although Walras allows for
exchanges at disequilibrium prices in his preliminary description of
the operation of markets, he overlooks this completely in his analytical

discussion of *tâtonnement*. The interpretation of Newman (1965) was somewhat different. Although he also claimed that Walras allows for trading at false prices, he maintained that Walras is aware of income effects but that he does not take their implications into account because he believes that the process of convergence is very rapid so that, in Newman's words, 'the vast bulk of transactions therefore occurs at "true" prices' (1965, p. 102).

The belief that Walras' conception of perfectly competitive markets allows for transactions at false prices is mistaken. This belief depends crucially on the interpretation of a single paragraph in the *Elements* – paragraph 42 – in which Walras discusses the operation of the market for *rentes*, the French equivalent of consols. But this discussion is ambiguous. Walras states that, if at the price initially cried out effective demand is not equal to effective offer, then 'trading' should come to a halt. Patinkin and Newman presumably interpreted the claim that 'trading' should stop as implying that actual exchanges must have been taking place. However, Walras, we suggest, is using the term 'trading' to refer simply to the process whereby, at the cried price, prospective traders search for and communicate with each other. Thus, in the preceding paragraph, Walras states that, in a perfectly organised market, 'an opportunity is given to sellers to lower their prices and to buyers to raise their bids' (p. 84). Furthermore, Walras' summary of his theory in the preface to the fourth edition of the *Elements* confirms that only when the equilibrium prices have been established does exchange 'effectively take place'. Accepting that Walras' conception of a perfectly organised market rules out transactions at disequilibrium prices means that all the convoluted attempts to explain his alleged failure to realise that such transactions would result in income effects are misconceived.[6]

To say that Walras' analysis of *tâtonnement* in production has been widely misunderstood would be an understatement. For example, Schumpeter (1954) and Hutchison (1953) purported to describe this process without even mentioning his quantity-adjustment rule.[7] The discussions by Patinkin (1965) and by Jaffé (1967) of Walras' rationale for introducing tickets in his production economy were marred by their belief that Walras' conception of perfect markets allows for transactions at disequilibrium prices. Patinkin (not surprisingly) was unable to find any meaningful rationale for introducing tickets in a production economy but not in an exchange economy. Jaffé's argument was rather odd: he claimed that Walras,

having allegedly completely overlooked the distributional implications
of transactions at disequilibrium prices in his exchange economy,
introduces tickets in his production economy to circumvent the
problem that the production of false quantities might have distributional effects and thereby result in path-dependence. As we have
seen, the introduction of tickets supplements the conception of
perfectly organised markets, thereby circumventing the problem of
path-dependence in an economy with production.

One of the more unfortunate misunderstandings is the claim by
Jaffé (1980, p. 540) – echoed by Walsh and Gram (1980, p. 160) –
that Walras' general equilibrium system assumes that production is
'instantaneous'. This claim is but one aspect of Jaffé's recent attempts
to portray Walras' general equilibrium analysis as essentially
'timeless'. In 'Another look at Léon Walras's theory of *tâtonnement*',
Jaffé has argued that the underlying purpose of the theory is 'to
portray an empirical possibility or feasible desideratum rather than
an empirical fact' (1981, p. 315). He has claimed that Walras' analysis
of *tâtonnement*, 'being consciously and deliberately confined within
a strictly statical framework, described no path at all' (1981, p. 327).
According to Jaffé, rather than depicting 'an actual process that
would require time to work itself out', Walras presents only 'a theory
of virtually timeless, simultaneous and mechanical adjustment
operation' (1981, pp. 327 and 321). This portrayal is a distortion of
what Walras is seeking to achieve. As Walker (1987) has shown,
Walras regards his theory of *tâtonnement* as 'dynamic', in contrast
to the 'static' exposition of the equilibrium conditions. Moreover,
as we have seen, whereas Walras does not purport to describe *the* path
to equilibrium, he is seeking to depict *a* path to equilibrium. The
artificiality of the sequences which Walras imposes on his *tâtonnement* processes has perhaps blinded Jaffé from recognising that the
quantity-adjustment process necessarily implies some form of
temporal order. As we have seen, the assumption of constant returns
to scale precludes 'instantaneous profit maximisation'. It is misleading
to invoke Walras' claim that, in reality, the processes of adjustment
operate simultaneously to justify the claim that there is no temporal
order: the fact that, at any point in time, both prices and quantities
may be adjusting is perfectly compatible with there being lags in the
adjustments of quantities. This applies even with the fiction of tickets.

Walker has recently distinguished between two theories of *tâtonnement*, namely, the 'disequilibrium-production model' of the first

three editions of the *Elements* and the 'pledges model' of the fourth
and definitive editions. Walker has claimed that the disequilibrium-
production model, 'depending as it does on the pricing and use of
disequilibrium quantities of labor and land and on the pricing,
production, and use of disequilibrium quantities of both capital and
consumer goods and services, is an attempt to model real dynamic
phenomena', but that, in contrast, the aim of the pledges model 'was
not realism but to devise a model that would have the solutions to
his equations as its equilibrium values, although he knew that the real
market mechanism did not' (1987, pp. 762 and 772). According to
Walker, Walras introduced the pledges model in 1900, 'at the very
end of the period in which he made theoretical contributions, and by
its characteristics revealed the weakening of his creative powers' (1987,
p. 769). Walker's contrast exaggerates the 'realism' of the earlier
model. It is one thing to assume that, for an individual market,
transactions do not take place until an equilibrium price has been
located. It is of a different order of abstraction to assume that, for
a network of inter-related markets, no transactions take place for any
commodity until a set of equilibrium prices has been identified.
Walras realises that, for this reason alone, the 'real market
mechanism' will not result in prices corresponding to the solutions
to his mathematical equations. The introduction of a phase of
preliminary *tâtonnement* with tickets should be described as a further
retreat from reality. Moreover, there is surely a tension between, on
the one hand, Walker's suggestion that Walras introduces the fiction
of tickets because he has finally realised the full significance of the
path-dependence problem and, on the other, his claim that the
introduction of such a fiction reveals the weakening of Walras'
creative powers. We will return to Walras' distinction between a phase
of preliminary *tâtonnement* and the stationary phase when we
examine Walras' conception of the 'continuous market'.

Capital formation

In order to understand Walras' temporal perspective, it is illuminating
to explore further his theory of capital formation. As Garegnani
(1960) argued, Walras' formal specification of the conditions for
equilibrium in capital formation is incoherent. Although the argument
also applies to circulating capital goods, we will focus on fixed capital
goods. To simplify the exposition, assume (as Walras, himself, does

in Appendix I of the *Elements*) that there is no depreciation or insurance of capital goods. The rate of (net) income for the kth capital good proper, i_k, is

$$i_k = r_k / P_k \qquad k = 1,...,K \qquad (1)$$

where P_k is the price of the kth capital good proper and r_k is the price of the service it yields. According to Walras, equilibrium requires a uniform rate of (net) income on all capital goods. Confining our attention to the K capital goods proper, this implies

$$i_1 = ... = i_k = ... = i_K = i \qquad (2)$$

where i is the uniform rate of (net) income. According to Walras, equilibrium also requires that

$$c_k = P_k \qquad k = 1,...,K \qquad (3)$$

where c_k denotes the cost of producing a unit of the kth capital good. From (1), (2) and (3), equilibrium requires

$$r_k / c_k = i \qquad k = 1,...,K \qquad (4)$$

The problem is that it will not be possible, in general, to satisfy simultaneously the conditions that there be a uniform rate of (net) income on all capital goods and that the selling prices of all the capital goods proper equal their respective costs of production. As a *first approximation*, assume (as Walras also does in Appendix I) that variations in the outputs of capital goods have no effect on the prices of productive services. Since these prices can then be taken as given when considering the capital goods market, this implies that both r_k and c_k are given in (4). Except by coincidence, the system of equations (4) will not be consistent, since there will *not* exist a uniform rate of (net) income which will enable all the equations to be satisfied. This inconsistency is not necessarily eliminated by allowing variations in the outputs of capital goods to have effects on the prices of productive services and on costs of production. The source of the problem is that the composition of the initial stock of capital goods, assumed to be random, will not, in general, be consistent with the satisfaction of the conditions.

Walras, in fact, appreciates that there is a problem with his formal analysis: 'In any economy like the one we have imagined, which establishes its economic equilibrium *ab ovo*, it is probable that there would be no equality of rates of net income. Nor would such an equality be likely to exist in an economy which had just been disrupted by a war, a revolution or a business crisis' (p. 308). This suggests that Walras does appreciate that the composition of the initial stock of capital matters. Indeed, in the same paragraph, Walras hints at a way in which the internal inconsistency could be eliminated: he refers to the 'order' in which capital goods might be produced over time. Invoking the 'first approximation', we can rank capital goods proper in terms of what we (as opposed to Walras) will call the rates of return on their supply prices, defined for the kth capital good as r_k/c_k. Equilibrium would involve only producing the capital good(s) with the highest rate of return on supply price, the remaining capital goods not being produced during the time period under consideration. The price(s) of the capital good(s) actually produced would be equal to the cost(s) of production. Since the (common) rate of return on the supply price(s) of the capital good(s) actually produced would determine the common rate of (net) income from the ownership of all capital goods, the prices of landed capital, of personal capital and of those capital goods proper which are not produced in the time period under consideration would adjust so that, in equilibrium, they would yield the same rate of (net) income from ownership as the capital good(s) actually produced. In terms of the equilibrium conditions, this reformulation would involve replacing the equality in (3) by a weak inequality; requiring that the kth capital good not be produced if $c_k > P_k$; and stipulating that (4) only apply to those capital goods actually produced. This reformulation is consistent with Walras' reference to the order in which capital goods would be produced. Moreover, additional evidence in the *Elements* to confirm that Walras recognised the need for this sort of specification is that, when discussing the *tâtonnement* process, he refers to 'the exclusion of those new capital goods which it was not worth while to produce' (p. 294); and to giving up the production of 'those capital goods whose cost of production exceeds their selling price' (p. 481).

Walras' reference to the order in which capital goods would be produced indicates how he would have responded to the inference which Garegnani has drawn from the inconsistency in Walras' equilibrium conditions. Garegnani claimed that, in the tradition of Smith and Ricardo, Walras is seeking to determine a 'long-period position', defined as involving a uniform rate of return on the supply prices of capital goods. Garegnani insisted, however, that, because of the inconsistency in his equilibrium conditions, Walras is 'simply incorrect in believing this to be compatible with treating each kind of "capital good proper" as a separate factor' (1976, p. 34). Garegnani contended that the only way in which it is possible to determine a long-period equilibrium by means of supply and demand analysis is to conceive of capital, not as heterogeneous capital goods, but as a single value magnitude which can freely assume the form of any physical capital good.

It is scarcely credible that Walras would have accepted such a reformulation of his approach. As we have seen, he does use an imaginary commodity (E) to reduce the whole complex of heterogeneous capital goods (including landed and personal capital) to a homogeneous income-yielding entity. The demand for new capital goods is thereby conceived of as a homogeneous value magnitude which is then allocated between the production of additional quantities of the various specific capital goods proper. However, to have forsaken the notion of inherited stocks of heterogeneous capital goods − to have treated capital in the same manner as J. B. Clark or Böhm-Bawerk − would have involved a fundamental change in his temporal perspective; it would have been totally incompatible with the way he 'enters' an economy at a particular point in time and conceives of a static phase which, once identified by a preliminary phase of groping, could commence immediately. That Walras wishes to hold fast to this conception is surely confirmed by the fact that, when he does acknowledge that the initial endowments of capital may be incompatible with a uniform rate of return, he refers to the order in which capital goods would be produced over time. He prefers to hold to the conception of a static phase which could commence immediately − albeit with some capital goods not being produced − rather than subscribe to a notion of equilibrium which could not commence immediately because its attainment would require a readjustment in the composition of the capital stock.

This argument applies *a fortiori* to the claims of Wicksell, who not only withdrew his earlier claim that Walras' theory is not applicable to an economy which is stationary in a thorough-going sense but also argued that, when applied to a stationary economy, it 'gains thereby in rigour'. According to Wicksell:

The underlying assumption is that the factors of production will have the same relative values or prices in the future as they have at the present moment. Actually this is true for the stationary state, but it does not hold for the progressive economy, unless we postulate a uniform increase in production, which is strictly speaking inconceivable, as the sum of natural forces cannot be increased (1977 [1934], p. 227, n.).

Although an understandable reaction to Walras' failure to take into account the future behaviour of prices, this argument — also advanced by Hicks (1934) — reflects a failure to understand the very essence of Walras' approach. To confine Walras' theory to a stationary economy would involve assuming that the conditions for stationariness have already been established by the beginning of the time period under consideration. But this would be utterly inconsistent with Walras' approach throughout the *Elements*. His approach — typified by the way he introduces 'the elements and mechanism of production' in Lesson 18, namely, by imagining 'the process of production in a given country to be momentarily arrested' (p. 218) — is to 'enter' an economy at an arbitrary point in time and to insist, which he does repeatedly, that the data may be any data whatsoever. To have assumed that the economy is already in a thorough-going stationary state, would have precluded his considering what he regards as a crucial question, namely, how equilibrium is established *ab ovo*.

Uncertainty

Whereas Walras clearly appreciates the importance of uncertainty in reality, he abstracts from uncertainty in constructing his model of general equilibrium. Consider first the decisions of entrepreneurs. In his model entrepreneurs face no uncertainty. They have perfect information about techniques of production. Moreover, the phase of preliminary *tâtonnement* involving tickets ensures that entrepreneurs do not need to predict future prices, since they can react to the prices currently being cried without any fear of incurring losses (or any prospect of making profits). Walras is well aware that, in reality, entrepreneurs do face uncertainty. It is worth noting parenthetically that he suggests that, in reality, entrepreneurs often do not know the cost-minimising techniques of production and that they grope for these by a process of trial-and-error. More significantly, Walras advances a pre-Knightian conception of profit as being ultimately attributable to uncertainty. Thus he criticises the 'English school' for not differentiating between interest on capital and the profit of enterprise; and for failing to realise that 'profit of enterprise ... is the correlative of possible loss, that it is subject to risk, that it depends upon exceptional and not upon normal circumstances, and that theoretically it ought to be left to one side' (p. 423).

We have seen that Walras takes for granted that no-one has perfect information about market supply and demand curves. Indeed, he supposes that an individual coming to market may not even 'know' his own trading schedules: an individual's trading schedules may be 'virtual', in the sense that he may not actually make up his mind what quantities to demand and offer until he knows what the prices are. Since no-one can calculate prices, everyone is reliant on the prices actually cried in the market.

Whereas it may be reasonable to suppose that, for certain types of decisions, 'current' prices are sufficient, for certain other types of decisions, individuals would, in reality, dearly like to know what 'future' prices will be. This applies, above all, to the acquisition of durable capital goods. In his theory of capital formation, Walras fudges this issue. In his economy, individuals acquire additional capital goods in order to increase their *future* net incomes. Given the absence of any forward markets, these future net incomes are uncertain. Walras, however, does not face up to this in formulating his model. Instead, he circumvents it by assuming that individuals base their decisions on current rates of net income – or on the equivalent notion of numbers of years' purchase, to which he also refers – so that investment decisions are based solely on prices currently being cried in the market. At best, assuming that individuals base their decisions solely on current rates of net income can be justified on the grounds that, in the real world, individuals might use this as a rule of thumb in the face of uncertainty.

Lest it be thought that Walras could have circumvented the problem of uncertainty more elegantly by assuming the existence of a complete set of markets of the Arrow-Debreu type, it is worth noting that this would not have been acceptable to him. Thus, in the preface to the *Elements*, he explains why he cannot accept Böhm-Bawerk's attempt to deduce the phenomenon of interest on capital from the difference between the value of a present good and that of a future good:

Let us open the first treatise on business finance that comes to hand, and we learn there that a thing worth A for spot delivery will only be worth

$$A' = A / (1 + i)^n$$

for future delivery n years from date, given the annual rate of interest i. Nevertheless, if we propose to use this formula as the basis of an economic theory of the determination of the rate of interest, we must first be told how A is determined, and then we have to be shown the market on which i is deduced from A' in conformity with the above equation. *I have looked in vain for such a market* (pp. 45–6, italics added).

This, according to Walras, is why he persists in determining the rate of interest on the basis of the supply and demand for new capital goods. It also highlights the fundamental dilemma which confronts him in formulating such a theory: on the one hand, he realises that he cannot assume known future prices when seeking to determine current prices but, on the other, he does not know how to incorporate uncertainty explicitly into his theory.

Walras does acknowledge somewhat belatedly that his formal analysis does not properly take uncertainty into account and that, as a consequence, it cannot explain certain types of transactions in capital goods. Thus, as a postscript to his pure theory of capital formation, he asks:

what reason is there to exchange net income against net income, to sell, for example, a house yielding 2,500 francs net in rentals for 100,000 francs, only to buy a piece of land for 100,000 francs yielding 2,500 francs in rent? Such an exchange of one capital good for another makes no more sense than the exchange of a commodity for itself. To understand why purchases and sales take place in the market for capital goods we have to fall back upon certain crucial facts of experience in the world of reality. Thus, we must remember that alongside of those who have an excess of income over consumption and who can buy capital goods there are others ... whose consumption exceeds their income and who must sell capital goods. We must remember, also, that the net income from new capital goods is not known to the same extent as the income from existing capital goods; the net income from new capital goods may prove to be larger or smaller, in short, it is attended with more risk. The result is that the more prudent and circumspect savers do not convert their savings into new capital goods but into existing capital goods; and then the sellers of these existing capital goods invest the proceeds in new capital goods. Applied economics studies the role of these *speculators* whose business it is to *classify* capital. In addition, we must remember that the price of capital goods varies not only by reason of past changes but also by reason of expected changes either in gross income or in rates of depreciation and insurance; and that especially with regard to future changes, expectations differ from individual to individual. It follows that numbers of people will sell the capital goods which, rightly or wrongly, they fear may be subject to a diminution in net income, and buy with the proceeds other capital goods which they hope, rightly or wrongly, will enjoy an increase in net income (pp. 310-11).[8]

Consider finally Walras' theory of circulating capital and money. Once again abstracting from uncertainty, he assumes that each consumer and each entrepreneur has at every moment a 'fairly exact idea' of what stocks of circulating capital goods and money he needs:

There may be a small element of uncertainty which is due solely to the difficulty of foreseeing possible changes in the data of the problem. If, however, we suppose these data constant for a given period of time and if we suppose the prices of goods and services and also the dates of their purchase and sale to be known for the whole period, there will be no occasion for uncertainty (p. 317).

A theory which abstracts from uncertainty cannot provide a wholly satisfactory basis for understanding the roles of money. However, this does not imply acceptance of Hicks'(1933) objection to Walras' theory on the alleged grounds that the phenomenon of money necessarily depends for its existence on uncertainty. As Marget has argued:

Even in a world in which everything was perfectly foreseen, a lack of synchronization between the receipt of income and its outlay would give rise to a need for cash balances so long as there are not perfect facilities for the borrowing of money in anticipation of receipts and the investment of money during the period elapsing between receipt and outlay (1935, p. 160).

Similarly, Niehans has asserted: 'While a time dimension and trans-actions costs are necessary ingredients of a meaningful monetary theory, uncertainty is not' (1978, p. 19). Even within these terms, however, Walras' theory is deficient, since he does not combine his allusion to a lack of synchronisation with any explicit reference to transactions costs or to any other frictions in the facilities for borrowing and lending money. Instead, he employs – indeed, perhaps initiates – what Niehans has called the 'metaphorical approach to monetary theory': Walras treats money *as if* it were a commodity whose services do not depend on market imperfections.

The conditions and consequences of economic progress

The neglect by most commentators of Walras' treatment of the 'conditions and consequences of economic progress' in Part VII of the *Elements* is lamentable. That some critics have ignored it is perhaps understandable, since it undermines their caricature of Walras as being obsessed with the 'timeless' allocation of resources and as having no 'vision' of a dynamic process through time. What is less easily explicable is that it is also ignored by Schumpeter who is certainly not anxious to belittle Walras' treatment of time. But what is particularly disconcerting is the recent attempt by Jaffé to dismiss Part VII as part of a structurally separate *coda*, 'tacked on' at the end of the *Elements* and intended as 'a link between his pure statical theory and his applied and "social" theories, which are intrinsically dynamic' (1980, p. 546).

In Lesson 35, Walras initially employs 'concrete numbers' to describe an economy in static equilibrium. For this purpose, it is necessary to specify a definite calendar duration: 'let us drop the assumption of an indefinite period and imagine, instead, a determinate period of, let us say a day, or better a year, in order to allow for seasonal variations' (p. 378). We have some misgivings about Walras' choice of a year, since such a choice is inconsistent with our claim that, once circulating capital is introduced into the analysis, the period of time under consideration needs to be thought of as 'short'. The only explanation we can offer for this is that, whereas Walras' concrete description of an economy over a year is repeated from earlier editions, it is not until the fourth edition that Walras distinguishes between a preliminary phase of groping, a static phase and a dynamic phase and that he assumes explicitly that newly-produced circulating capital goods are not 'put to use' until after the static phase. In any event, Walras immediately proceeds to consider the implications of supposing that there is no stationary phase at all. He states:

Finally, in order to come still more closely to reality, we must drop the hypothesis of an annual market period and adopt in its place the hypothesis of a continuous market. Thus, we pass from the static to the dynamic state. For this purpose, we shall now suppose that the annual production and consumption, which we had hitherto represented as a constant magnitude for every moment of the year under consideration, change from instant to instant along with the basic data of the problem (p. 380).

Walras likens circulating capital to 'so many shoots that are continually being pruned at one end while they are constantly growing at the other' (p. 380). Producers are constantly drawing on and replacing their stocks of raw materials. Final products are constantly being sold to consumers, only to be replaced by new products placed on display. Consumers are constantly depleting and replenishing their stocks of commodities in cupboards and larders: 'Every hour, nay, every minute, portions of these different classes of circulating capital are disappearing and reappearing. Personal capital, capital goods proper and money also disappear and reappear, in a similar manner, but much more slowly. Only landed capital escapes this process of renewal' (p. 380). Such a process is consistent with an economy being in a thorough-going stationary state. But this is not what Walras has in mind. He is concerned with a progressive economy, for which the quantities of fixed and circulating capital are inexorably changing over time. Moreover, he takes for granted that, in reality, utility functions and production functions are likely to be changing autonomously over time. The process whereby capital goods disappear and reappear is also consistent with an economy always being in momentary equilibrium but where the equilibrium state is changing over time. Indeed, in an earlier lesson, when examining the theory of bimetallism, Walras does consider 'a *variable* or *moving* equilibrium, which reestablishes itself automatically as soon as it is disturbed' (p. 318 and Lesson 32). However, this is not what Walras has in mind in his description of the continuous market. He is emphatic not simply that the equilibrium state is constantly changing but also that the processes of adjustment necessarily take time. Consequently, the market is forever chasing, but never reaching, a moving target:

Such is the continuous market, which is perpetually tending towards equilibrium without ever actually attaining it, because the market has no other way of approaching equilibrium except by groping, and, before the goal is reached, it has to renew its efforts and start over again, all the basic data of the problem, e.g. the initial quantities possessed, the utilities of goods and services, the technical coefficients, the excess of income over consumption, the working capital requirements, etc., having changed in the meantime. Viewed in this way, the market is like a lake agitated by the wind, where the water is incessantly seeking its level without ever reaching it. But whereas there are days when the surface of a lake is almost smooth, there never is a day when the effective demand for products and services equals their effective supply and when the selling price of products equals the cost of the productive services used in making them (p. 380).

It must be emphasised that, for Walras, the different adjustment processes operate at different speeds. In his discussion of exchange in a single market, he asserts: 'It is a matter of daily experience that even in big markets where there are neither brokers nor auctioneers, the current equilibrium price is determined within a few minutes, and considerable quantities of merchandise are exchanged at that price within half or three quarters of an hour' (p. 106). Walras has in mind what, in Marshallian terms, is a partial equilibrium pertaining to the market day. In contrast, adjustment to 'full' equilibrium is considerably slower:

The diversion of productive services from enterprises that are losing money to profitable enterprises takes place in various ways, the most important being through credit operations, but at best these ways are slow. It can happen and frequently does happen in the real world, that under some circumstances a selling price will remain for long periods of time above cost of production and continue to rise in spite of increases in output, while under other circumstances, a fall in price, following upon this rise, will suddenly bring the selling price below cost of production and force entrepreneurs to reverse their production policies. For, just as a lake is, at times, stirred to its very depths by a storm, so also the market is sometimes thrown into violent confusion by *crises*, which are sudden and general disturbances of equilibrium. The more we know of the ideal conditions of equilibrium, the better we shall be able to control or prevent these crises (pp. 380-1).

In Lesson 36, Walras considers the systematic implications of 'economic progress'. This involves an entirely different temporal perspective, the complications highlighted in the description of the continuous market being set aside. Walras seeks to derive what he calls the 'laws of the variation of prices in a progressive economy'. These systematic variations arise because the quantity of land cannot be increased. Thus, in the absence of technical progress, economic progress requires the substitution of the services of capital goods proper for the services of land. This, of course, involves relaxing his earlier assumption of fixed input-output coefficients. The nature of the 'laws' themselves need not detain us. What is of interest here is Walras' method. In essence, he examines the implications for equilibrium prices of assuming that, 'at the end of a certain period of time', population and the quantities of capital goods proper are increased. A particular, if not peculiar, feature of his analysis is that he defines economic progress as 'nothing but a diminution in the intensities of last wants satisfied, i.e. in the *raretés* of final products, in a country with an increasing population' (p. 383). Consequently, he is obliged to assume that, if population doubles, the quantities of capital goods more than double, 'as is necessary to enable entrepreneurs utilizing the original quantity of land and land-services and twice the amount of personal faculties and labour to produce at least twice as much of each of the products' (p. 389).

One commentator who has attached considerable significance to Part VII is Morishima. In *Walras' Economics: A Pure Theory of Capital and Money*, he claimed that the whole of the *Elements* may be regarded as providing a general equilibrium foundation for a Ricardian-like model of economic growth. According to Morishima, Walras' 'theory of growth' focuses on 'the temporary equilibrium that will be established in a particular period, provided that prices, outputs and investments are all perfectly flexible' (1977, p. 78). This equilibrium is based on the initial endowments of capital. The productive activities during that period will result in new initial endowments at the beginning of the next period:

The new Walrasian equilibrium which will be established in the second period by the same principle as that which ruled in the first will be different from the temporary equilibrium established in the first period, because of changes in the initial endowments; it will result in further changes in the initial endowments in the third period. Continuing in such a manner, we have a dynamic movement through periods (1977, p. 79).

It should be stressed that (leaving aside Walras' digression on bimetallism) such a sequence of 'temporary equilibria' does not appear explicitly in the *Elements*. It is not self-evident what Walras would have made of the 'Walrasian sequence'. It would involve regarding the equilibrium prices for any period as more than simply 'normal' values. Moreover, his description of the continuous market – in particular, his observation that the diversion of productive services between unprofitable and profitable enterprises operates, at best, slowly – suggests that he might well have had misgivings about such a sequence being taken too literally.

Morishima's *Walras' Economics* has been described by Blaug (1978), with some justification, as 'profoundly *a*historical'. Nevertheless, Morishima shows much greater feeling for Walras' dynamic vision than does Jaffé. Whereas Jaffé's attempt to discount the significance of the continuous market is contrived, his portrayal of Walras' analysis of economic progress is simply untenable. Jaffé has asserted:

Walras's strict adherence to the statical hypothesis on which the whole general equilibrium edifice rested led him to relegate his discussion of the 'Conditions and Consequences of Economic Progress' to Part VII, toward the end of the *Elements* where it was tacked on, along with Part VIII, as a *coda* structurally separate from the preceding self-contained pure theory. That Walras meant the preceding Part VI to top off his all encompassing model of general equilibrium is shown at the very outset of that part by his declaration that he intended his theory of circulation and money 'to *complete* the general problem of economic equilibrium'[my italics] (1980, p. 545).

This claim − in particular, Jaffé's italicisation of the word 'complete' − is, at best, misleading, since it supposes that Walras' pure theory is synonymous with his analysis of economic equilibrium. However, in the preface, Walras asserts: '*Pure Economics* is, in essence, the theory of the determination of prices under a hypothetical régime of perfect competition' (p. 40). And, at the very outset of Lesson 36, Walras introduces the laws of the variation of prices in a progressive economy as being 'essential to the *completion* of the theory of the determination of prices' (p. 382, *our* emphasis). This shows conclusively that, whilst Lesson 36 is manifestly not part of his static general equilibrium model, it *is* an integral part of his pure theory.

Jaffé's conception of Walras' pure theory as being synonymous with his static general equilibrium model is bound up with his claim that the ultimate aim of the *Elements* is *not* to examine how a capitalist system works. He contends that the *Elements* is designed 'to portray how an imaginary system *might* work in conformity with principles of [commutative] "justice", rooted in traditional natural law philosophy, though the system remained subject to the same forces, the same "passions and interests", and the same material and technological constraints that govern the real world' (1980, p. 530). Whilst not denying that there is a significant normative dimension to the *Elements*, we are not persuaded by this argument. Certainly, this thesis has led Jaffé to make the superficial claim that, because Walras' purpose was to formulate a static model of commutative justice, he 'deliberately and explicitly left the flow of time out of account (assuming, for example, all production to be instantaneous)' (1980, p. 540). Moreover, Jaffé's characterisation of Part VII has led him to assert that there is no place for growth in Walras' economic theory. He has claimed: 'Since capital formation, once carried out, entails dynamic changes in the data, Walras confined his attention to decisions made at a given moment of time, without following up the consequences of the decisions' (1980, p. 540). Obviously enough, when Walras focuses on a particular period of time, he is not concerned with the consequences for some subsequent period of time. However, he *is* concerned with the implications for 'current' equilibrium prices of decisions to accumulate. And in Lesson 36 – which, we repeat, is part of his pure theory – Walras does consider the 'historical effects' of capital accumulation, albeit in an idiosyncratic way.

Jaffé's claims have already misled. Thus Walsh and Gram (1980, p. 160) have portrayed Walras' analysis as involving 'the timeless allocation of a given set of resources'. Like Jaffé, they have claimed that, in Walras' model, all production is 'instantaneous'. They have explicitly invoked Jaffé's claim that there is 'no room for growth' in the model; his distinction between 'mere' decisions to accumulate and their consequences; and his assertion that Walras' discussion of economic progress forms part of a separate *coda*. Furthermore, they have asserted that, in alleged contrast to classical theories, 'unidirectional time plays no role in the model'. All this amounts to a misleading caricature. As we have seen, the claim that production is 'instantaneous' involves a fundamental misunderstanding of the final stage of Walras' development of his static theory of general equilibrium. As we have also seen, his discussion of economic progress is an integral part of his pure theory. Moreover, it is difficult to understand the precise meaning of the charge that 'unidirectional time plays no role', when it is directed at an analysis in which the quantities of capital goods at the beginning and at the end of the period are necessarily different.

Some concluding comments

What can we conclude about Walras' treatment of time? Clearly in formulating his static general equilibrium model Walras does not get to grips with many of the real implications of the passage of time. His model is primarily concerned with the time of succession: he invokes what Jacques calls 'our capacity mentally to make time stand still' (1982, p. xii). The most disconcerting feature of his approach is that he 'enters' his economy at a particular point of time but does not, or cannot, accommodate the implications which follow from this, particularly the implications of the uncertainties which agents face. In seeking to set aside the complications posed by behaviour in the face of an unknown future, Walras thereby ignores the complex interrelationships between memory, perception, expectation and desire.

Nevertheless many of the caricatures of Walras are unfair and inept. Critics of Walras sometimes seem to rest their case on the observation that actual economies are never in equilibrium. But this misses the point. He makes it perfectly clear — first when introducing equilibrium in production and again when describing the continuous market — that he believes that actual economies are never in equilibrium. Critics who berate Walras for invoking 'analytical time' perhaps fail to appreciate that he conceives of a preliminary phase of *tâtonnement*, not because he thinks that adjustment processes operate rapidly, but because he *knows* that, in reality, they operate slowly. Walras' discussion of the continuous market — we quoted virtually the entire passage — is extremely brief. Nevertheless, as we have insisted, an appreciation of it is essential to a proper understanding of the *Elements*. In essence, Walras' conception of reality is that of a process in which there are equilibrating forces at work but where the attainment of equilibrium is invariably frustrated by both endogenous changes and exogenous disturbances. Walras' contribution should be evaluated in that light. At the risk of stating the obvious, any conception of a process involving interaction between equilibrating and disequilibrating forces must involve some notion of equilibrium; this Walras seeks to provide by adopting a *point de vue statique*. In attempting to analyse the various processes of adjustment, Walras is obliged to imagine a stationary target — namely, the equilibrium state implied by the 'current data' — because the notion of an economy forever chasing a moving target is analytically intractable. Rightly or wrongly, Walras regards his analysis of equilibrium and of adjustment processes, albeit in some fictional preliminary phase, as a way of understanding those processes which take place in 'real time'.

But Walras is perhaps entitled to the last word. Having complained that 'practically all the criticisms levelled against me have consisted in calling my attention to complications which I had left to one side', he continues:

I find it very easy to reply to these criticisms. So far as I am concerned, since I was the first to elaborate a pure theory of economics in mathematical form, my aim has been to describe and explain the mechanism of production in terms of its bare essentials. It is for other economists who come after me to introduce one at a time whatever complications they please. They in their way and I in mine will then, I think, have done what had to be done (p. 478).

Notes

1 Unless otherwise indicated, page references in this chapter relate to Walras (1954).
2 See for example Appendix 1: Dimensions, stocks and flows.
3 Walras is not consistent with his conception of roles when discussing his (emasculated) theory of credit. As we have seen, he assumes that the demands for new capital goods come, not from entrepreneurs, but from capitalists. He asserts that, in reality, the demands for new capital goods typically come from entrepreneurs using funds borrowed from capitalists. However, to be consistent with his distinction between roles, he should suppose that a producer who uses borrowed funds to acquire ownership of capital goods does so in the role of capitalist, and that he then leases the services to himself as entrepreneur. It is surprising that he does not acknowledge this, particularly since he has previously claimed that an individual who buys a house 'must be resolved by us into two individuals, one making an investment and the other consuming directly the services of his capital' (p. 267).
4 Walras did not succeed in allaying misgivings. See, in particular, the debate between Morishima (1977, 1980) and Jaffé (1980).
5 One of the difficulties in interpreting Walras is that he often refers to the products market in the singular and to the services market in the singular. In the present context, he might be interpreted as meaning that it never happens that the effective demands and supplies of all products are absolutely equal or that it never happens that the effective demand and supply of any one product are absolutely equal. Elsewhere, in fact, he does refer to a price in an individual market actually being located – 'within a few minutes' – at which effective demand and effective supply are equal (p. 106).
6 In this context, it is perhaps worth mentioning something which puzzled Patinkin. In 'Léon Walras', published in 1934, Hicks rebuked Walras for not making it clear whether or not transactions do take place at disequilibrium prices. However, in *Value and Capital*, published in 1939, Hicks took for granted that Walras assumes that they do not. The explanation for this change of mind is that, in the interim, Hicks received a letter from Keynes arguing that Walras 'assuredly' does suppose that transactions do not take place except at equilibrium prices: 'For that is the actual method by which the opening price is fixed on the Paris Bourse even today' (cited in Hicks, 1976).

7 It should be clear that the 'textbook' distinction between the 'Marshallian adjustment rule' and the 'Walrasian adjustment rule' is *not* derived from the *Principles* and the *Elements*. Both Marshall and Walras invoke both price-adjustment and quantity-adjustment rules.

8 We observed in note 3 that Walras' discussion of credit is not consistent with his conception of roles. This may be because, in the context of his analysis, it would make 'no more sense than the exchange of a commodity for itself' for a producer, in his capacity as capitalist, to borrow funds from some other capitalist in order to acquire physical capital goods so that he can lease their services to himself as entrepreneur. To explain such an activity it would again be necessary 'to fall back upon certain crucial facts of experience in the world of reality' – such as differences in expectations between individuals or, perhaps more significantly in the present context, the fact that new capital goods frequently loose some or all of their mobility by being 'installed'.

4

Lindahl *1929*

The assumption, that in a given period of time people perfectly foresee the price level that will prevail in this period as a result of their actions during the period, is, strictly speaking, a necessary condition for an explanation of a price situation as a state of equilibrium, in the sense that there exists a mutual connection between supply and demand on the one hand and actual prices on the other, and that, therefore, at existing prices exchange can continue until full satisfaction has been attained (p. 339, n*[1]).

'The Place of Capital in the Theory of Price', originally published in Swedish in 1929 and translated into English in 1939 as Part Three of *Studies in the Theory of Money and Capital*, is a remarkable work. Like Marshall and Walras, Lindahl is acutely conscious of the complications posed by time. But, whereas it might be argued that both Marshall and Walras, in their different ways, sought to circumvent these difficulties, Lindahl attempts to confront them directly.

His approach is to develop a sequence of models which increasingly approximate reality, each stage forming the basis for the next. His starting-point is what he calls the 'traditional setting of the pricing problem', that is, a general equilibrium analysis which abstracts from time. His next stage is to develop 'the pure "static" problem of price determination' by examining a stationary economy in which individuals have perfect foresight. Although this static problem has 'little or no connection with the phenomena determining prices in the real world', it provides the foundation for the next stage in which Lindahl retains the assumption of perfect foresight but allows for the economy to be changing over time. Thus, although he does not use the term, Lindahl introduces the notion of inter-temporal equilibrium.[2] The analysis of inter-temporal equilibrium — involving, as it does, the assumption of perfect foresight — is, for Lindahl, but a stage in the development of a more realistic theory. Accordingly, in the final section of the essay, devoted to how imperfect foresight might be accommodated, Lindahl develops what may be called a sequence of temporary equilibria. The sequence he considers entails assuming that individuals have the same ideas about the future, that they are subjectively certain that these ideas will be realised and, further, that they *would* be realised were it not for the periodic occurrence of unforeseen events. Lindahl is not satisfied with this. But he acknowledges that dispensing with these assumptions is attended with 'such considerable difficulties' (p. 348) that he is only able to offer a few suggestive comments.

For Lindahl, time is intimately bound up with capital and interest. As the title of the essay implies, he is particularly concerned to integrate capital and interest into the general theory of price. Specifically, he seeks to generalise Walras' analysis by incorporating insights provided by the Austrian theory of capital. Thus he considers roundabout processes of production and the idea of the original services invested in the production of a durable capital instrument 'maturing' as that instrument renders services of its own. Interesting though these notions may be, we cannot be drawn into examining their usefulness. Nevertheless, there is much in the essay which is of considerable interest to us.

Lindahl maintains certain assumptions throughout the essay. Although he does not explicitly discuss the nature of the agents and their roles, it is evident that entrepreneurs perform the same role as in Walras' economy, each entrepreneur seeking to maximise profit. Technology is characterised by constant returns to scale, though not necessarily by fixed input-output coefficients, and all factors of production and products are perfectly mobile. Lindahl does not consider the decisions of individuals with respect to their supplies of factor services and their demands for products; following Cassel rather than Walras, he starts from market supply functions for productive services and market demand functions for products. All markets are competitive, so that 'at every moment of time there is a uniform price for productive services and goods of any specified type' (p. 275). All agents have perfect information about the relevant prices currently prevailing on the various markets.

The traditional setting of the pricing problem

According to Lindahl, the 'traditional setting of the pricing problem'
– he has in mind Cassel and Bowley, not Walras – abstracts from
time. Lindahl seeks to elucidate the assumptions which are implicit in
such an approach, the rationale for this being to identify the complications which have to be confronted in the development of a more
realistic theory. Lindahl considers an economy over a certain period of
time. His purpose, in effect, is to specify the circumstances under
which the period in question is *strictly self-contained*, so that 'the
formation of prices in each period is an independent process, and there
is no connection between the prices prevailing during successive
periods' (p. 274). Although he does not specify the calendar duration
of the period, he seems to envisage it as being 'very short'. It is worth
noting, however, that, for Lindahl, there must be a duration and that
it would be meaningless to postulate a self-contained moment in time:

> The assumption of the non-importance of time can hardly be said to mean
> that production does not require time. For production implies the utilisation
> of productive services for the attainment of certain ends, and since these
> services, in Irving Fisher's words, are a flow in time, it follows that time must
> enter as a dimension in the concept of production. 'Timeless production' is
> thus, strictly speaking, impossible. The assumption should therefore be
> formulated by saying that everything has a time dimension, but that this time
> factor has no economic relevance (p. 272).

For the time factor to have no economic relevance, the production
which takes place during the period must be for use within that same
period. Furthermore, for the period to be strictly self-contained,
individuals must not even contemplate exchanging present and future
incomes among themselves; if they did, the problem of interest would
arise.[3]

Lindahl acknowledges that there is a tension between, on the one
hand, the fact that production necessarily takes time and, on the other
hand, the fact that, if the period is to be strictly self-contained, it must
be supposed that 'individuals have no ideas of the future and so only
think of satisfying the desires of the moment' (p. 273). Thus he
cautions:

> This limited outlook should naturally not be stressed too strongly: a certain
> minimum of thought for the future must necessarily be assumed if productive
> co-operation is to be possible. But individual economic plans must be regarded
> as so short sighted that the relation between the present and the future

remains obscure, and there is therefore no process by which the price of the time factor is determined (p. 273).

Although Lindahl's purpose is to highlight complications, he does not explicitly acknowledge them all. Consider the claim that production during the period must be solely for use within the period. What sorts of technologies would be consistent with identifying a discrete period of time which can be treated as self-contained? Produced means of production must be ruled out. Furthermore, from an Austrian perspective, there must be no opportunity for varying the 'quantity of time' used in producing any commodity. Moreover, the only possible technologies are ones where, in Georgescu-Roegen's terms, elementary processes are arranged in line or in parallel; elementary processes cannot be arranged in series, as in factory production. A further complication, resulting from the fact that production takes time, is that, since individuals must wait until production has been completed, purchases and consumption cannot be conceived of as constant rates of flow over the period. Lindahl cannot avail himself of Walras' assumption of inherited stocks of final commodities to tide the community over, since each period would no longer be self-contained. Indeed, pushing the notion of self-containedness to the limit, it is necessary to suppose that the productive effort which individuals are capable of providing in any period is strictly independent of what they have consumed in previous periods.

All prices within the period are 'determined jointly and simultaneously' (p. 274). These prices are determined by given supply functions for productive services, given demand functions for products and the given technical conditions for production. In equilibrium, the price of each product is equal to its cost of production; and the total supply of each productive service is equal to the total quantity used in the production of the goods demanded. These are, of course, Walras' equilibrium conditions for an economy with production but no capital formation. What ensures that an equilibrium will actually be realised? Whereas one of Walras' basic objectives was to analyse the spontaneous tendency towards equilibrium under free competition, Lindahl never even alludes to this question. Instead, he seeks to circumvent it by assuming that individuals have perfect foresight.

We must examine carefully the precise nature of this assumption of perfect foresight, partly because it is central to the entire essay and partly because Lindahl acknowledges a tension which must have troubled many economists. Consider the way in which he introduces this assumption:

Since the determination of prices involves time, the individual actions that give rise to a certain price level must be assumed to take place before prices are settled. If individuals cannot foresee correctly what price level will be the result of their combined activities, they must base their actions on ideas which are more or less uncertain. Here, evidently, a risk factor enters, giving a dynamic stamp to the pricing problem, even though the economic plans of individuals are assumed to cover only very short periods of time. In order to eliminate such dynamic aspects of the problem due to the time factor, it must therefore *in addition* be assumed that individuals in every concrete instance have such a knowledge of the conditions determining prices that they can let their sales and their demand be governed by the prices that are the result of these conditions. Then all prices within a certain period will be determined jointly and simultaneously, and the time factor will give rise to no complications (pp. 273–4).

As we have seen, Lindahl assumes that, at any moment in time, individuals know the prices prevailing at that moment. He is now making an assumption involving a different degree of abstraction: he is assuming that, at the beginning of the period, individuals know what the prices of the period will turn out to be. For Lindahl, this requires assuming that, when individuals make their plans at the beginning of the period, they are able to formulate and solve the equilibrium conditions: they know the conditions determining prices and they can base their decisions on 'the prices that are the result of these conditions'. Why does Lindahl not simply assume that individuals 'know' what prices will be? He could reasonably object that, without knowledge of all the relevant conditions, individuals could not know what prices will be. It would be only *superficially* weaker to assume merely that individuals know what prices will turn out to be rather than to assume that they know the conditions determining prices. Indeed, there would be no rational basis for such an assumption. Furthermore, Lindahl would argue that, if individuals do not base their decisions on knowledge of these conditions, it would be inappropriate to claim that prices are being 'determined jointly and simultaneously' by the forces of supply and demand. We will return to this argument later.

In one crucial respect, Lindahl's analysis is seriously flawed. Consider an entrepreneur, at the beginning of the period, contemplating how much of some commodity to produce. Suppose that he does know 'the conditions determining prices' and that he has unlimited computational ability. It does not follow that he can let his plans 'be governed by the prices that are the result of these conditions'. Since, by assumption, production involves constant returns to scale, there is not a unique profit-maximising production plan at those prices. How is this entrepreneur to decide how much of this commodity to produce? What ensures that the manufacturers of this commodity will produce precisely the equilibrium total quantity? Lindahl's assumption of perfect foresight – heroic though such an assumption may be – does not ensure that each entrepreneur, acting independently, will behave in the manner needed to bring about equilibrium: perfect foresight is *not* sufficient to 'pre-reconcile' plans. Lindahl's failure to recognise this – he is by no means alone in doing so – is a crucial weakness of the entire essay, not simply of his study of the traditional setting of the pricing problem.

Perfect foresight and stationary conditions

Lindahl's next step is to develop 'the pure "static" problem of price determination' by combining the assumption that individuals have perfect foresight of the future and the assumption that the economy is stationary. For Lindahl, stationarity does not logically imply perfect foresight, since there is no necessity that individuals learn from their experiences: 'The fact that everything actually remains unchanged in a community does not prevent its members from continually fearing or hoping that certain changes will take place' (p. 287). Since analysing a stationary economy where there is uncertainty would, for Lindahl, be more complex than analysing a non-stationary economy where individuals have perfect foresight, he suggests that the assumption of perfect foresight involves a greater simplification than does the assumption of stationarity *per se*.

Consider first the assumption of perfect foresight. For an individual to formulate a plan which he will not subsequently wish to modify, he needs to know 'his own productive power and the size of his wants during the relevant future periods' (p. 285). Moreover, individuals need to know when a future technical change will take place and what its 'implications' will be, so that they can 'take steps to secure that the apparatus of production will at the time in question be completely adjusted to the new technique' (p. 285). But they must not know the 'nature' of the technical change, since, if they did, it would be introduced immediately. This is patently disquieting: it is difficult to conceive of individuals knowing the 'implications' of a change, whose 'nature' they do not know. In addition to needing to know future changes directly relevant to their own wants and production possibilities, individuals must also know the conditions determining prices for all relevant future periods. Although Lindahl does not specify what is the 'relevant' number of periods, we infer that, in contrast to the previous economy, the time-horizon is to be thought of as 'long', certainly sufficiently long for Lindahl to be concerned about future technical changes.

Lindahl is clearly not comfortable with the assumption of perfect foresight:

The assumption of Perfect Foresight implies that individuals have full knowledge of all future data which they take into consideration in their economic planning .... Although individuals must therefore be supposed to be aware both of future prices and of the forms of functions that determine the dependence of supply, demand and the technical coefficients on these prices, economic developments must nevertheless be regarded not as determined beforehand, but as the result of the actions of individuals (p. 285).

There clearly *is* a tension between, on the one hand, supposing that, when they decide on their actions, individuals know what will happen and, on the other hand, insisting that what will happen is the result of those actions. Lindahl is justified in being troubled by this. He would, we suggest, have been even more troubled had he recognised the complications which arise from constant returns to scale.

Given perfect foresight, the assumption of stationarity − defined as the absence of change − naturally affords an additional simplification. However, the nature of the assumption must be properly understood. Lindahl stresses that the analysis involves the assumption that the conditions for stationariness have already been established. He initially considers the simplest case of a stationary economy where production within any period is solely for use within that period but where 'the time factor has economic relevance, since individuals can exchange present for future income among themselves' (p. 288). Such exchange may give rise to a rate of interest: 'This case is instructive. It shows with all desirable clarity that the influence of the time factor in increasing productivity is not a necessary prerequisite for the creation of a rate of interest' (p. 289). He then considers an economy in which productive services in the current period may be used to produce durable capital goods which will last for a given number of future periods, the production of any capital good requiring only one period. For such an economy to be stationary, the rate of interest must be such that the production of capital involves only replacement. In the final stage of his analysis of stationarity, Lindahl assumes that 'productive services from various periods of time are used up in the manufacture of a particular article'; and that 'a process of production requiring more time often brings larger results than one that needs less time, owing to the productive influence of the time factor itself' (p. 296). Although we cannot explore the issue of roundabout processes of production or the related question of Lindahl's treatment of capital, we must consider his observations on 'the difficulties inherent in the assumption of stationary conditions', since these are of general importance.

Lindahl is emphatic that the analysis must not be interpreted as determining the stationarity state which would be approached in the long run given certain assumptions regarding supply functions, demand functions and technical coefficients. Such a problem involves dynamics. He argues:

In a study of the pricing problem under stationary conditions it is presumed, as has already been stated, that a condition of equilibrium already exists, and the investigation proceeds to show how the prices, the rate of interest, the time-structure of capital, etc., then prevailing are determined by certain given factors. This relation may be expressed by saying that the values in question are a necessary condition for the continuation of the stationary state, but not that they are a necessary consequence of certain given functions concerning supply, demand, etc. (p. 310).

This clearly has implications for the validity of comparative statics. Suppose that an economy is in a stationary state with certain prices, interest rate, time-structure of capital, etc. Suppose that there is a change in, say, the technical coefficients for producing some commodity. It would not be legitimate simply to introduce the new coefficients into the model, solve for a new set of equilibrium prices, etc. and then claim that this indicates what the implications of the technical change would be. The reason is that the technical change would give rise to a dynamic process, 'concerning which nothing definite can be said without more precise assumptions as to anticipations and planning' (p. 311).[4]

Lindahl concludes his discussion of stationarity by asserting: 'On account of its artificial and very special assumptions the static problem has little or no connection with the phenomena determining prices in the real world' (p. 317). Together with his strictures on the use of comparative statics, this would seem to imply a very severe indictment of the usefulness of analyses of stationarity. However, Lindahl is not dismissive of such analyses. Recall his claim that the study of a stationary economy with no capitalistic production is instructive. More significantly, the analysis of a stationary economy provides the foundation for the next stage.

Perfect foresight and dynamic conditions

Lindahl's next stage is to examine an economy which is *changing* over time in a way which is perfectly foreseen by the individuals in the economy. Lindahl explains his temporal framework:

In contrast to the stationary case, which is in fact a series of repetitions of one and the same state, we now obtain a series of states differing more or less from one another with regard both to the factors determining prices and to the prices themselves. This dynamic process is in reality continuous, but its analysis will be facilitated if it is subdivided into relatively short periods of time during which prices are assumed to remain unaltered. The changes are accordingly assumed to take place at the points of *transition* between the different periods, and in each period the average state is assumed to last during the entire period (p. 318).

Lindahl enters his economy at a particular point in time, this constituting the beginning of the first period. Previously produced capital goods are treated as 'original' factors. The time-horizon of the analysis encompasses v periods:

We regard the period v as so far distant that conditions in the periods following it are of no importance for the price situation in the periods that are chosen for investigation. The situation in these earlier periods of the dynamic process would accordingly not be changed, if the community reached stationary conditions in period v. In order to simplify the analysis we *imagine* this to be the case (p. 322).

This enables Lindahl to impute terminal values to fixed capital goods in existence at the end of the period v.[5]

The essence of Lindahl's approach is to characterise an intertemporal equilibrium over the time-horizon of the analysis. Endowed with perfect foresight, individuals make plans at the beginning of the first period, plans which encompass all the periods. For each period, there are given supply functions for productive services, given demand functions for consumption goods and given production functions. For each period, equilibrium requires that the price of a consumption good equal its cost of production (where this cost includes accrued interest charges on original services invested in previous periods and 'maturing' in the production of the commodity in the period under consideration); and that the total supply of each productive service equal the total quantity used in the production of the goods demanded. An inter-temporal equilibrium involves simultaneous equilibrium in all periods. In this context, it is worth emphasising that the demand for a particular consumption good in, say, period 4 depends not only on all prices in that period and in the subsequent periods (5, 6, ..., v) but also on all prices in the *previous* periods (1, 2, 3). It is evident from this that all actions for the entire time-horizon are determined at the beginning of the first period. These actions are supposedly pre-reconciled, not by a complete set of forward markets, but by the perfect foresight with which individuals are endowed.[6] Lindahl's inter-temporal equilibrium does not constitute a sequence in any essential sense.

Lindahl claims that the analysis of an inter-temporal equilibrium can provide insights into change:

Under the assumption that the future is perfectly foreseen, all prices in all periods in the dynamic system thus become linked together in a uniform system. The equilibrium of the system is maintained by the same laws as under stationary conditions. Costs of production and prices coincide, and supply and demand are also equal, both for productive services and for consumption goods. The real difference from the stationary case lies in the circumstance that the primary factors, there regarded as given, are assumed to undergo change from one period to another. In this way a movement arises in the system. The task of theory is to elucidate more closely the general conditions on which this movement depends and to give exact expression to its course under all conceivable assumptions (p. 330).

Lindahl's general reflections on this are somewhat obscure. He suggests that 'the general connection not only between prices in a certain period but also between the different successive price situations has a marked tendency to smooth out and damp down all price movements in comparison with a community where the future is not completely foreseen' (p. 330). This relative stability is enhanced 'by a certain regularity to be found in the changes of the functions for supply, demand and technical coefficients, which we have regarded as primary factors determining prices and as data in the problem' (p. 330). Lindahl claims that the various functions would adjust continuously in the light of 'current and expected future price developments' (p. 330); and that, 'if this tendency were alone operative, the community would in time reach stationary conditions' (p. 331). However, any such tendency will be disrupted by 'changes of a more spontaneous character, not directly due to the economic situation'. Lindahl continues:

This is because the development of human nature is regulated not by mechanical but by organic laws, that give rise to new impulses and new acts breaking away from the stationary tendency. Furthermore, man does not control the external conditions of his existence. He cannot influence climatic conditions and so forth to any great extent, and changes of this kind therefore represent continually disturbing factors in economic life. But if all these changes, really primary in relation to price developments, were known beforehand (the angle from which we are discussing the problem), both the factors determining prices and the prices themselves would have the opportunity of adjusting themselves to the new conditions in good time (p. 331).[7]

Imperfect foresight

In the final section of the essay, Lindahl considers, in two stages, how imperfect foresight might be accommodated. The first stage involves assuming that all individuals have the *same* ideas about the future, that they are *subjectively certain* that these ideas will be realised and, further, that 'these views regarding the future have such a character that they would be completely fulfilled if it were not − and there lies the difference from the previous case − that unforeseen events occurred from time to time' (p. 338). These unforeseen events take place *only* at the points of transition from one period of time to another: 'This appears not unreasonable when dealing with short periods' (p. 339).

Suppose, for the moment, that the only unforeseen changes take place at the end of the tth period. Lindahl's method involves setting up two systems of equations. The first, which encompasses all the periods $(1, ..., v)$, relates to the beginning of the first period. During the first t periods, actual prices will correspond with the anticipated prices, the prices actually realised during the first t periods, of course, being dependent on the individuals' initial anticipations relating to periods $(t + 1, ..., v)$. However, because of the unforeseen events, these anticipations relating to periods $(t + 1, ..., v)$ will not actually be realised. A second system of equations must be set up corresponding to the beginning of the $(t + 1)$th period.[8] These embody the individuals' new anticipations relating to periods $(t + 1, ..., v)$. A comparison of the two systems of equations can elucidate the impact of the unforeseen changes on anticipations: 'This brings out the way in which one pricing situation is *transformed* into another, and also the importance of unforeseen changes for the actual development of prices' (p. 340). Unforeseen events may, of course, occur at the end of each period. But since the earliest any unforeseen events can occur is at the end of the first period, this method involves assuming that individuals do at least have perfect foresight for the first period. More generally, at the beginning of any period, individuals are assumed to have perfect foresight for that period.

Lindahl's model of an economy where individuals have imperfect foresight does constitute a genuine sequence. For Lindahl, the attraction of assuming that individuals have the same subjectively certain ideas about the future and that these ideas would be fulfilled were it not for unforeseen events is that it enables him to exploit the preceding analysis of a dynamic economy in which individuals have perfect foresight. Moreover, such assumptions about anticipations at least have a rational basis! He stresses:

The assumptions made as to the anticipations of individuals in every particular case are evidently of decisive importance for the character of the process. In a theoretical case these assumptions should not be arbitrary in any way. The most natural assumption from the theoretical point of view is *either* that anticipations are such that they will be realized (as assumed above), *or* that in each period people are certain that the price situation then existing will be maintained in the future (p. 344).

This belief that assumptions regarding anticipations must not be arbitrary is central to Lindahl's views as to how imperfect foresight might be accommodated.

Lindahl's final 'stage' is no more than suggestive. He observes: 'We have now brought our investigation to a point at which a further approximation to reality is associated with such considerable difficulties that we shall restrict ourselves to a few comments on a special setting of the problem' (p. 348). His main argument is that 'the assumption previously made, that a particular future development appears quite certain to everyone, must evidently be replaced by the assumption that people's ideas regarding the future have the character of probability judgments' (p. 348). He continues: 'The character of *these ideas regarding the future* depends upon two factors: people's power of making judgments regarding future developments, and their tendency to let their ideas be influenced by emotional considerations. How they act under the influence of these ideas depends in turn on a third factor, their evaluation of the risk believed by them to be associated with alternative courses of action' (p. 348). Lindahl has little to offer on how to proceed. He does hint that an appropriate starting-point might be an economy which is stationary 'in spite of the fact that people do not fully foresee the future and therefore must reckon with risks' (p. 349). More significantly, he stresses that it would be necessary 'to descend to *individual* functions, since the special mark of the fully dynamic problem is the difference between different individuals' (p. 349).

Some concluding comments

Lindahl's 1929 essay did not attract the attention which it deserved, even after its translation into English in 1939.[9] There have, however, been two highly significant references to Lindahl's influence. Hicks has acknowledged that the dynamic analysis of *Value and Capital*, published in 1939, was based on conversations with Lindahl. Moreover, in the *Theory of Value*, Debreu has credited Lindahl with providing 'the first general mathematical study of an economy whose activity extends over a finite number of elementary time-intervals under conditions of perfect foresight' (1959, p. 35, n. 1). We will consider both *Value and Capital* and the *Theory of Value* in subsequent chapters.

Lindahl's 1929 essay is a remarkable work for its time. However, he is clearly not satisfied with his attempts to incorporate uncertainty. He seems to be particularly uncomfortable that, even at the final stage, he is obliged to assume that, at the beginning of any period, individuals have perfect foresight for that period. He provides an extremely revealing footnote:

The assumption, that in a given period of time people perfectly foresee the price level that will prevail in this period as a result of their actions during the period, is, strictly speaking, a necessary condition for an explanation of a price situation as a state of equilibrium, in the sense that there exists a *mutual* connection between supply and demand on the one hand and actual prices on the other, and that, therefore, at existing prices exchange can continue until full satisfaction has been attained. The assumption thus underlies most theories of price determination. If this abstraction is dropped, another method of analysis must be used. It must be imagined that people anticipate a certain price situation and therefore decide upon a certain volume of supply and demand, and that these decisions give rise to a price situation *different* from that anticipated. (Even if there should be agreement with regard to prices, the two situations differ with regard to the relation between supply and demand.) The new situation causes people to alter their decisions, and this in turn gives rise to still another situation, again with new decisions, etc. In this case there is no mutual dependence between prices and the factors affecting prices at a given moment, but instead a *one-sided* causal connection in one direction or the other. A 'zigzag' movement of this kind in the determination of prices exists in reality, above all in transactions unusually sensitive to price change, especially on the stock and produce exchanges (pp. 339–40).

In this footnote, Lindahl is arguing that it is *only* in the case where, at the beginning of any period, individuals are assumed to have perfect information about the supply and demand functions for that period, that we can meaningfully claim that 'there exists a *mutual* connection between supply and demand on the one hand and actual prices on the other'. A curious feature of the essay is that Lindahl never alludes to Walras' preliminary phase of *tâtonnement*, since such a phase provides a way in which the equilibrium prices can be located *ex ante* without individuals having such perfect information. Presumably Lindahl would be prepared to say that, in that case, a mutual connection does exist between supply and demand and prices. It may well be that, in 1929, Lindahl had not understood the nature of the *tâtonnement*.[10] If he had, it seems likely that he would at least have qualified the claim that his own assumption of perfect foresight for the period 'underlies most theories of price determination'. Naturally, given that the assumption of a preliminary phase of *tâtonnement* is patently unrealistic, Lindahl would still be entitled to stress the need for another method of analysis. And, as we will see, Lindahl himself develops another method of analysis during the 1930s.

Notes

1 Unless otherwise indicated, page references in this chapter are to Lindahl (1939a).

2 Hayek (1928) is generally credited with first introducing the notion of intertemporal equilibrium.

3 As Lindahl notes, stipulating that the question of interest does not arise is not the same as assuming that the rate of interest is equal to zero. A zero rate of interest would involve a particular price for the 'time factor' and, indeed, depending on their time preferences, would be consistent with individuals exchanging present and future incomes between themselves. For the period to be strictly self-contained, the possibility of such exchanges must not even occur to them.

4 Lindahl notes that seeking to circumvent this problem by comparing 'independent stationary communities which are conceived to exist in isolation and which, in respect of the factors determining prices, show both resemblances to and differences from each other' is 'also beset with methodological difficulties' (p. 311).

5 In Chapter 7, we consider in some detail the implications of assuming a finite time-horizon.

6 We should perhaps repeat that, given constant returns to scale, perfect foresight is not sufficient to pre-reconcile plans.

7 Lindahl emphasises that his analysis of inter-temporal equilibrium ignores various complications which arise in a monetary economy. He stresses that, without 'more specific assumptions with regard to the monetary system and the ruling principles of monetary policy', 'no general rules can be laid down for the movements of the general price level in a community with perfect foresight' (p. 336). The reason is that, when prices are expressed in an arbitrary monetary unit, 'the problem is determined except for a multiplicative factor for each period' (p. 327).

8 Lindahl is not explicit as to whether, as one moves forward in time, the analysis still encompasses v future periods. Moreover, as we have seen, when discussing the case of perfect foresight, Lindahl 'imagines' that the economy will become stationary in period v. He does not reassess this assumption when he introduces imperfect foresight.

9 Lindahl's 1929 essay has been considered by Milgate (1979) in his study of the roles of Hayek, Lindahl and Hicks in the origin of the notion of inter-temporal equilibrium. Milgate's study is marred by a failure to distinguish between an inter-temporal equilibrium and a sequence of temporary equilibria. Moreover, Milgate presents a distorted picture of Lindahl's essay. Milgate claims that, whereas Lindahl advertises his contribution as an attempt to bring economic theory into closer contact with reality, underlying his analysis is a desire to circumvent the problem of defining the quantity of capital. In our view, there can be no doubt

that the fundamental impetus for Lindahl is a desire 'to bring the theory of price into closer contact with reality' (p. 271). This desire permeates the entire essay. But, leaving that aside, Milgate's story is flawed. For Milgate, the notion of inter-temporal equilibrium is necessarily bound up with the idea of a multiplicity of commodity own-rates of interest. But Lindahl's essay makes no reference to such own-rates. His analysis of inter-temporal equilibrium involves just one rate of interest for any period – a money rate of interest. It is worth noting that, whereas Lindahl claims that certain concepts – for example, capital value, income, saving – 'are not indispensable for a theoretical treatment of the pricing problem, they are only of secondary importance' (p. 328), the rate of interest is definitely not included among such concepts. Furthermore, Lindahl does not seek to circumvent the problem of measuring capital. Thus he states: 'We can, for example, try to determine the rate of interest as a function of the size of capital, keeping the basic thesis of the modern theory of capital in view, namely that with an increased amount of capital and a falling rate of interest longer investments are on the whole increased in a greater degree than the short ones' (pp. 309–10). Although he does not undertake 'this important and extensive task' in the essay, Lindahl does, for his more modest purpose, compare two alternative measures of capital. In a footnote added in 1939, he notes that both 'have the disadvantage that the measure of capital is made dependent on the prices of the services invested and on the rate of interest – which belong to the unknown factors of the problem' (p. 317). But, far from seeking to circumvent the problem of measuring capital, Lindahl continues: 'Since no better method seems to be available, we must, however, choose one of the two measures of capital' (p. 317). In the case of Lindahl at least, Milgate's arguments are patently false.

10 In 1939, when discussing Walras, Lindahl does allude to 'negotiation at the beginning of the period' (p. 66).

5

Lindahl *1939*

In the following statement of the general dynamic problem we have only made use of *one basic assumption* about the behaviour of the individuals concerned, namely, that their actions, for a shorter or longer period in the future, represent merely the fulfilment of certain plans, given at the beginning of the period and determined by certain principles which it is possible to state in one way or another. These principles should in general state that the plans are made for the attainment of certain aims ... and that they are based on individual expectations concerning future conditions, expectations which in turn are influenced by individual interpretation of past events (p. 36[1]).

It is extraordinary – indeed, lamentable – that so little attention has been accorded to Lindahl's 'The Dynamic Approach to Economic Theory'. This essay, published in 1939 as Part One of *Studies in the Theory of Money and Capital*, is even more remarkable than his 1929 essay. Although both essays have in common a preoccupation with time and, in particular, a manifest desire to develop a more realistic theory of price determination, their methods of approach are fundamentally different. As we have seen, the essence of the 1929 essay is, starting with the simplest case, to develop a sequence of increasingly complex models. In contrast, the essence of the 1939 essay is to start with a *general* theory which can then form the basis for more specific theories designed for particular purposes.

Although the 1939 essay makes only passing reference to the 1929 essay, it is evident that dissatisfaction with the latter provides the impetus for the new approach. As we have seen, the 1929 essay culminates in an acknowledgement by Lindahl of the 'considerable difficulties' which confront further progress in his sequential approach. It is reasonable to surmise that Lindahl's inability to see a way through these difficulties explains, at least in part, his search during the 1930s for an entirely different approach. Moreover, the 1929 essay acknowledges that dispensing with the assumption that individuals have perfect foresight at least for a short period will entail a new conception of the pricing process. The 1939 essay provides one.

The nature and aim of economic theory

For Lindahl, the role of the economic theoretician is to provide 'theoretical structures' which can be used 'either to explain the past or to forecast the economic events that will, under given conditions, probably occur in the future' (p. 21). The key to the essay is the desire to develop a theoretical system sufficiently general for it to serve the purposes of economic historians and applied economists. Given this desire to develop a general theoretical system, Lindahl's statement of the aim of economic theory is remarkably specific. He claims that explaining the past and forecasting the future both involve 'the demonstration of causal connections between the phenomena studied'. He continues:

The first step in this analysis is *to explain a certain development as a result of certain given conditions* prevailing at the beginning of the period studied. These given conditions must be stated in such a way that they contain *in nuce* the whole subsequent development. Thus they should embrace not only the external facts and the plans in existence at the initial point of time, but also, as latent propensities of the economic subjects taking part in the system, their subsequent reactions to what happens during the period. If all this is known, it will be possible to give a theoretical construction of the development in question (p. 21).

Lindahl further insists that it is an integral part of the causal-genetic approach to economic theory to examine the implications of *alternative* initial conditions: 'We do not fully understand the importance of the initial conditions for the resulting development, unless we have undertaken a *comparison with hypothetical developments* that might be the result of an assumed variation of these conditions' (p. 21). Establishing the relationships between initial conditions and subsequent developments is necessary for explanation, prediction and control. For example, if some future development is regarded as desirable, one could seek to determine which 'initial conditions' would need to be 'established', that is, one could seek to identify those actions of the relevant public bodies which would give rise to the desired development.[2]

Lindahl's ambitious conception of the aim of economic theory implies that it is inescapably dynamic:

> In mathematical phrasing, the object is to determine certain variables as functions of time (or time curves) with the help of equations, based on what is known as to the initial values of these variables and the conditions which determine their fluctuations. A theory of this type must be called *dynamic*. If our definition of economic theory is accepted, it is then impossible to avoid the somewhat perplexing conclusion that *all* economic theory that fulfils its purpose must have a dynamic character (p. 31).

Dynamics is thus defined to encompass statics: 'static theory represents a special application of general dynamic theory for stationary conditions' (p. 32).

Whereas it is commonplace for authors presenting 'dynamic' theories to be dismissive of analyses of stationary economies, Lindahl offers a more measured evaluation of such analyses. He suggests that, in some circumstances, stationarity may be a reasonable approximation to real conditions. Furthermore – and more significantly for Lindahl – the analysis of stationarity can provide insights into change: 'If we can state under what conditions the variables studied do not change, we can better understand the course of their actual fluctuations. Such comparisons between real and hypothetical cases are often very instructive' (pp. 34–5). Lindahl also suggests that, in the *exposition* of a theory, it may be appropriate to start with the case of a stationary economy. However, he is insistent that, in *working out* the theory, there are considerable disadvantages to doing so: 'If we begin with the static assumption as an isolated premiss, formulated as "abstraction from the time factor" or something of that sort, we are easily led astray, as is shown by the laborious but not always very successful attempts "to introduce the time factor in the Walrasian system of equations"' (p. 33). Lindahl has in mind, in particular, his own 1929 essay, the weakness of the latter, from his new perspective, being that, lacking a general dynamic theory, it proceeds from a static theory to a 'special' dynamic theory.

Taken out of context, Lindahl's statements of the objective of economic theory might suggest a misplaced confidence in the ability of economists to make precise predictions of the future. The context, however, involves a sharp distinction between the theory itself and its application:

The study of economics is largely concerned with human actions or the result of human actions. Leaving aside the question whether man can exercise free-will or not, it is of course not possible to determine the causes of his behaviour in the same way as those of the events of the external world. We cannot prove that certain human actions will *necessarily* be the result of a definite situation at a given point of time. We can only state that they do *probably* result from it and that a variation of the data will probably cause the individuals to act differently.

There lies in this a serious limitation to the possibilities of our analysis of historical and practical problems in the economic field. This deplorable inexactitude, however, affects only the application of economic theory, not the theory itself. In the construction of economic theories whose aim, as already indicated, is to determine certain developments on the basis of certain data, all inexactness can be avoided by explicit *assumptions* about all these phenomena which in the real world cannot be definitely determined. We can thus assume that individuals, under given conditions, do act in a certain manner, and the adoption of this assumption makes it possible to determine exactly what results will develop from any given situation (p. 35).

This should not be interpreted as meaning that theorists can be cavalier in choosing their assumptions. For Lindahl, it is self-evident that the usefulness of a theoretical structure will depend on the realism of the assumptions: 'It is of course essential that the assumptions which are the data of the theoretical system should be related as much as possible to empirical phenomena. Only in this way can the theoretical structures acquire relevance for the solution of actual problems' (p. 24). The choice of assumptions thus involves balancing the need for simplification and the desire for realism. Whereas in developing his *general* theory, Lindahl wishes to employ 'generally acceptable assumptions', he emphasises that analyses of actual problems will necessarily involve formulating *special* theories, involving more specific assumptions appropriate to the tasks in hand. He argues: 'The claim that can be made on economic theory in its proper sense can therefore be formulated in the following way: *it should give as much assistance as possible in the elaboration of the special theories*' (p. 25).

Lindahl's general dynamic theory

The emphasis of the essay is on the purposeful behaviour of individuals in the face of uncertainty; it is concerned with what Jaques called the time of intention and, in particular, with the interaction between memory, interpretation, expectation and desire. The essence of Lindahl's general dynamic theory can be explained in terms of Figure 5.1.

Figure 5.1

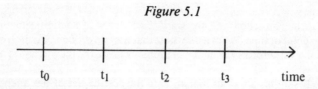

At t_0, some arbitrarily chosen initial instant, public bodies, private enterprises and private individuals form expectations of future conditions on the basis of their interpretations of past events and, on the basis of these prognoses, they formulate plans to achieve their objectives. Since, in general, these plans will not be consistent with one another or with external conditions, the attempts of at least some of the economic subjects to implement their plans will be frustrated. At t_1, they modify their prognoses of future conditions in the light of their experiences and revise their plans accordingly. During the period from t_1 to t_2, they seek to carry through their new plans. At t_2, they again revise their plans. And so on.

For the theorist to be able to deduce the future course of economic development from the 'given conditions', he must specify these conditions sufficiently comprehensively. According to Lindahl:

The statement of 'the given conditions' that represent the data for the explanation of the development can now be made more explicit. If we know (1) the *plans* of the economic subjects concerned at the initial point of time, if we further know (2) how these individuals are likely to *change their plans* in the future under different assumptions, and if we have (3) enough knowledge of *external conditions* to make definite statements with regard to future changes in plans, and the results of the actions undertaken then it should be possible to provide a theoretical construction of the developments that will be the outcome of the initial position (pp. 37–8).

Note, in particular, that the initial conditions – which are supposed to 'contain *in nuce* the whole subsequent economic development' – must include not only any latent propensities on the part of the economic subjects to react to what happens to them but also the future occurrence of relevant *non-economic* events, such as climatic and political events. Whilst known to the theorist, such future non-economic events are, of course, not supposed to be known to the economic subjects at t_0.

In his 1929 essay, Lindahl employs a discrete temporal framework, almost apologetically, to facilitate the analysis. In contrast, a major theme of the 1939 essay is a deliberate emphasis on discontinuities, a discrete temporal framework being invoked to highlight these discontinuities. Central to Lindahl's dynamic theory is the idea that there will typically be *lags* in the reactions of agents to their experiences:

The division of the planned development into definite periods has deep-lying grounds in the imperfection of human knowledge. Man cannot register all that happens around him. He can only take account of it *intermittently*, observing the total result obtained for certain time periods, or registering more important events that can be referred to definite points of time (p. 42).

These 'registration lags' – which may vary from individual to individual – influence the frequency of plan revision and, thereby, the theorist's choice of elementary periods. Specifically, the duration of the elementary periods must be sufficiently short for it to be reasonable to assume that no relevant changes in any plans take place *within* any period.

Lindahl is concerned about the realism of postulating that the various economic subjects formulate plans to attain their aims on the basis of prognoses of future conditions. Whereas explicit planning is obvious enough in the cases of public bodies and of private enterprises, he suggests that, for a private individual, the notion of a 'plan' may be interpreted broadly:

It can hardly be pretended that every individual has a clear conception of the economic actions that he is going to perform in a future period. Nevertheless, in the greater number of cases it will certainly be found that underlying such actions there are habits and persistent tendencies which have a definite and calculable character comparable to the explicit plans already mentioned. We may accordingly without danger proceed to generalize our notion of 'plans', so that they will include such actions. Plans are thus the explicit expression of the economic motives of man, as they become evident in his economic actions (p. 37).

Thus Lindahl does not have a purely mechanistic conception of the activity of planning. Nor does he suppose that all human actions are necessarily the result of conscious deliberation.

Lindahl suggests that it is convenient to divide a systematic exposition of a general dynamic theory into three stages. The first involves considering 'the *technical, institutional* and *psychological* conditions with regard to which the economist must make certain definite assumptions in explaining the principles of planning and the effects of the endeavours to realize the plans' (p. 39). The second involves the theory of *economic planning,* which encompasses not only the formulation of plans but also 'the principles valid for the alteration of plans with the lapse of time' (p. 39). The final stage is the theory of *economic development* whose purpose is 'to explain the dynamic process on the basis of certain assumptions regarding planning and external conditions made in accordance with the theories developed in the two first parts of the system' (p. 40). Lindahl does not elaborate on the first stage since it involves 'well-known theories'. He does, however, explore in some detail the second and third stages. We will consider these in turn.

The general theory of planning

Lindahl distinguishes two phases in an individual's planning at a given point in time. The first phase involves 'the intellectual *prognoses* of future developments' (p. 40). The individual must identify the 'field of choice', that is, the set of courses of action perceived to be open to him, where each course of action − or 'path of action' − would involve specified actions in each of the periods encompassed by the planning process. Since the future is uncertain, the individual must allow for different possible outcomes corresponding to any course of action. He must assign *subjective* probabilities to these possible consequences: 'The crux of the problem will lie in the calculation of the probability values, but this can of course be carried out more or less summarily' (p. 42).

Having completed this prognosis of future developments, the individual must choose between the alternatives open to him: 'In the *second* phase of planning a valuation of the relative advantages of these different alternatives is made, with due regard to the uncertainty factor in each case' (p. 42). The plan results from this co-ordination of anticipation and valuation: 'The actions of the individual prescribed in the selected alternative represent the "plan" in the strict sense' (p. 40).

Lindahl stresses that 'if we take a given plan as a whole, there exists a *mutual* interconnection between the present and future actions included in the plan' (p. 44). Just as the individual's field of choice at t_0 may well be constrained by past actions, he must take into account in his planning that his actions in the first period will typically limit the set of feasible actions in the second period, that his actions in the first two periods will typically restrict the set of feasible actions in the third period, and so on. Thus, even though the planner may be primarily interested in deciding upon his *immediate* behaviour, he needs to take a long-term perspective and to consider alternative actions, and their likely consequences, beyond the immediate future:

Only by taking account of this whole complex of alternatives and their respective probabilities, can the individual fully realize the consequences of his immediate choice. As a matter of fact, the primary purpose of the whole scheme is merely to provide a rational basis for this immediate choice, since the actions required in future periods can be determined by new or revised plans. Only if the anticipations turn out to be correct and if the valuation-attitude is unaltered, will the original plan retain its relevance for the succeeding periods (p. 44).

Lindahl emphasises the *diversity* of plans. They may be more or less definite. Whereas actions may be specified in some detail for the immediate future, they may be specified only in general terms for more remote periods. Plans may determine uniquely the intended actions or they may simply specify the intended actions between limits. Plans may also differ in the degree to which individuals deliberately maintain some leeway to modify them in the future. For Lindahl, the most important distinction is between planned actions which are *unconditioned* and those which are *conditioned*: 'The actions planned are unconditioned, if their realization does not depend on what happens in the intervening period, and they are conditioned in the opposite case when they are performed after the realization of a certain condition, either *immediately* or *with a certain time lag*' (p. 45). For example, a manufacturer's planned production levels of various types of shoes over the first period may be unconditioned, whereas his planned production levels for the second period may be conditioned, being contingent on his sales during the first period.

Having examined planning at a given point in time, Lindahl considers the even more complicated issue of the amendment of plans over time. He again emphasises the importance of registration lags: 'even in cases where the course of actual development is continuous, it cannot usually be assumed that our planner's apprehension of them also changes without discontinuity' (p. 49). In addition to the lag between events and their registration, there may be a further lag between the registration of events and changes in planned actions. For example, an individual's registration at t_1 of the events of the first period may only affect planned actions from, say, t_2 onwards since his actions during the first period may have determined his actions during the second period, t_1 to t_2. Lindahl continues:

Also, since it is reasonable to assume that the individual will not make frequent alterations in plans that do not refer to current periods but to more distant ones we may conclude that the intervals between relevant changes of plans, that is the 'periods with fixed relevant plans', will usually be considerably longer than the 'periods of registration' (p. 50).

Certain changes in plan may fall within the framework of the original plan, merely making the planned actions more definite. For example, planned actions previously specified between limits may be uniquely determined. Moreover, planned actions contingent on some particular event will become unconditioned once the event has occurred. With respect to more fundamental changes in plans, Lindahl differentiates between changes due to altered anticipations and those due to altered valuation-attitudes: 'It is hardly necessary to mention that changes of the former type are the commonest, both in actuality and in economic theory. The latter changes are usually of a more irregular character, and hence they present a more difficult subject for theoretical treatment' (p. 47). Lindahl also differentiates between changes in plans occasioned by economic events and changes prompted by non-economic events, the former being of more interest since they are explicable in terms of prior economic developments. He further stresses that the economist is primarily interested in changes in the actions planned in the immediate future rather than for more remote periods: 'Since the plan can be altered many times before these more distant periods are reached, this part of the planning is of importance only in so far as it facilitates the understanding of the plans actually put into practice' (pp. 47–8). He concludes that 'the economist is primarily concerned with immediately relevant changes in plans (those which are more fundamental than the mere increase in the definiteness of earlier plans) when they have their ground in changes in expectations, occasioned by the course of events during earlier periods' (p. 48).

Lindahl's discussion of the impact of events on expectations is uncharacteristically feeble. He merely identifies three simple assumptions which might be invoked:

(a) the change (e.g. the raising of a price) is assumed to continue at the same rate (an equal rise is expected for the next period), (b) the new conditions are expected to continue (the higher price is expected to remain unchanged), and (c) the change is regarded as temporary, so that in the next period a return to the original position is anticipated (here the rise is assumed to be followed by an equal fall in price) (p. 49).[3]

The main deficiency in Lindahl's treatment of this issue is his failure to acknowledge that there may be changes in the *ways* in which individuals formulate their expectations. Thus suppose that an individual is conceived to have some *subjective* model, of which he may or may not be conscious, of the workings of the relevant sectors of the economy. New experiences may be fed into this model leading him to revise his expectations. However, some events may be sufficiently surprising for him to change the model itself. Such changes over time in the individual's subjective model are likely to be irregular and potentially dramatic, rather than smooth and predictable. Consequently, changes in anticipations may present just as difficult a subject for *satisfactory* theoretical treatment as changes in valuation-attitudes.[4]

Lindahl is perhaps not sufficiently explicit in distinguishing between what is 'known' to the individual agents and what is 'known' to the theorist. At any point in time, the 'plan' of an individual refers to what he intends to do under various contingencies which he himself identifies. In general, the plan is *not* a complete specification of what the individual will do under every conceivable contingency which the *economic theorist* might identify. Some event may occur which the individual has not even contemplated. Thus the economic theorist needs to know more than the individual's plan. The 'given conditions' – which, as we have seen, 'contain *in nuce* the whole subsequent development' – must be sufficiently comprehensive to enable the theorist to determine how the individual *will* react under every conceivable circumstance. This can be illustrated with respect to registration periods. Such periods are embodied in the plans of individuals: an individual plans in terms of discrete periods because he recognises his own limited capacity to register what happens to him or because it would not be worthwhile to keep track of moment-to-moment variations in, say, his sales. The *ex post* registration periods need not correspond to these *ex ante* registration periods. Thus an individual may be prompted by some surprising event to review his experiences sooner than he had planned. For example, a newsagent may plan to 'take stock' at the end of each week. However, an unexpected boom in sales may lead him to do so on Wednesday evening. Therefore, the theorist needs to know not only how frequently the individual intends to review his experiences but also the circumstances which will prompt him to do so at other times. Similarly, although the individual will typically not know *ex ante* how he will amend his prognoses of future conditions in the light of new experiences, the theorist does need to know this.

The general theory of development

According to Lindahl, economists are generally interested in 'macro-economic processes'. He uses the term 'macro-economic' to embrace more than does its modern usage: whereas a micro-economic analysis is, for Lindahl, confined to the study of a *single* economic subject, a macro-economic process consists of 'acts and the results of acts carried out by a number of economic subjects, together constituting a *group* of a certain definite character' (p. 52). In the study of a macro-economic process, the variables will usually be aggregates (e.g. the quantities of services used in the production of a particular commodity) or averages (e.g. the average of the prices for a particular commodity):

All these variables can be regarded as functions of time. But it should be observed that they cannot conveniently be determined as continuous functions of time. Some of the actions considered, for example the announcement of prices and sales and other transactions, have, strictly speaking, no time dimension. They must therefore either be correlated with definite points of time or with certain time periods for which the total result is calculated. Other variables, e.g. the amounts of services put into production, have undoubtedly a time dimension. But even in this case only the total result for certain definite periods is usually of interest, and not the continuous variation from moment to moment (p. 53).

Thus the specification of the temporal framework involves differentiating carefully between those actions which are to be related to definite points in time and those which are not. For example, if the analyst wishes to highlight the precise points in time at which announcements of prices are made but not the precise points in time at which transactions take place, price announcements would be related to those points in time which constitute the boundaries between periods, whereas transactions would only be referred to periods of time. The analysis would merely involve determining, for each time period, the total results of the transactions taking place during that period, the variations in transactions from moment to moment within each period being ignored. Lindahl calls the elementary period – the shortest period taken into account – 'the "period of registration" with respect to the variables studied by the economist' (p. 54).

Since the most significant events in Lindahl's general dynamic theory are relevant changes in the plans of individuals, these are necessarily related to the points in time which demarcate the various periods. Consequently the maximum duration of the period of registration of the analysis will be the longest period for which it can reasonably be assumed that there are no relevant changes in any plans. If all plan changes were *synchronised* – if all individuals were to amend their plans at precisely the same points in time – the elementary period of the analysis would correspond to the period for which individual plans are fixed. But as Lindahl notes: 'In reality, however, the synchronization is very incomplete, and the period during which the relevant plans of all members of the group are retained unchanged, must therefore be taken to be *fairly short*' (p. 54). Although Lindahl does not (at this stage[5]) specify what 'fairly short' might mean in calendar terms, he does elaborate on why the period of the analysis will need to be 'fairly short':

In the greater number of instances studied we then find in operation a great variety of plans that have been drawn up, not only by public authorities and individual consumers, but also by private and more or less independent entrepreneurs who do not know very much about one another's intentions. One cannot count upon all these plans being kept wholly unaltered during any long period. The attempts to realize the plans must quickly reveal that they are more or less incompatible. The actual course of events cannot correspond to all the anticipations of the individuals about the behaviour of the others. The result must therefore be a modification of some of the plans (pp. 54–5).

This justification implicitly acknowledges that the lengths of time for which individual plans will be unchanged are endogenous, such intervals depending on the degree to which plans are incompatible and on how quickly individuals realise that they need to amend their plans. Lindahl insists that, although the elementary period needs to be fairly short, the amendment of plans is *not* to be regarded as a continuous process: 'since the decisions to apply new plans can be allocated to certain moments, some time must always elapse between these moments in any given case, during which all plans are unaltered' (p. 55). He concludes:

Our scheme can therefore, even from a strictly logical point of view, be directly applied, as long as the time periods used are made sufficiently short. It should further be observed that, in applying our scheme to practical problems, it is quite a justifiable simplification to assume that the intervals elapsing between alterations of plans are not impossibly short, but long enough to be of practical interest. This represents only a slight modification of what really happens, and it helps us to get a clearer insight into the nature of the economic process (p. 55).

In assessing Lindahl's discussion of the appropriate temporal framework, there is a tension between doing so from the perspective of theoretical economist and doing so from the perspective of applied economist. Rather than saying that the initial conditions are given to the theoretician, it would be more appropriate to say that the conditions are what he assumes them to be. In principle, the theoretician could determine the precise points in time at which plans will be amended, so that discrete periods, during which all plans are unaltered, could emerge from an analysis which treats time as continuous. In contrast, an applied economist must specify periods *ex ante*. Lindahl does not elaborate on precisely why economists are not likely to be interested in 'the continuous variation from moment to moment' in the variables being studied. Perhaps he has in mind that, if the elementary period was, say, of one second's duration, the results of the analysis would be so overwhelming as to be uninformative. A compelling argument for employing time periods which are 'not impossibly short' might be that, *like the economic subjects whose behaviour he studies*, the applied economist cannot continuously register all that happens and that 'he can only take account of it *intermittently*, observing the total result obtained for certain time periods, or registering more important events that can be referred to definite points of time'.

Lindahl discusses briefly the data required for the analysis of a macro-economic development. To determine the developments which will take place over the *first* period, it is necessary for the economist to know the totals of all unconditioned and uniquely determined plans for that period (a knowledge of each individual plan not being necessary). Lindahl suggests that, to determine the 'totals' of the unconditioned plans specified within limits, the probability calculus

may be invoked: 'Even though the acts of each individual may be supposed to vary within a narrower or wider margin, the probable result
of the totality of their acts may be deduced by means of the law of
large numbers' (p. 56). In addition, it is necessary to know the totals of
the conditioned plans, where the planned actions are contingent on
external factors or on the results of the unconditioned acts:

The realization of these plans may be supposed to take place either immediately upon the fulfilment of the condition or, if the latter is realized at
the beginning of the period, with a time lag which may not exceed the length
of the period. The conditioned plans must evidently enter into the data as
functions of the conditions valid in each given case (p. 56).

In order to determine the economic developments over the first period,
it is also necessary to know the relations between actions and their
outcomes: 'For example, if in a given ca . the acts consist of certain
kinds of inputs of productive services, and the output resulting from
these inputs is included among the variables studied, we must naturally
know the true relation between input and output' (p. 57). Finally it
is necessary to have the required information on external conditions,
such as climatic or political events: 'For instance, if we know that
the members of the group are prepared to act in a certain way on a
sunny day and in a different way on a rainy day, the determination
of their actions presupposes knowledge of which alternative is
realized' (p. 57).

   In order to determine developments during the *second* period, it
is necessary to know how individuals will modify their plans in the
light of endogenous developments during the first period and in the
light of relevant non-economic events. Having established the plans
for the second period, the developments for the second period are
analysed on the same principles as for the first period. And so on.

   Lindahl notes that the analysis may be simplified by invoking
various assumptions (e.g. that non-economic events may be
neglected). He also stresses that it will normally be impossible for the
economist to analyse a macro-economic development − based on
'fairly short periods' − in detail from period to period: 'In spite of
this, it is quite feasible to give a picture of the course of events during
a fairly long stretch of time. If by the analysis of certain selected
typical periods, one can determine the directions of movement during
these stretches, the character of the intervening periods may also be
understood' (p. 59). This indicates that Lindahl would not wish the

notion of the analyst working out the implications for macro-economic processes of certain initial conditions to be taken too literally. Nor should the notions of explaining the past or forecasting the future be interpreted too mechanically. Lindahl is, above all, seeking for ways in which macro-economic developments may be *understood*. It should also be recalled that Lindahl appreciates that his general theory is very general and that 'special' theories are needed for examining specific economic problems, 'thus permitting a certain division of labour, not only between economics as a whole and the other social sciences, but also between the various branches of economics itself' (p. 60).

The pricing process

Lindahl's general dynamic theory provides the basis for a radically different conception of the pricing process. He insists that conceiving of this process as a series of disequilibria is more realistic than the usual approaches:

The pricing problem is often treated under the assumption of free competition, whereby the prices operating in a certain period can be regarded as the *result* of the operation of certain given demand and supply functions during the period. This construction is quite appropriate when used for the analysis of the *equilibrium* position of a price or a system of prices. But it is not always so appropriate when the pricing problem is analysed from a more realistic point of view. In an actual dynamic case, there is no necessity for equality of demand and supply. But the opposite concept of price as *continuously changing* under the influence of the demand and supply functions is equally not correct (p. 60).

Lindahl's analysis involves a sharp distinction between *offers* to trade and *acceptance* of those offers. His representation of the pricing process is designed to highlight the precise moments at which prices are announced: price changes *only* take place at the points in time which demarcate the periods. In contrast, the precise moments at which price offers are accepted are not identified, so that only the period in which a particular transaction takes place is relevant. Thus consider again Figure 5.1. Suppose that, at t_0, it is *sellers* who announce prices at which they are willing to trade until further notice, these prices being based on anticipated sales. During the period t_0 to t_1, transactions are carried out at those prices and 'the more or less continuous processes of production and consumption take place'

(p. 62). At t_1, sellers calculate their actual sales over the first period and take account of their stocks and of any outstanding orders. On this basis, they revise their plans and, in particular, they announce any changes in prices, these new prices remaining in force for the duration of the second period. The 'motive force' behind price movements is the divergence between actual sales and anticipated sales.

The weakness of this conception of the pricing process is that much happens at the points in time which demarcate the time periods. As Lindahl concedes:

The announcement of new prices, for example, by certain sellers, will generally induce other firms or persons who for some reason (as buyers or competing sellers) are directly interested in these prices, to modify their own plans of action, and eventually the prices they themselves offer. In applying our scheme we must assume that either these alterations follow the original price changes immediately and can therefore be allocated to the same points of time, or that they are allocated to a transition point between certain later periods (p. 61).

Although Lindahl claims that the first of these assumptions is the more convenient for his purpose, he does not elaborate on why. It is worth exploring these alternatives further.

Lindahl does acknowledge in a footnote that the first assumption imposes a strain on the notion of individuals formulating their plans at the same moment in time:

This assumption involves of course a simplification, as in reality some time must always elapse between the moment when a seller alters his price and the moment when a buyer decides for that reason to buy more or less of the article in question. But if no bargains are transacted during this short interval (which is quite a reasonable assumption, as the buyer may be waiting for the new price before he decides how much to buy), this is of no economic importance (p. 61, n*).

It is not disquieting to have to conceive of, say, t_1 as a very short interval (rather than as a strict point in time) to allow buyers time to formulate plans in response to the announced prices. However, this does not get to the heart of the problem – Lindahl does not acknowledge the complications which arise in the case of *competing sellers*. Suppose that certain manufacturers of (more or less differentiated) shoes announce new prices. The other manufacturers may well wish to modify the prices they themselves offer. The original manufacturers may then wish to alter their prices yet again. And so on. Lindahl's preferred alternative seems to imply that all these reactions are to be assigned to a short interval during which no bargains are transacted. Although *per se* that need not be disquieting, what *is* disconcerting is that this process of interaction between the shoe manufacturers is an essential element of the pricing process. Yet Lindahl has nothing to say on how the process of interaction might be analysed. Treating shoe manufacturers as a 'group' would simply evade the problem.

Consider Lindahl's second – and less convenient – alternative. This would presumably involve supposing that each shoe manufacturer decides on what prices to offer (at, say, t_1) without knowing what prices other manufacturers are planning to offer and without having any opportunity to revise his prices until the end of the following period. It is not at all evident that his pricing decision could reasonably be assumed to be governed, in some relatively simple way, by the relationship between his actual sales and his anticipated sales over the previous period. His pricing decision would be dominated by his anticipations as to the price changes the *other* manufacturers are likely to announce, rather than being governed by his anticipations of the general state of demand for shoes. This second approach would clearly raise, in acute form, questions about the degree of homogeneity of commodities and the amount of information prospective buyers have about the prices on offer. In the extreme case, if all pairs of shoes were perfectly homogeneous and if prospective buyers knew all the prices on offer, they would all concentrate on the seller(s) offering the lowest price.[6]

Lindahl and others

In the introduction to this chapter, we suggested that Lindahl's 1939 essay has not received the explicit recognition which it deserved. However, it has perhaps had a highly significant *indirect* influence on the economics profession. Lindahl undoubtedly had a profound effect on Hicks. We have already noted that Hicks has acknowledged that *Value and Capital* was based on conversations with Lindahl. That *Value and Capital* was also published in 1939 does not mean that it could not have been affected by Lindahl's 1939 essay, since, as we will see in a moment, Lindahl had formulated the ideas underlying the 1939 essay some years earlier. It seems likely that his conversations with Hicks would have embraced not only his 1929 essay but also his 1939 approach. Moreover, it seems that Hicks' 'fix-price' method, presented in *Capital and Growth*, was largely inspired by Lindahl's 1939 essay.

Furthermore, Shackle, who cannot be accused of littering his works with references to other economists, has often referred to Lindahl. In particular, he has acknowledged an early indirect influence of Lindahl: 'Hayek's *Economics and Knowledge* was of course of classic and inspiring importance, but although this appeared just after my time as a research student under Hayek, my inoculation with ideas of the fundamental and central importance of expectations came from the lectures I attended in my first term at the LSE given by Brinley Thomas, just back from a year in Sweden where he had absorbed ideas from Myrdal and Lindahl' (1981, p. 60). Moreover, Shackle reviewed *Studies in the Theory of Money and Capital* for the *Economic Journal*. He was particularly impressed by Lindahl's 1939 essay.[7] One can only speculate on the impact which this essay had on Shackle's subsequent thoughts.

The relative neglect of Lindahl's 1939 essay is in stark contrast to the plaudits bestowed, albeit somewhat belatedly, on Hayek's 'Economics and Knowledge', published in 1937. The reader may be struck by a certain affinity between the two works. However, it should not be supposed that Hayek's article provided the inspiration for Lindahl's new approach. Hansson (1982) has located a draft chapter of Lindahl's which formed the basis for the 1939 essay. This was written in 1935 at a time when Hayek was still clearly insisting on the indispensability, for all economic theorising, of the assumption that prices provide an automatic mechanism for equilibrating supply and demand. *Indeed, it would be a mistake to exaggerate the affinity between Lindahl's essay and Hayek's article.* It is true that Lindahl observed that Hayek's ideas were 'quite in harmony' with his own (p. 38, n*). However, in his review of *Studies in the Theory of Money and Capital* for *Economica*, Hayek claimed that the *1929* essay − not the 1939 essay − 'will prove to be of the greatest permanent value' (1940, p. 333). There was no suggestion that Hayek approved of Lindahl's new approach. The explanation for this, we suggest, is that Hayek's 1937 article was much less 'radical' − in a methodological sense − than commonly portrayed. Certainly it was much less radical than Lindahl's 1939 essay. Whereas Lindahl emphasised the complexity of the individual's planning problem, Hayek asserted that an individual's choice of plan follows tautologically from his subjective data by the so-called 'pure logic of choice'. Whereas Lindahl focused on uncertainty, Hayek spoke of knowledge. Whereas Lindahl was proposing a disequilibrium method – his only reference to equilibrating forces being the observation that the process of price formation might *conceivably* result in an equilibrium – Hayek was fundamentally concerned with equilibrium analysis – and, indeed, suggested that experience shows that, in reality, equilibrating forces are at work, 'since the empirical observation that prices do tend to correspond to costs was the beginning of our science' (1937, p.49). Given that in the 1930s many notable economists were questioning traditional equilibrium analysis, Hayek's 1937 article was not as radical as some 'modern Austrians' (Lachmann is an exception to this) would have us believe.

Notes

1 Unless otherwise indicated, page references in this chapter are to Lindahl (1939a).
2 It should be clear that Lindahl is using the expression 'initial conditions' – 'which contain *in nuce* the whole subsequent development' – to embrace much more than the usual usage of the term.
3 Lindahl refers to Hicks' notion of the 'elasticity of expectations'. We will consider this in the next chapter.
4 In principle, the theorist could specify a latent rule whereby the individual's subjective model might be amended in the light of sufficiently surprising events. The theorist might also specify a latent rule whereby *that* latent rule might be altered in the light of sufficiently surprising events – and so on! There is clearly a problem of infinite regress.
5 Lindahl subsequently uses a day as his elementary period.
6 Lindahl discusses briefly the relationship between his conception of the pricing process and those methods which involve equilibrium between supplies and demands (see pp.64–9 of his essay). In part, this discussion relates to Hicks' *Value and Capital*, to be considered in the next chapter.
7 Shackle argues: 'There is only one respect in which this chapter is not completely satisfying: Professor Lindahl is content to use the word "probability" where the future outcome of a present action is not felt by the individual concerned to be definitely known to him. In this he seems to be turning aside from *the* central problem of dynamic economics: how to give risk and uncertainty precise meaning and fit them into our analysis' (p.104). *If* Shackle has in mind Knight's

distinction between risk and uncertainty, he has misunderstood it. Contrary to a very widespread belief, Knight actually confined the term 'risk' to the case of objective probabilities and used the term 'uncertainty' to encompass the case of subjective probabilities. Lindahl is concerned with uncertainty in the Knightian sense.

6

Hicks

The economic system has now to be conceived of, not merely as a network of interdependent markets, but as a process in time (p. 116[1]).

Sir John Hicks has, throughout his career, been preoccupied with the treatment of time. In this chapter, we will focus on *Value and Capital: An Inquiry into Some Fundamental Principles of Economic Theory*, in which he presents his conception of a process in time as a series of temporary equilibria, each temporary equilibrium being dependent on individuals' expectations of the future. Published in 1939, this work constitutes one of his most influential contributions to economic theory.

Value and Capital reflects both Marshallian and Walrasian influences. Although Hicks rejects what he describes as Marshall's 'rigid' division between the day, the short period and the long period, the influence of Marshall is nevertheless evident. As we will see, Hicks' motive for rejecting Marshall's temporal framework is that it is inappropriate for analysing an economic system as a whole. In emphasising the interdependence between markets, Hicks follows Walras and Pareto. Indeed, one of his stated objectives is to rescue the Lausanne analysis from the Marshallian reproach of sterility. The major influence on *Value and Capital*, however, was Lindahl. As we have seen, Hicks has acknowledged that his conception of a process in time was inspired by conversations with Lindahl. As Lindahl observed in a letter to Frisch in 1934, an attraction of conceiving of a process in time as a sequence of temporary equilibria is that static analysis can be applied to the single period.[2] Hicks exploits this to the full.

Value and Capital is divided into four parts. The first two parts focus on the interdependence between markets without any reference to time. Hicks refers to this analysis as his 'statics', since 'we do not trouble about dating' (p. 115). The final two parts – on which we will focus – present his conception of a process in time. Hicks describes this as his 'dynamics', since 'every quantity must be dated' (p. 115). In the next section, we will summarise the essential features of Hicks' process in time. In subsequent sections, we will explore in more detail certain aspects of his analysis.

Hicks' process in time

Hicks enters his economy at a particular point in time. The economy has given stocks of 'material equipment', comprising land, buildings, machines, raw materials, final products ready for sale and consumer durable goods: 'From now on, the economic problem consists in the allotment of these resources, inherited from the past, among the satisfaction of present wants and future wants' (p. 130). Certain resources – designated 'entrepreneurial resources' – cannot be disposed of on markets. Hicks does not specify precisely the nature of these resources. He does not seem to have in mind inherently non-marketable personal attributes. More mundanely, it seems that some individuals – prospective entrepreneurs – own relevant material resources which are non-marketable, but which can be productively combined with resources for which there are markets. Whether or not it will be profitable for a prospective entrepreneur to become an actual entrepreneur will depend on prices. Entrepreneurs demand factors and supply products on their business accounts, returns from these entrepreneurial activities constituting part of their incomes on their private accounts. Whereas all entrepreneurs are thus private individuals, not all private individuals are entrepreneurs, since some individuals may not possess entrepreneurial resources and others may do so but elect not to use them.

Hicks assumes that all markets are perfectly competitive, all prospective traders being price-takers with 'perfect contemporaneous knowledge' about current prices. Commodities are differentiated not only on the basis of their physical attributes but also according to date. Thus units of wheat to be delivered at different dates are different commodities. Hicks distinguishes between spot markets, forward markets and loan markets. A spot transaction involves the 'immediate' execution of both sides of the contract. A forward transaction involves the 'simultaneous' execution of both sides of the contract at some stipulated time in the future. The distinguishing characteristic of a loan transaction is that 'its execution is divided in time'. According to Hicks, the dominant type of loan transaction is one which involves money on both sides: any other form of loan transaction – such as one involving money payment in advance for a commodity or one involving deferred money payment for a commodity or one involving the exchange of current wheat for future wheat – can be reduced to a money loan combined with a spot transaction and/or a forward transaction. Hicks acknowledges that own rates of interest can be defined but argues that they are 'of little direct importance for us' (p. 142).[3]

The nature of Hicks' economy cannot be separated from his temporal framework. Specifically, he assumes that markets are *only* open on 'Mondays'. Thus, on the Monday of any 'week', individuals enter into spot contracts, loan contracts and, where appropriate, forward contracts. The 'spot' contracts would include contracts to be fulfilled during the week, that is, fulfilment during the week must be interpreted as 'immediate' fulfilment. Although Monday is differentiated from the rest of the week, the analysis does not differentiate between different times during the rest of the week. Thus, when Hicks suggests that assuming that markets are open only on Mondays provides 'a convenient way of visualising the assumption of constant prices during the week' (p. 122), this has to be interpreted as meaning that the prices determined on Monday are independent of delivery times during the week. Moreover, when Hicks refers to allowing for variability in the output of a commodity 'during' the week, this must be interpreted as referring not to *intra*-week variations in instantaneous rates of flow but to variations in the total output of the week, that is, in the week's accumulated flow of output. Hicks emphasises that the week must not be confused with its calendar counterpart and that its duration will depend on the purposes of the analysis.

The week represents the planning interval. The plans of entrepreneurs and private individuals, which are formulated or revised each Monday, normally encompass planned transactions not only on that Monday but also on subsequent Mondays. According to Hicks:

It is fundamentally important to realize that the decisions of entrepreneurs to buy and sell (and to some extent also the similar decisions of private persons) nearly always form part of a system of decisions which is not bounded by the present, but has some reference to future events. The current activities of a firm are part of a plan, which includes not only the decision to make immediate purchases and sales, but also the intention to make sales (at any rate, and usually purchases as well) in the more or less distant future (p. 123).

These plans must be based on expectations of the prices and rates of interest which will prevail on future Mondays. By assuming that these expectations are single-valued, Hicks is able to exploit his static analysis of a multi-product firm.[4] Such expectations will, in general, depend on the prices established on previous Mondays. Hicks does not discuss the nature of that dependence − let alone postulate any formal relationship − on the grounds that, as far as the current Monday is concerned, what happened in the past is a datum. In contrast, he does emphasise that a change in the 'current' price of a commodity may affect an individual's expectations of the future prices of that commodity. Thus Hicks defines an individual's elasticity of expectations of the price of a particular commodity as the ratio of the proportional change in expected future prices of the commodity to the proportional change in its current price (which, of course, involves the assumption that a change in the current price will result in the same proportionate change in expected future price whatever the future date to which the expectation relates). Hicks distinguishes the cases where the elasticity of expectations is negative; zero; positive but less than one; one; and greater than one. If the elasticity of expectations is zero, expectations are strictly given: we can visualise the individual forming expectations on the Monday morning before the markets open and not revising them whatever may transpire when they do open. If the elasticity of expectations is unity, a change in the current price of a commodity will change expected prices in the same direction and in the same proportion.

Each entrepreneur plans ahead over a finite period, any plant which would be left over at the end of that period being regarded as a particular type of output, one which is only produced in the last week of the planning period. An entrepreneur's technology is represented by an inter-temporal production function. Corresponding to each feasible production plan is a stream of expected surpluses of revenues over costs. The entrepreneur is assumed to choose the one with the highest present value. In identifying the corresponding marginality conditions and in deriving the effects of changes in current or expected prices on the optimal production plan, Hicks is able to draw on his static analysis of a multi-product firm.

Hicks expresses some reservations about extending the notion of planning to private individuals:

But when we turn to the case of the private individual, whose 'plan' (if he has a plan) must be directed solely to the satisfaction of his wants in the present and in the future, then the fact that he will ordinarily not know what his future wants are going to be (and will know that he does not know) becomes very upsetting (pp. 227–8).

He allays his misgivings, however, in a characteristically Hicksian manner:

If we assume the individual to have a complete plan of expenditure, extending over a considerable future period, and complete in every detail, we are falsifying his actual behaviour quite absurdly; but if we merely use this assumption, not to determine the details of the purchases which may (or may not) be planned to be made in the future, but to determine the details of current expenditure alone, we are not involved in anything which is at all absurd. The determination of current expenditure will proceed just as if there was such a complete plan; if we assume the existence of a complete plan we can proceed to determine current expenditure with the minimum of trouble (p. 229).

Having stipulated an inter-temporal budget constraint which takes into account the possibility of borrowing and lending, Hicks again invokes his static analysis: 'Just as in the case of production, we have only to make a distinction between transactions due to be made at different dates, and to replace actual prices by discounted prices; when we have made these changes, the whole static theory of value becomes directly applicable' (p. 230). Hicks suggests that private individuals (and entrepreneurs) might choose to demand money, rather than interest-yielding securities, because of a lack of synchronisation between receipts and expenditures, because of uncertainty over future receipts and expenditures and because of the costs of effecting transactions.

Temporary equilibrium, which requires that 'current demands and supplies have been rendered equal' (p. 155), pertains only to those spot, forward and loan markets which are open on the current Monday; it does not require that plans pertaining to transactions on future Mondays be consistent with each other or with the economy's resources. In a spot economy with short lending, current supplies and demands must be equal for all commodities, for loans of one-week duration and for 'money' (i.e. that 'good' used as *numéraire*).

If there are n commodities (excluding money), there are (n + 1) prices to be determined, i.e. the n prices of commodities in terms of the *numéraire* plus the rate of interest. The (n + 2) equations − namely, n equations of supply and demand for commodities, one for loans and one for money − provide (n + 1) independent equations. In a spot economy with long lending, Hicks, by regarding the promise to pay £1 per annum as a unit of 'security', reduces all old and new securities to a homogeneous commodity whose price is the reciprocal of the current interest rate.[5] As before, there are (n + 2) equations − for commodities, for securities and for money − of which one can be eliminated. These (n + 1) independent equations determine the n prices of commodities and the rate of interest (or equivalently the price of a security).

Hicks assumes that trading continues on the Monday for however long is necessary for a temporary equilibrium to be established: 'this is essential in order for us to be able to use the equilibrium method in dynamic theory' (p. 131). He postulates just one adjustment process, whereby prices respond to excess demands and excess supplies:

The plans which people adopt depend upon current prices and on their expectations of future prices; but current prices are themselves determined by current demands and supplies, which are part of the plans. Thus, if a set of prices is fixed on the first Monday which does not equate demand and supply in all markets, there will have to be an adjustment of prices; prices will fall in those markets where supply exceeds demand, rise in those markets where demand exceeds supply. This change of current prices will induce an alteration of plans, and consequently of supplies and demands; through the alteration of plans supplies and demands are brought into equilibrium (pp. 130-1).

Hicks acknowledges that, as a result of trading at 'false' prices, the final equilibrium would typically be path-dependent. To circumvent this, he suggests that 'we need ... to try and bring ourselves to suppose that price-changes are negligible during market hours on the Monday, when the market is open and dealers have to fix market prices by higgling and bargaining, trial-and-error. This implies that the market (indeed, all markets) proceeds quickly and smoothly to a position of temporary equilibrium' (p. 123).

Having considered Hicks' week, his conception of plans, his treatment of expectations and his notion of temporary equilibrium, we are now able to appreciate his own description of his approach:

By using the week, we become able to treat a process of change as consisting of a series of temporary equilibria; this enables us still to use equilibrium analysis in the dynamic field. By using the plan, we become able to bring out the relation between those actions devoted to present ends, and those actions which are directed to the future. By supposing plans to unroll themselves during the week, we find ourselves able to conceive of the situation at the end of the week being different from the situation at the beginning; thus the new temporary equilibrium which is established in a second week must be different from that which was established in the first; going on in like manner, we have a process under way.

By the device of definite expectations, we are enabled to use the same analysis as we used in statics to set out the equilibrium of the private individual and the firm, to determine the dependence of plans on current prices *and* expected prices. Taking this together with the fact that we have preserved the concept of market equilibrium, the essentials of static analysis are still available to us (p. 127).

Hicks' analysis of the 'working of the dynamic system' consists primarily of examining the impact on temporary equilibrium of changes in the data. He emphasises that these are purely *hypothetical* changes: 'We seek to compare the system of prices actually established in a particular week with that system which would have been established in the same week if the data (tastes, resources, or expectations) had been rather different' (p. 246). He argues that such an analysis can provide useful insights into 'what immediate alteration in the course of events will follow from a particular change in data' (p. 246). Invoking the elastic nature of the week, he suggests that the term 'immediate' can be interpreted more or less strictly.

The attainment of temporary equilibrium on each Monday does not ensure that the economy is, in any meaningful sense, in 'equilibrium over time', since the economy might be staggering from one temporary equilibrium to the next, with individuals constantly finding that their expectations are being disappointed and that they are unable to fulfil their plans. In seeking a criterion for equilibrium over time, Hicks rejects the notion of stationarity as too restrictive: 'the stationary state is, in the end, nothing but an evasion' (p. 117). In the context of his process in time, the relevant consideration is whether or not expectations are realised. Consider, as Hicks does, two successive Mondays. The most exacting requirement for equilibrium over time is that individuals' point expectations on the first Monday concerning the prices of the second Monday are actually realised. On this basis, he identifies several possible causes of disequilibrium.

First, individuals may have different expectations. Second, even if their expectations are consistent, their plans may not be. For example, for some commodity, total planned demand may be less than total planned supply, so that price turns out to be lower than expected. Finally, even if both their expectations and their plans are consistent, individuals may fail to foresee changes in their own preferences or in techniques of production, so that, on the second Monday, they may be unwilling or unable to carry out their original plans. Hicks is, in fact, prepared to invoke a considerably less demanding − and vaguer − requirement for equilibrium over time: 'when we remember that the expectations of entrepreneurs are in fact not precise expectations of particular prices, but partake more of the character of probability distributions, then it becomes evident that the realised prices can depart to some extent from those prices expected as most probable, without causing any acute sense of disequilibrium' (p. 133). Hicks' primary motive for considering disequilibrium over time is not to examine how the disappointment of expectations will induce individuals to revise their plans but to enable him *ex post* to identify possible causes of 'waste' and, on this basis, to compare alternative institutional arrangements. He suggests that a point of reference may be provided by a 'pure futures economy' in which everything is arranged in advance 'for a considerable period ahead'. Although he emphasises that, because of transactions costs and uncertainty, such a complete set of markets never exists, he does suggest that the pure futures economy may have some theoretical uses:

By examining what system of prices would be fixed up in a futures economy, we can find out what system of prices would maintain equilibrium over time under a given set of changing conditions. Economists have often toyed with the idea of a system where all persons trading have 'perfect foresight'. This leads to awkward logical difficulties, but the purpose for which they have invented such systems can be met by our futures economy (p. 140).

Hicks does not elaborate on the nature of the 'awkward logical difficulties' associated with the assumption of perfect foresight but he may well have in mind the difficulty which troubled Lindahl in 1929, namely, that of reconciling the assumption that individuals know what future prices will be with the idea that future prices will be the result of the actions of those individuals.[6]

The week

We must now explore certain aspects of Hicks' temporal framework
in more detail. Hicks introduced the Monday and the week in 'Wages
and Interest: the Dynamic Problem', published in 1935.[7] Like
Lindahl in his 1929 essay, Hicks justified a discontinuous treatment
of time on grounds of analytical tractability:

> We are accustomed to thinking of economic magnitudes as continuous 'flows',
> but the convenience of this is limited to the static case, when the flows are
> constant through time. A flow which varies through time is very difficult to
> handle. Consequently it seems best to cut up the varying flows into short
> sections, each of which can be treated as constant. We can do this by supposing
> changes to take place, not continuously, but at intervals (1935, p. 68).

In *Value and Capital*, Hicks insists that the week, being the 'shortest
period' allowed for in the analysis, 'needs to be clearly conceived and
clearly defined'. He continues:

> I shall define a week as that period of time during which variations in prices
> can be neglected. For theoretical purposes this means that prices will be
> supposed to change, not continuously, but at short intervals. The calendar
> length of the week is of course quite arbitrary; by taking it to be very short,
> our theoretical scheme can be fitted as closely as we like to that ceaseless
> oscillation which is a characteristic of prices in certain markets. I think we
> shall find, however, that when the week is supposed to be very short, our
> theory becomes rather uninformative; I believe that it is better to think of
> it as being fairly long, though that means we have to be content with a fairly
> loose approximation to reality (p. 122).

However, this is hardly illuminating. It is not evident why it would
be 'rather uninformative' if one really could approximate closely 'that
ceaseless oscillation which is characteristic of prices in certain
markets'.[8] Nor is it clear what Hicks means by 'very short' or by
'fairly long'.

To get any real insights into the nature of the week, it is necessary
to consider Hicks' observations on Marshall. His characterisation of
Marshall's treatment of time is dubious. Thus Hicks seems to regard
Marshall's day, his short-period and his long-period as operational
concepts, an interpretation which we have challenged. Moreover,
whereas we have stressed that, for Marshall, these periods merge into
one another, Hicks refers to Marshall's 'rigid tripartite division'. In
any event, he rejects Marshall's periods: 'These categories are suitable

enough for Marshall's isolated market, but they hardly fit the analysis of the whole system' (p. 122).

Hicks' week is certainly 'shorter' than the 'Marshallian long-period'. Of the latter, he claims that 'there is scarcely any nameable period of time so long that the supply of all commodities can be "fully adjusted" within it' (p. 122). To have taken the Marshallian long-period as his unit time period would have effectively undermined his conception of a process in time. How does the week relate to the 'Marshallian short-period'? Hicks does not say explicitly. We can infer, however, that the week is normally to be thought of as 'shorter' than the Marshallian short-period. Hicks is no doubt aware that Marshall refers to 'short periods of a few months or a year'; the term 'week' clearly connotes a shorter period.[9] More significantly, Hicks' temporary equilibrium has much in common with Marshall's equilibrium for the market day but very little in common with his short-period equilibrium. In particular, in contrast to Marshall's short-period equilibrium, Hicks' temporary equilibrium does not involve the notion of 'normal' values.[10]

Hicks' week is to be thought of as normally 'longer' than the 'Marshallian day'. He argues that the Marshallian day, involving strictly given quantities available for sale, is inappropriate for analysing the whole system on the grounds that 'there is scarcely any period of time so short that it can give us temporary equilibrium (in Marshall's sense) for all commodities; there will nearly always be some products whose supply can be increased within the period' (p. 122). Hicks' desire to 'admit some small variability of output into our shortest period' (p. 122) should have led him to be particularly explicit about timing. In fact, the elastic nature of his week results in a degree of vagueness. This is most easily seen by considering 'Wages and Interest: the Dynamic Problem', since this involved a community which produces just one homogeneous good, 'bread'. Hicks assumed explicitly that, at the beginning of the first week, there is a certain stock of finished bread. He also stated that each output is 'to be reckoned at the date at which it is to be sold' (1935, p. 71, n. 3). This could be interpreted as meaning that sales on the first Monday would include the production of the first week. But he then claimed that each entrepreneur has to determine, 'not only how much labour he will employ in the first week, but how he will employ that labour, whether in the production of bread for the *next* market day, or in the production of bread for the more distant future' (1935, p. 71, italics added).

This implies that the production of the first week would not be sold until the second Monday, so that the quantity available for sale on the first Monday would be limited to the inherited stock of bread. The obscurity was compounded by the fact that, when considering equilibrium on the first Monday, Hicks treated the terms 'output' of bread and 'supply' of bread as synonomous. A more careful analysis would have differentiated between the initial stock of bread, the production of bread during the first week, the quantity available for sale on the first Monday, the quantity actually supplied on the first Monday and the stock of bread held at the end of the week. Given Hicks' failure to draw these distinctions in a one-commodity model, it is perhaps not surprising that he did not do so in the much more complex multi-commodity model of *Value and Capital*.

In contrast to Marshall's periods, Hicks' week is an operational time concept. However, in contrast to the 'textbook' Marshallian periods, the week is not explicitly defined in terms of those 'forces' which are operating to determine prices. In particular, the Hicksian week lacks the analytical sharpness of the Marshallian day. In this respect, *Value and Capital* also compares unfavourably with the *Elements*. The difference between Hicks' easy style of writing and Walras' cumbersome presentation can detract from the fact that Walras makes much more effort to be explicit about the assumptions which he is making.

The Monday

It is curious that Hicks, who was sufficiently familiar with the *Elements* to write a review of it in 1934, makes no explicit reference in *Value and Capital* to Walras' distinction between phases. Yet Hicks' Monday serves a similar purpose to Walras' phase of preliminary *tâtonnement*, at least in one respect. We have seen that Walras assumes such a preliminary phase so that he can conceive of a subsequent phase involving stationary current prices. Similarly Hicks, having assumed that prices are constant during the week, introduces the assumption that markets are open only on Monday, as 'a convenient way of visualising this assumption of constant prices during the week' (p. 122).

Walras' preliminary phase and Hicks' Monday are both artificial devices designed to allow the process of price determination to take time and yet to permit a conceptual distinction between the determination of equilibrium prices and the actual implementation of contracts based on those prices.[11] However, there is an essential difference between their preoccupations. Walras *is* interested in understanding the process whereby prices are determined in the market by trial-and-error. In contrast, Hicks does *not* attempt to analyse the process of price determination on any Monday. Thus, he states:

We are supposing that trading continues, on the Monday, until supplies and demands are brought into equilibrium; this is essential in order for us to be able to use the equilibrium method in dynamic theory. Since we shall not pay much attention to the process of equilibration which must precede the formation of the equilibrium prices, our method seems to imply that we conceive of the economic system as being always in equilibrium. We work out the equilibrium prices of one week, and the equilibrium prices of another week, and leave it at that (p. 131).

Since Hicks is not really interested in the process of price determination on any Monday, he is extremely vague both about the way in which markets are organised and about the time-sequences involved. Indeed, he is not entirely explicit about his conception of temporary equilibrium.

In 'Equilibrium and the Cycle' (1933) and in 'Léon Walras' (1934), Hicks had questioned the conceptions of equilibrium of both Walras and Pareto, accusing the former of 'sheer confusion' (1933, p. 33) and the latter of being 'almost deliberately ambiguous' (1933, p. 29). In an attempt at clarification, Hicks had distinguished between two conceptions of equilibrium in the context of an exchange economy. First, one might assume that individuals come to market on some particular day with given endowments of goods which they exchange among themselves until there is no incentive for further exchange, such a state being described as an equilibrium. Hicks had objected to this notion of equilibrium on the grounds of path-dependence: 'Neither Walras nor Pareto faced up to this difficulty; when we do so, it is impossible to avoid the conclusion that the "Lausanne equations" are of rather less significance than they imagined' (1934, p. 91). Second, one might assume a 'continuing market' in which on every day (with no carry-over of stocks) new transactions are concluded involving the supplies of that day: 'We then ask the question: What are the maintainable prices, i.e. what prices under unchanging conditions of demand and supply can be maintained indefinitely, so that no one needs to sell tomorrow at prices different from those attained today?' (1933, p.30). At that time, Hicks had definitely favoured this second conception: 'When it is understood in the last sense, the theory of static equilibrium of exchange takes its place as a step towards the development of a complete theory with which future exposition is unlikely to dispense' (1934, p.91).

By the time of *Value and Capital*, Hicks has evidently changed his mind. There are no accusations of ambiguity levelled at Walras or Pareto. More significantly, there is no reference to the second conception of equilibrium involving a 'continuing market'.[12] Hicks' notion of a process in time obliges him to employ the first conception of equilibrium on any Monday: 'Temporary equilibrium implies that current demands and supplies have been rendered equal' (p.155). Thus equilibrium on any particular Monday is achieved when there is no reason for the markets to remain open.[13]

How does Hicks confront the issue of path-dependence? How can it be possible to 'work out' the equilibrium prices without analysing the trading process itself? Is it meaningful to think of the equilibrium prices as being given by the solution to a set of conditions which an omniscient observer might formulate at breakfast-time before the markets even open[14] – since that is what Hicks' equilibrium conditions amount to? As we have seen, Walras sought to ensure that the solution provided by the market would correspond to his 'theoretical solution' by assuming that actual transactions do not take place until the equilibrium set of prices has been identified during the phase of preliminary *tâtonnement*. Hicks rejects this as 'not very convincing' (p.128). He further admits that Marshall's justification for ignoring income effects cannot legitimately be extended to a general equilibrium analysis. Consequently, almost in desperation, he suggests that 'we need ... to try and bring ourselves to suppose that price-changes are negligible during market hours on the Monday, when the market is open and dealers have to fix prices by higgling and bargaining, trial-and-error. This implies that the market (indeed all markets) proceeds quickly and smoothly to a position of temporary equilibrium' (p.123).

It is difficult to know what to make of this. Walras perhaps goes to an extreme in assuming that traders have no information whatsoever about market conditions and in supposing that the initial prices in the process of *tâtonnement* are determined completely at random. In reality, agents are not likely to start negotiations at prices very different from the previous period's prices. But what exactly is Hicks supposing? One interpretation is that he is requiring that there be 'negligible' differences between the prices which solve his equilibrium conditions for the current Monday and the prices of the previous Monday. Given that dealers start from last Monday's prices, one could envisage 'negligible' price changes during the course of trading. Another interpretation is that Hicks is allowing for 'non-negligible' differences between the prices which solve his equilibrium conditions for the current Monday and the prices of the previous Monday but that he is endowing dealers with sufficient information about the changed conditions so that the prices at which trading *starts* will be 'close' to the new equilibrium prices. Hicks' claim that the degree of indeterminacy can be reduced by shrinking the calendar duration of the week suggests that he is, in fact, relying on there being negligible differences between the new equilibrium prices and the previous Monday's prices.[15] Placing such a restriction on the week-to-week variations in equilibrium prices is not particularly appealing, since it severely limits the nature of the process in time. Moreover, it is not easily reconciled with Hicks' references to the activities of speculators.

It is by no means evident that Hicks appreciates all the complications which are circumvented by Walras' assumption of perfectly organised markets. He does acknowledge that income effects from 'false trading' can result in path-dependence, this being the reason he assumes negligible price changes during the course of the day's trading. However, his suggestion that it is reasonable to assume that few transactions take place at 'very false prices', so that the indeterminacy imparted by income effects is unlikely to be serious, is hopelessly vague. Transactions at false prices for labour services are likely to be more troublesome in terms of income effects than transactions at false prices for salt, thereby complicating any attempt to provide a meaningful definition of 'very false' (unless, tautologically, a very false price is defined as one which involves a 'very significant' income effect). Moreover, assuming that few transactions take place at 'very false prices' does not guarantee that 'very false quantities' can be ignored; in other words, 'very false quantities' could result from transactions at prices which, according to some criterion, are not 'very false'.[16]

But there is a much more fundamental issue. What if Hicks had simply said that he was allowing for any amount of higgling and bargaining with no restrictions on price changes and that he was quite prepared to accept that the resulting equilibrium would be path-dependent? Would this have made any real difference to his process in time? Of the assumptions of an 'easy passage to temporary equilibrium' and of 'perfect contemporaneous knowledge', Hicks claims: 'As far as I can see, these simplifications do not make any real difference to the sort of results we may expect to obtain by our analysis' (p. 123). However, matters are not so simple. The possibility of path-dependence would have undermined his comparative-static analyses of the implications for temporary equilibrium of hypothetical changes in the data. More significantly, allowing for trading at disequilibrium prices would have undermined his conception of the formulation of plans by agents: *the plans of agents would not be independent of the organisation of markets.*

To treat Monday's trading itself as a 'process in time' involving genuine higgling and bargaining would present formidable difficulties. For example, it would be necessary to recognise that an agent could not be in *each* market at the *same* instant in time. Thus an entrepreneur might have to borrow money *before* entering, say, the markets for different types of labour services. He would, in general, have to base his decision of how much to borrow on his expectations as to subsequent prices in those markets. Having borrowed money, he would have to decide on the *order* in which to enter the various input markets. Even if we were to suppose that each individual would formulate some plan before any markets opened, then – short of that plan being so complex as to exceed the bounds of rationality – we would want to allow that he might well revise the planned order in which to enter the various markets in the light of experiences in any of those markets. He might, of course, decide to re-enter some particular market. Moreover, the trading opportunities open to him at any particular moment in some market would, in general, depend on which other individuals *happened* to be in that market at that time.

Hicks, himself, has subsequently expressed misgivings about his failure to be sufficiently precise about timing. In particular, he has criticised the analysis of *Value and Capital* for treating equilibrium prices and price expectations as being reciprocally determined: 'Such reciprocal determination is, however, a piece of telescoping; in dynamic analysis, telescoping is dangerous. It is essential to keep the time-sequence right. Though changes in actual prices do affect expectations, and changes in expectations do affect actual prices, cause precedes effect' (1965, p. 66). More generally, he has criticised the temporary equilibrium method on the grounds that

it is necessary to assume that prices remain unchanged through the single period; and that these prices are equilibrium prices which, within the single period, equate supplies and demands. In order to visualise this, some such construction as my 'week' and my 'Monday' appears to be necessary; but the artificiality of such constructions is only too obvious. They do deliberate violence to the *order* in which in the real world (in *any* real world) events occur (1965, p. 73).

He has also subsequently conceded that the analysis of *Value and Capital* lacks a satisfactory theory of markets:

How – just how – are prices determined? In *Value and Capital* (even in the dynamic part of *Value and Capital*) I had been content to be what is now called neo-Walrasian; prices were just determined by an equilibrium of demand and supply. And I am afraid that for many years I got no further, or very little further.... Walras himself, it is true, had been much less obtuse. He had seen that for a market to work in his way (the way in which so many others have followed him) some market *structure* was necessary. But the market structure which he posited was very special (1976, p. 296).

Walras' assumption that transactions do not take place until the equilibrium prices have been identified not only indicates how markets are organised; it also has the attraction that its artificiality is (or should be) transparent. In contrast, Hicks' reference in *Value and Capital* to 'higgling and bargaining' conveys a spurious air of realism, since assuming that price changes are 'negligible' during Monday's trading is tantamount to assuming that there is no real need for any higgling and bargaining. It bears repeating that, although the notion of Monday allows trading to take time, trading is *not* treated as a 'process in time'. The 'method' which Hicks proposes involves *assuming* that, on any Monday, trading results in the set of prices which would solve the equilibrium conditions which an omniscient observer could formulate before trading even begins. Obvious though it may be, it is worth stressing that the assumption of an 'easy passage' to temporary equilibrium in a network of countless inter-related markets is of a different order of abstraction compared to a similar assumption for an individual market.[17]

Before leaving Hicks' Monday, it is instructive to compare briefly his temporary equilibrium conditions with Walras' equilibrium conditions. First, whereas Walras' general equilibrium involves zero profits for entrepreneurs, Hicks' temporary equilibrium does not. Thus, whereas Walras assumes that all factors of production are perfectly mobile and that technology is characterised by constant returns to scale, Hicks assumes that, at the beginning of any week, entrepreneurs have fixed inputs determined by transactions on previous Mondays. Second, whereas Walras' equilibrium involves a uniform rate of net income on the ownership of all capital goods, Hicks' temporary equilibrium does not. This difference is scarcely surprising, since Walras arrives at this condition by ignoring uncertainty. However, there is a more fundamental point: Hicks does not even consider the inter-relationships between the markets for existing capital goods, the markets for new capital goods and the markets for the services which those capital goods provide (or the related question of the allocation of investment between the production of new capital goods).[18] Indeed, notwithstanding the title of *Value and Capital*, Hicks does not define what he means by the term 'capital'. He even seems to have a preference for the term 'equipment'.

The essential difference between the analyses of Walras and Hicks is that the former's conception of equilibrium involves more than 'supplies equal demands'. Walras is seeking to *characterise* equilibrium in terms of meaningful relationships between prices, relationships which would obtain under 'normal conditions'. Though perhaps less explicitly than Walras, Marshall is also seeking to characterise both his short-period equilibrium and his long-period equilibrium in terms of relationships between prices, relationships which would obtain under 'normal conditions'. Walras' equilibrium, Marshall's short-period equilibrium and Marshall's long-period equilibrium can all be interpreted as 'centres of gravity', albeit ones which are changing over time. Hicks' temporary equilibrium, involving simply 'supplies equal demands', is not designed to elucidate any particular relationships between prices and cannot meaningfully be interpreted as a centre of gravity.

The process

In essence, the reader of *Value and Capital* is presented with a vision of a process in time. The reader is invited to visualise such a process, to 'conceive of the situation at the end of the week being different from the situation at the beginning' (p. 127). However, aside from the final two chapters on the accumulation of capital and the trade cycle (both of which have to be described as anti-climactic), *Value and Capital* is concerned with a particular week. Thus Hicks' analysis of the 'working of the dynamic system' primarily involves examining the implications for temporary equilibrium in a given week of hypothetical changes in the data. He acknowledges that this falls far short of identifying the full consequences over time of such changes:

Even when we have mastered the 'working' of the temporary equilibrium system, we are even yet not in a position to give an account of the process of price-change, nor to examine the ulterior consequences of changes in data. These are the ultimate things we want to know about, though we may have to face the disappointing conclusion that there is not much which can be said about them in general (p. 246).

Why does Hicks' conception of a process in time turn out to be rather limited? The explanation relates to the 'links' between weeks. The individual week cannot, of course, be taken in isolation – or, in the terminology of *Capital and Growth*, as 'self-contained'. The initial resources are determined by productive activities in previous weeks; the productive activities in the current week will affect the resources available in future weeks. Moreover, the current decisions of individuals are oriented towards future weeks; these decisions will be based on expectations which, in general, will depend on experiences in previous weeks. Nevertheless, the links between successive weeks are not specified sufficiently concretely to permit any form of sequence analysis. In particular, although Hicks points out at various stages that the accumulation of capital provides the primary link between successive periods, his analysis of temporary equilibrium, focusing, as it does, on the determination of prices, simply does not confront the issue of capital accumulation sufficiently directly. Moreover, although the reader may visualise current expectations depending on the experiences of previous weeks, the form of that dependence is not specified, the only explicit relationship being that of the dependence of expectations of future prices on *current* prices. Hicks, acknowledging his failure to show how the individual weeks link on, has since described his analysis as 'quasi-static' (1965, p. 65). The essential point is that *Value and Capital* does not provide an analysis of an economy as it 'moves through time'.[19] The deficiencies in *Value and Capital* relate to inherently formidable difficulties. These difficulties no doubt explain why the 'dynamic' section of *Value and Capital* was largely neglected for thirty years, at least by economists who prefer formal analysis to impressionistic visions. Indeed, it was no doubt recognition of these same difficulties which led both Walras and Marshall to concentrate primarily on 'normal' conditions.

Notes

1 Unless otherwise indicated, all page references in this chapter relate to Hicks (1946 [1939]).
2 Lindahl's letter is referred to by Hansson (1982).
3 Hicks discusses in detail the relationships between 'long' and 'short' money rates of interest.
4 Hicks appreciates that individuals seldom have precise expectations and suggests that their expectations typically take the form of subjective probability density functions. Recognising that the behaviour of a risk-averse individual will depend not simply on the mean of the probability density function but also on its dispersion, he suggests that the 'expected' price be interpreted as involving an allowance for riskiness.
5 Note the similarity to Walras' commodity (E).
6 In the next chapter, we will examine in detail a 'pure futures economy' – the so-called Arrow-Debreu economy.
7 It is worth noting that, in 'Wages and Interest: the Dynamic Problem', Hicks' economy comprised labourers, entrepreneurs and rentiers. *Value and Capital* – in which there is no sign of such groups – may well have been influential in their displacement by 'consumers' and 'producers' in so much of economic theory.
8 Hicks does not subsequently say explicitly why it would be rather uninformative.
9 At one point, Hicks suggests that, for certain purposes, it may be legitimate to 'spin out' the week into 'something like a Marshallian "short-period" – the time during which existing equipment (in a broad or narrow sense) can be taken as given' (p. 247). This sets an upper limit on the duration of the week. It implies that the only 'equipment' which can be used in production during the week is that which exists at the beginning of the week; any capital goods produced during the current week cannot be 'put to use', to use Walras' phrase, until some subsequent week.
10 In *Capital and Growth*, Hicks states explicitly that the week of *Value and Capital* is 'shorter' than the Marshallian short-period (1965, p. 74).
11 We do not wish to exaggerate the similarities between Hicks' Monday and Walras' preliminary phase. In particular, whereas Walras supposes that actual transactions take place during the 'static phase', Hicks supposes that all transactions are concluded on Monday, so that the markets are closed for the rest of the week. A significant implication of this is that, whereas it is meaningful to think in terms of transactions demands for

money in Walras' economy, it is *not* meaningful to do so in Hicks' economy, that is, individuals would have no transactions motive for holding money at the cessation of Monday's trading. This is why Patinkin, in his *Money, Interest and Prices*, incorporated a modification to the Hicksian framework. Specifically, Patinkin assumed that payments for the final contracts are made, not at the close of Monday's trading, but at randomly determined hours during the ensuing week. According to Patinkin, the lack of synchronisation between payments and receipts gives rise to a transactions demand, and the uncertainty as to the timing of the payments gives rise to a precautionary demand for money.

12 In the 'static' section of *Value and Capital*, Hicks' definition of equilibrium – relegated to a footnote – is essentially atemporal: 'A market is in equilibrium, statically considered, if every person is acting in such a way as to reach his most preferred position, subject to the opportunities open to him. This implies that the actions of the different persons trading must be consistent' (p. 58, n. 1).

13 At one point, Hicks claims: 'There is a sense in which current demands and supplies are always equated in competitive conditions. Stocks may indeed be left in the shops unsold; but they are unsold because people prefer to take the chance of being able to sell them at a future date rather than cut price in order to sell them now .... In this (analytically important) sense the economic system (or at least all those systems with which we shall be concerned) can be taken to be always in equilibrium' (p. 131). This conception of equilibrium is scarcely illuminating: for the notion of equilibrium to be useful, one must be able to conceive of not being in equilibrium. Moreover, Hicks makes no attempt to reconcile the claim that markets are always in equilibrium with his earlier reference to equilibrium being established through 'higgling and bargaining'.

14 In formulating the conditions, the omniscient observer would have to take into account the dependence of individuals' expectations of future prices on 'current' prices.

15 Hicks' claim that the shorter the calendar duration of the week the less the degree of indeterminacy does presuppose that equilibrium prices were established on the Monday of the previous week. However, in reality, the shorter the calendar duration of the week, the less likely it would be, *ceteris paribus*, that the previous Monday's actual prices were equilibrium ones.

16 To assess the implications of 'false' transactions for, say, labour services, it would be necessary to know whether entrepreneurs could 'resell' labour services without the permission of the workers concerned.

17 In *Capital and Growth*, Hicks conveys a misleading impression of the analysis of *Value and Capital*, when he claims that the latter allows for 'a good deal of "false" trading' before prices are established (1965, p. 66).

18 In 'Léon Walras', Hicks had suggested that Walras' theory of capital, when suitably amended, would possibly provide a better basis for extending in a dynamic direction than the capital theories of either Wicksell or Böhm-Bawerk. Moreover, in the Introduction to *Value and Capital*, Hicks announces his intention to examine capital and interest in much greater detail than did Walras in his 'sketch of a theory of capital' (p. 6). However, there are no subsequent references to Walras' treatment of capital (or to his theory of money or to his discussion of the continuous market). Like Lindahl in his 1929 essay, Hicks devotes more attention to Böhm-Bawerk's theory of capital.

19 Recall that Hicks suggests that the theory would be 'rather uninformative' if the week was taken to be 'very short'. He might well not have suggested this if he had been able to show how the weeks 'link on'.

7

Debreu

The theory of value is treated here with the standards of rigor of the contemporary formalist school of mathematics.... Allegiance to rigor dictates the axiomatic form of the analysis where the theory, in the strict sense, is logically entirely disconnected from its interpretations (p. x[1]).

Most economic theorists, invited to expound on general equilibrium theory, would describe the Arrow-Debreu model. To simplify the exposition, they might well begin by leaving time (and space) out of the account. They would then explain that the theory can accommodate time (and space) provided only that the concepts of commodity and price are appropriately interpreted. They might then suggest (perhaps with some misgivings) that a further reinterpretation of the concepts permits the extension of the analysis to incorporate uncertainty.

The Arrow-Debreu model was developed largely by Kenneth Arrow and Gerard Debreu during the 1950s. Other notable economists played a part; mention might be made of Allais, Koopmans, Malinvaud and McKenzie. In this chapter, we will focus primarily on Debreu's *Theory of Value: An Axiomatic Analysis of Economic Equilibrium*, published in 1959 and usually regarded as the canonical work. Debreu acknowledges the influence of Lindahl, crediting him with providing 'the first general mathematical study of an economy whose activity extends over a finite number of elementary time-intervals under conditions of perfect foresight' (p. 35, n. 1). In his 1929 essay, as we have seen, Lindahl introduced the concept of an intertemporal equilibrium involving simultaneous equilibrium in all the periods encompassed by the analysis. All actions for the entire time-horizon are thereby determined at the beginning of the first period, plans being 'pre-reconciled' by the perfect foresight with which individuals are endowed. In the Arrow-Debreu economy, all actions for the entire time-horizon are also determined at the beginning of the first period. However, plans are 'pre-reconciled' by the existence of current markets for *all* commodities, where a good or service available in some period constitutes a different commodity from that same good or service available in some other period.[2]

In the next section, we will summarise the salient features of the Arrow-Debreu model. In the subsequent sections, we will explore in greater detail certain features pertaining to the treatment of time. It is worth noting that, as the quotation at the beginning of the chapter indicates, Debreu emphasises that the formal theory is 'logically entirely disconnected from its interpretations'. This applies, in particular, to the temporal interpretation of the theory. In this chapter, we will focus on Debreu's own interpretation. In Appendix 2, we consider alternative temporal interpretations placed on the Arrow-Debreu model. In Appendix 3, we consider the somewhat different temporal framework employed by Malinvaud in his *Lectures on Microeconomic Theory*.

The Arrow-Debreu economy

The economic agents, characterised by the constraints on their choices and by their choice criteria, comprise given numbers of producers and consumers. A producer, in choosing a plan of action involving the transformation of inputs into outputs, is constrained to choose a plan from a known production set, defined as the set of technically possible production plans. His objective is to maximise profit. A consumer, in choosing a plan of action specifying the quantities of all his inputs and outputs, is constrained to choose from his known consumption set, defined as the set of plans which are *a priori* possible, a plan which is consistent with his wealth constraint. Subject to these restrictions, he chooses a consumption plan to which no feasible plan is preferred.

In a private ownership economy, the profits of producers are distributed among the consumers according to their shareholdings, so that the wealth of any consumer includes any shares in profits to which he is entitled. Debreu suggests that all producers be conceived of as corporations, a sole proprietor thus playing two roles, that of president, for which he receives a salary, and that of sole shareholder, for which he receives the profit. Debreu also supposes: 'An individual who buys a house, a car, ... for his own use and sells it back later plays two roles: that of a *producer* who buys and sells houses, cars, ... in order to sell their services, and that of a *consumer* who buys the service, use of that house, of that car, ...' (p. 51).

The key to Debreu's accommodation of time and space into the model lies in the interpretation of the concept of a commodity as a good or service completely specified physically, temporally and spatially. Since the theory assumes a finite number of commodities, time has to be treated discontinuously. Debreu describes succinctly his conception of both time and space:

The interval of time over which economic activity takes place is divided into a finite number of compact *elementary intervals* of equal length. These elementary intervals may be numbered in chronological order; the origin of the first one is called the present instant. Their common length, which may be a year, a minute, a week, ... is chosen small enough for all the instants of an elementary interval to be indistinguishable from the point of view of the analysis. An elementary interval will be called a *date*, and the expression 'at date t' will therefore be equivalent to 'at some instant of the tth elementary interval'.

Similarly the region of space over which economic activity takes place is divided into a finite number of compact *elementary regions*. These elementary regions, which may be arbitrarily numbered, are chosen small enough for all the points of one of them to be indistinguishable from the point of view of the analysis. An elementary region will be called a *location*, and the expression 'at location s' will therefore be equivalent to 'at some point of the sth elementary region' (p. 29).

Debreu exhorts the reader to bear in mind the 'full generality' of the concept of commodity: 'By focusing attention on changes of dates one obtains, *as a particular case* of the general theory of commodities ..., a theory of saving, investment, capital and interest. Similarly by focusing attention on changes of locations one obtains, *as another particular case* of the same general theory, a theory of location, transportation, international trade and exchange' (p. 32).

Debreu enters his economy at the 'present instant', or 'now', this being the beginning of the first period. The economy's resources — the land, mineral deposits, buildings, equipment and inventories of goods — existing at the present instant and available to the agents are a legacy of the past. The pattern of private ownership of these resources and the shareholdings of consumers are also *a priori* given. Each agent selects now a plan 'for the entire future', that is, for all the elementary periods encompassed by the model. All transactions take place at the present instant. The price of a commodity is the amount which has to be paid *now* for one unit. This price differs from the price on a futures market, in that a futures contract entered into now stipulates the price to be paid at the delivery date. According to Debreu, the difference in the timing of payment is inessential. He continues: 'A difference of another kind clearly exists. Organised futures markets concern only a small number of goods, locations and dates (not too distant in the future), whereas it is implicitly assumed here that markets exist for *all* commodities' (p. 33).

The economy functions without any medium of exchange. Debreu explains the institutional arrangements and, in particular, the role of prices:

With each commodity is associated a real number, its price. When an economic agent commits himself to accept delivery of a certain quantity of a commodity, the product of that quantity and the price of the commodity is a real number written on the debit side of his account. This number will be called the amount paid by the agent. Similarly a commitment to make delivery results in a real number written on the credit side of his account, and called the amount paid to the agent (p. 28).

Each agent treats market prices as parameters. According to Debreu, for a producer, this may be 'because, for example, his output or input of any commodity is relatively small and he thinks his action cannot influence prices' (p. 43). All agents face the same prices. It is worth noting that Debreu never employs the term 'competitive' or any cognate term.

Equilibrium for a private ownership economy requires that the plans of agents be compatible with each other and with the economy's total resources. Given the price system and the plans of the other agents, no agent has an incentive to choose a different plan. Specifically, a set of prices and of plans constitutes a market equilibrium provided that (i) each producer's plan maximises his profit at those prices given the constraints on his choice; (ii) for each consumer, there is no preferred plan at those prices given the constraints on his choice; and (iii) the associated excess demands for all commodities are zero. Assuming aggregate free disposal, the last condition can be replaced by stipulating that the associated excess demands for all commodities are non-positive. If equilibrium involves a strictly negative excess demand for some commodity, its price would be zero. Note that the definition of an equilibrium does not refer to a set of prices but to a set of prices *and* plans. This is to allow for excess demands which are not single-valued functions of prices, that is, to allow for excess demand correspondences, this being necessary to accommodate, for example, technologies which exhibit constant returns to scale.

Debreu has two objectives. The first is 'the explanation of the prices of commodities resulting from the interaction of the agents of a private ownership economy through markets' (p. ix). This 'explanation' consists in proving an existence theorem which he calls the 'fundamental theorem of the theory of value'. Specifically, assuming that the numbers of producers, consumers and commodities are all given positive integers and that the quantities of all commodities are perfectly divisible, certain axioms relating to production sets, consumption sets, consumer preferences and consumer resource endowments are sufficient to ensure that an equilibrium exists for a private ownership economy. Debreu's other objective is 'the explanation of the role of prices in an optimal state of an economy' (p. ix). Essentially, this involves proving the theorem that, given certain assumptions, a market equilibrium is a Pareto optimum; and proving the 'deeper' theorem that, given certain (different) assumptions, a Pareto optimum is a potential market equilibrium.

So far we have considered the interpretation of the Arrow-Debreu model which assumes that there is no element of uncertainty confronting agents. However, an imaginative reinterpretation of the concepts of commodity and price enables the same theory to accommodate uncertainty arising from the future 'choices of Nature'.[3] Commodities are now defined by their physical characteristics, by location, by date and *by stipulated choices of Nature up to and including the specified date.* Delivery of a good or service at the specified location and date takes place if and only if Nature makes the stipulated choice. In contrast, payment for a commodity is not contingent, the price being paid at the present instant.

Consider a case of one location and two dates, where, at each date, Nature has two choices: 'rain' and 'no rain'. Consider wheat (of a specific quality). In relation to date 1, there would be two commodities: wheat to be delivered (at date 1) in the event of rain at date 1; and wheat to be delivered (at date 1) in the event of no rain at date 1. In relation to date 2, there would be four commodities, each defined by a *sequence* of choices by Nature: wheat to be delivered (at date 2) in the event of rain at date 1 *and* rain at date 2; wheat to be delivered (at date 2) in the event of rain at date 1 *and* no rain at date 2; and so on. A farmer could sell delivery commitments in each of these markets. Subject only to the restriction that the number of commodities is finite (so that Nature can be permitted only a finite number of choices), this sequential specification can, in principle, accommodate the complete impact of the weather from planting to harvesting on the yield of wheat obtained from any given set of inputs.

Each producer is assumed to know how the choices of Nature will affect his possible input-output combinations. Given that payment for a commodity is not contingent, the producer does not 'face' uncertainty and simply maximises profit, which (as before) is the difference between his receipts and outlays *at the present instant*. In contrast, a consumer does face uncertainty. His utility function (or, more generally, his preference preordering) is interpreted as reflecting both his assessment of the likelihood of the various choices of Nature and his attitude to risk. With these new interpretations of the concepts of commodity and price, the theory developed for certainty can accommodate uncertainty. According to Debreu, the assumption that markets exist for all the contingent commodities is 'a natural extension of the usual assumption that markets exist for all the certain commodities' (p. 102, n. 2).

Time horizon

The Arrow-Debreu model raises sharply a number of the difficulties involved in the treatment of time. We must explore these difficulties in some detail. Since the theory presupposes a finite number of dated commodities, the number of elementary time intervals must be finite.[4] Suppose that the model encompasses T elementary time intervals. The beginning of the first period, which we will denote by I_p, is the present instant; the end of the last period, which we will denote by I_T, is the terminal instant. If, following Koopmans (1957, p. 106), we use the term 'time horizon' to mean the union of all time periods encompassed by the model, the time horizon is from I_p to I_T. Debreu's own expression – 'the interval of time over which economic activity takes place' – might suggest that no economic activity takes place prior to the present instant or after the terminal instant. Indeed, at least one commentator has, presumably ironically, interpreted the beginning of the first period as relating to the Garden of Eden (Davidson, 1980, p. 157). However, Debreu does suppose that economic activity has been taking place prior to the present instant. In particular, as noted earlier, he postulates that the land, mineral deposits, buildings, equipment and inventories of goods in existence at the present instant and available to the agents are a legacy of the past. Whether this is an adequate representation of the influence of the past on the present and future will be considered later.

Is the model consistent with there being economic activity after the terminal instant? Although Debreu acknowledges that there are 'conceptual difficulties in postulating a predetermined instant beyond which all economic activity either ceases or is outside the scope of the analysis' (p. 36), he does not elaborate on the nature of these difficulties. Suppose that there will be economic activity after the terminal instant. The complication is that, whereas the analyst is entitled to treat what is past relative to I_p as given, he *cannot* meaningfully treat what is future relative to I_T as given. And yet it is not clear that the theorist can ignore the fact that there will be economic activity after I_T. Presumably some of the decisions of some of the agents in the economy would involve considering time intervals subsequent to the terminal instant. Presumably some of the agents would have an interest in the land, buildings, mineral deposits, equipment and inventories of goods which will exist at the terminal instant and be available to them. However, the Arrow-Debreu model does not accommodate such considerations. By assuming implicitly that resources existing at the terminal instant have no value, the model effectively assumes that all economic activity ceases at the terminal instant.

Debreu makes no reference to calendar durations in relation to the time horizon of the model. The implicit assumption that the terminal values of commodities are zero surely implies that the calendar duration of the time horizon cannot meaningfully be thought of as being 'short'. However, interpreting it as being 'long' – or as 'very, very long', as some economists seem to do – raises other conceptual difficulties. Patently disquieting is the assumption that producers know at the present instant what input-output combinations will be technically possible over the time horizon of the model. This assumption is not rendered any more palatable by Debreu's claim that for a producer to know what input-output combinations will be possible in the future does not require that he know the details of the technical processes which will make them possible. Indeed, Debreu's claim that it is not necessary for producers to know the technical details does not get to the heart of the matter: as Lindahl observed, it is necessary to *require* that they do not know such details since, if they did, the technical changes could be implemented at once. And yet, as we suggested in Chapter 4, it is difficult to envisage how producers could know *precisely* the 'implications' of future technical changes but not the 'details' of such changes.

The notion of an individual consumer taking lifetime decisions imposes a considerable strain on the imagination. It is worth recalling Hicks' reservations about the idea of an individual formulating an expenditure plan complete in every detail: 'the fact that he will ordinarily not know what his future wants are going to be (and will know that he does not know) becomes very upsetting' (1946, p. 228). Moreover, it is hardly coherent to assume that a consumer knows what utility he will derive from products which have not yet been introduced. It surely has to be acknowledged that the Arrow-Debreu model effectively rules out any significant conceptual developments in techniques of production or in the characteristics of commodities. As MacIntyre has observed: 'The notion of the prediction of radical conceptual innovation is itself conceptually incoherent' (1985, p. 93).

The Arrow-Debreu model also denies the influence of experience, at least over the time horizon of the analysis. Although this applies to consumer preferences generally, it is most easily seen by considering individuals' subjective expectations regarding the likelihoods of future states of Nature. We are entitled to suppose that the subjective expectations of individuals at the present instant may depend on their experiences prior to the present instant. However, the model does not allow for any changes in expectations during the time horizon. Thus, for example, the model does not allow the experiences of individuals over the first t periods to change their original expectations relating to, say, the $(t + 1)$th period. In like manner, the theory effectively denies the possibility that the experience of actually consuming commodities may alter individual preferences. To assume that individuals know fully the implications of future 'experiences' would deprive the term of any real meaning.

Interpreting the time horizon of the Arrow-Debreu model as 'long' also raises the question of how consumers not yet born and producers not yet in existence are to be represented at the present instant. According to Koopmans: 'Choices for production and consumption units not yet in existence at the beginning of the period must be made by proxy' (1957, p. 61). Debreu does not say who is to represent them. Arrow and Hahn concede that the notion of consumer decisions by proxy is disquieting:

To suppose that I now contract for the delivery of a pair of shoes to my grandson, whom I expect to be born twenty years from now, is itself somewhat fanciful. To suppose further that I have correctly foreseen the situation in which my grandson will find himself and that in these circumstances he will value the shoes in a way correctly known by me now is certainly dubious. Even if we allow contingent future contracts such as, 'For a price to be paid now, deliver a pair of shoes to my grandson if he exists and is twenty years old in forty years' time, and if not, deliver nothing', we would certainly expect such markets to be pretty narrow and to become narrower as the future recedes; quite apart from anything else, it is not clear how far the benevolence of an individual of a given generation extends to future generations (1971, p. 34)

The notion of decisions being taken now on behalf of producers who do not yet exist is even more disconcerting, if not incoherent. Recall that Debreu conceives of all producers as corporations. But what can it really mean to say that a corporation does not yet 'exist' − given that there exists 'now' both some decision-taker endowed with the technical knowledge defined by the production set and some *a priori* given basis for distributing 'now' the profits of the corporation?

Granular time and the specification of commodities

We must now consider in more detail the nature of the elementary time intervals and the corresponding specifications of commodities. To his credit, Debreu devotes far more attention than most economists to the specifications of commodities, discussing, for illustrative purposes, various examples of goods and services − wheat, trucks, land, labour services, the use of an hotel room, storage services and transportation services. For most goods and services, the commodity specification involves just one date. For wheat, the commodity specification would involve its grade, the location at which it will be available and *the date at which it will be available*. Recall that the expression 'at date t' is equivalent to 'at some instant of the tth elementary interval'. Thus the economic agents are, by assumption, indifferent as to the precise instant of availability within the stipulated time interval. Time is thus endowed with a granular structure, all the instants of an elementary interval being 'indistinguishable from the point of view of the analysis' (p. 29).

For the service of an electrician, the commodity specification would involve location and *the date at which the service is to be rendered.*

The quantity of such a service would be expressed in terms of time. For example, if the length of the elementary time interval is twenty-four hours, the quantity might be eight hours, this being the time to be worked during the stipulated twenty-four hour period. It should be stressed that this involves the assumption that the electrician and the party for whom the service is to be performed are both indifferent as to which particular 480 minutes he would actually work – whether this would be the first twenty minutes of every hour or every third minute of the day or from 8.00 a.m. to 5.00 p.m., with an hour's break for lunch. Since it is difficult to visualise circumstances in which this would not be a patently unrealistic assumption, one might be tempted to stipulate a shorter elementary time interval.[5] However, in principle, this limitation remains given that quantity, that is, the time to be worked, is permitted to be less than the duration of the elementary time interval.

A granular representation of time has other disquieting implications which Debreu does not acknowledge. Consider a producer contemplating acquiring ownership of a new or second-hand truck during some specified time interval.[6] The assumption that he is indifferent as to the precise instant of delivery to him of the truck is disconcerting, in that the precise instant of delivery would determine what quantity of services would be available to him during the rest of the elementary time interval. If he intends to lease the services of the truck, he will not be able (at the present instant) to enter into any leasing contract relating to the elementary time interval under consideration, since he would not be able to guarantee to fulfil his side of the contract. A similar problem arises in relation to land. Suppose that an individual enters into a contract to transfer ownership of a particular plot of land to another individual, the transfer to take place at date t. Which individual is entitled to offer the services of the land on the appropriate rental market for date t? To mitigate these complications, it would seem necessary to assume explicitly that a durable good does not provide services until the interval after the one in which a new owner accepts delivery and then to postulate a 'very short' duration for each elementary interval (since if the length of the interval was, say, a year, the assumption could scarcely be justified).[7]

For some services, the commodity specification involves more than one date. For example, the commodity specification of a storage service includes the type of warehouse, its location and *the dates from which to which it is rendered.* The quantity of a storage service is expressed, not in terms of time, but in terms of, say, cubic feet. Consider Figure 7.1, in which we have identified two successive dates, t and t + 1, and four 'instants', I_1 to I_4.

Figure 7.1

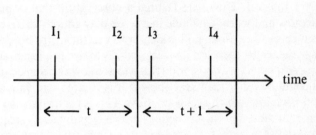

Whereas a storage service from I_1 to I_4 is the *same* commodity as one from I_2 to I_3, storage from I_1 to I_2 does not constitute a commodity, since the analysis does not discriminate between different instants within the same elementary time interval. To accommodate the latter as a commodity, it would be necessary to stipulate a shorter elementary time interval.

The commodity specification for a transportation service also involves more than one date. Specifically it includes a complete physical description of the services rendered, the locations involved and the dates involved. The quantity of a transportation service for a good is expressed, not in terms of time, but in terms of the weight or volume transported. Since the analysis does not differentiate between different points within the same elementary region, a transportation service must involve more than one location. Moreover, since a transportation service requires 'a time longer than an elementary time interval', it must involve more than one date. This implies that the division of the time horizon into elementary intervals is not independent of the delineation of the elementary regions: the duration of the elementary time interval must be less than the minimum time required for any transportation service between any two elementary regions. Thus, if the elementary regions are defined to accommodate transportation services involving 'short' distances, the duration of the elementary time intervals would have to be 'short'.

What emerges from this section is a presumption in favour of 'very short' elementary intervals. Recall that, according to Debreu, the calendar duration of the elementary time interval, 'which may be a year, a minute, a week, ... is chosen small enough for all the instants of the elementary interval to be indistinguishable from the point of view of the analysis' (p. 29). We must confess that we are not clear as to the precise meaning of 'the point of view of the analysis' and what criterion this really implies for determining the length of the elementary interval. However, Debreu's observation that 'wheat available now and wheat available in a week play entirely different economic roles for a flour mill which is to use them' (p. 29) does encourage the reader to reflect on what matters to *real* producers and to *real* consumers. If we do, it is difficult to see how the elementary interval could be other than very short if it is to accommodate the sorts of distinctions which agents do draw. This is particularly so to the extent that the temporal distinctions drawn by individuals are not 'synchronised'. Consider four-star petrol at a particular location on a particular day. If one consumer discriminates between petrol received between 9.00 a.m. and 9.10 a.m. and petrol received between 9.10 a.m. and 9.20 a.m., whereas another consumer discriminates between petrol received between 8.55 a.m. and 9.05 a.m. and petrol received between 9.05 a.m. and 9.15 a.m., the elementary time interval could not exceed five minutes.

The question of realism of assumptions, however, cuts in more than one way in the context of the Arrow-Debreu model. Whereas the desire to capture the sorts of temporal discriminations which agents make leads in the direction of very short elementary intervals, we also know quite well that markets in real economies do not cater for such fine distinctions. However, reflecting on actual institutional arrangements is scarcely in the spirit of the Arrow-Debreu approach, since this approach does not involve elaborating a model of the operation of actual market economies.

That there is a certain symmetry between the treatments of time and space in the Arrow-Debreu model is evident from Debreu's interpretations of commodities. There are disconcerting implications of the discrete representation of space analogous to those resulting from the discrete representation of time. Moreover, just as we have argued that there is a presumption in favour of 'very short' elementary time intervals, we could argue that there is a presumption in favour of 'very small' elementary regions (which would reinforce the presumption for 'very short' time intervals). It is worth noting, however, that, as the elementary regions become 'very small', it would be difficult to sustain the assumption that there are competitive markets for the ownership of land or for the services of land.

In emphasising the symmetry between time and space in the Arrow-Debreu model, we are *not*, of course, suggesting that time *should* be treated like space. One of the most persistent criticisms of the model has been that it 'reduces' time to space. For example, Bliss, referring specifically to the *Theory of Value*, has argued that the analogy between time and space is ultimately a false one:

A manager decides that a certain coal mine in Pennsylvania will produce 50,000 tons of coal. Where is the manager who makes this decision – what point of space does he occupy? A moment's consideration will convince the reader that this is a matter of no importance provided only that the manager has the relevant information, which might be transmitted to him in New York, Acapulco or Bangkok .... If the manager decides upon the output of coal somewhere else than the pit-head he might in principle be anywhere else – provided only that he can communicate his decision to his subordinates. He may be 'up the railway line' or 'down the railway line'; and if in some particular case he must be down the railway line because the only train that will take his message travels up the line, we could equally well imagine a situation in which the train will travel in the opposite direction, in which case he would have to be up the line. In short, space has no direction independently of the objects that occupy it.

With time a new consideration enters in .... To decide upon an action of yesterday is not to decide upon anything; it is either to mentally confirm an action or else it is day-dreaming .... We may quite reasonably treat decision makers as if they did not, for the purposes of the theory, occupy any particular point in space – although we might get a better theory if we took into account this feature and its possible consequences for tastes, knowledge and so forth. But we cannot meaningfully treat our decision-makers as so 'disembodied' that they do not occupy even a moment of time (1975, pp. 42–3).

Without denying Bliss' basic point, it might be countered that Debreu does not treat time and space in precisely the same way. Thus, whereas the focus of the analysis is the present instant, the present location of an agent is not emphasised. Indeed, it might be argued that, for *consumers*, present location *should* be emphasised. Whereas, for a managerial decision, the manager may not need to be at the pit-head at the time the decision is taken or at the time it is implemented, an individual who commits himself to provide the services of a coal-miner *does* have to be there at the appropriate time. Thus the analogy between time and space is 'ultimately false' for another reason: whereas it is possible to be in the same place at two different times, it is not possible to be in two different places at the same time. As we will see, this has implications for the properties of consumption sets, implications which have not been generally appreciated.

Consumption sets

The temporal and spatial interpretation which Debreu assigns to the theory inevitably has implications for the plausibility of the various assumptions relating to consumption sets, consumer preferences and production sets. Although we cannot examine all these assumptions, we must consider consumption sets and, in particular, the assumption that they are convex. As Debreu acknowledges: 'this convexity assumption is crucial because of its role in all the existing proofs of several fundamental economic theorems' (p. 53).

For a consumer, certain plans will be physiologically impossible: 'for example, the decision for an individual to have during the next year as sole input one pound of rice and as output one thousand hours of some type of labour could not be carried out' (p. 51). Consider now an example involving one location and two dates, where rice at date 1 is the first commodity and rice at date 2 is the second commodity. Suppose that the minimum quantity of the first commodity which must be available to the consumer to enable him to survive until the end of the first elementary time interval is 5. It would seem that a consumption plan (4, 6) involving 4 units of rice at date 1 and 6 units of rice at date 2 would not be possible, since the consumer would not be alive to consume the rice at date 2. In that case, the consumption set would not be convex (since (4, 6) is a linear combination of (2, 0) and (6, 12), both of which would be possible). However, Debreu seeks to salvage convexity of the consumption set by a somewhat artificial device. He invokes free disposal of commodities: if the consumer chooses a plan (4, 6), this means that 4 units of rice at date 1 *'are available to him* and he will actually consume at most that much of it' and that 6 units of rice at date 2 *'are available to him* and he will actually consume none of it'.

Consider now an example involving two locations. Consider rice at Manchester at date t and rice at London at date t. Suppose that a consumer could acquire the prior transportation services needed for him to be *either* in Manchester *or* in London at date t. Since a transporation service requires a time longer than an elementary time interval, he could not be in both Manchester and London at the same date. It would seem, at first sight, that a consumption plan involving strictly positive quantities of rice in both locations at date t would not be possible, implying a non-convex consumption set. Debreu does not discuss such an example. However, he would presumably again argue that free disposal would restore convexity: both quantities would be *available* to the consumer, even though the consumer could not be in a position actually to consume both.

Whatever one makes of this argument, however, it cannot be invoked to circumvent an analogous complication which arises in relation to an individual's supplies of labour services. Assume that it would be possible, with the appropriate prior transportation services, for an individual to deliver either a fifty minute lecture in London or a fifty minute lecture in Manchester during some stipulated hour. A plan which would involve the individual in delivering a twenty-five minute lecture in London and a twenty-five minute lecture in Manchester during that same interval must be impossible, so that the consumption set cannot be convex. Convexity *cannot* be salvaged by invoking free disposal, since it is an essential feature of the Arrow-Debreu model that agents are able to (and do) carry out their commitments to other agents. Violation of the convexity of consumption sets is of decisive importance, since that convexity is invoked in all of the theorems propounded in the *Theory of Value*.

Producers and production sets

We noted earlier the problems which arise with respect to producers who do not yet exist at the present instant. At least these problems are transparent. Even more disturbing – since they are not so immediately transparent – are problems with respect to producers who do 'exist' at the present instant. If we enter any *real* economy at a point in time, some of the economy's resources will be owned by firms, such resources being owned only indirectly and jointly by the owners of those firms. The resources owned by firms will determine their production possibilities: the standard distinction between fixed and variable inputs may be excessively sharp, but it does refer to something real. Moreover, many firms will already have entered into contractual commitments which relate to dates *which are still in the future*, such commitments also constraining their activities.

In contrast, in the Arrow-Debreu model, each producer starts with a clean sheet, the only constraint on a producer's choice of plan being that it be an element in his production set. According to Debreu, this set represents 'essentially his limited technical knowledge' (p. 37). Producers do not own any resources, since, at least *prior* to the transactions at the present instant, all resources are owned directly and separately by consumers.[8] Producers have neither fixed inputs nor any commitments which are a legacy of the past but which relate to future dates. In short, the firms in the Arrow-Debreu economy are not, in any meaningful sense, 'going concerns'. This is particularly disturbing in a 'general' model which involves entering an economy at some (arbitrary) point in time and designating that the 'present instant'.

We should perhaps anticipate an objection to our argument. It might be thought that the production set of a producer could be construed as taking into account any fixed inputs and any inherited commitments. With such an interpretation, however, it would be hard to justify the assumption that inaction is possible for a producer (in formal terms, that the origin is an element in his production set).[9] This axiom plays a crucial role in the theory, since it ensures that maximum profit for a producer is non-negative. Debreu, who lists his assumptions about production sets in an order which 'corresponds approximately to decreasing plausibility', places this axiom second in a list of eight. Arrow and Hahn describe the possibility of inaction as a 'trivial assumption' (1971, p. 59). However, this can only be a trivial assumption if the production set relates solely to limited technical knowledge. It surely has to be concluded that the Arrow-Debreu model, by assuming simply that there are *a priori* given resources owned by consumers, provides only the feeblest of representations of the effects of the past on the present and future. Particularly disconcerting is that we are invited (explicitly) to suppose that there exists 'now' a complete set of markets which encompasses the entire time horizon of the analysis and (implicitly) to suppose that at no date in the past did any producer enter into any contract relating to a date which is still in the future.

Durable goods and their services

Walras' conception of general equilibrium involved more than simply simultaneous clearing of all markets: it entailed certain relationships between prices. The most familiar are the conditions which result from the proposition that, in equilibrium, entrepreneurs make neither profit nor loss. However, as we saw in Chapter 3, Walras' equilibrium conditions also involved relationships between the prices of capital goods and the prices of their services.

In contrast, the Arrow-Debreu conception of equilibrium is solely one of simultaneous clearing of all markets, no attempt being made in the *Theory of Value* to identify relationships between equilibrium prices. Perhaps a preoccupation with 'generality' accounts for this. In any event, it is instructive to consider, in the context of the Arrow-Debreu model, the relationships between the prices of durable goods and the prices of their services. Consider then land at a stipulated location with specified physical properties which, for simplicity, are assumed to be unaffected by its use. Consider a producer who plans to buy and sell land in order to sell its services. Specifically suppose that he plans to buy one unit of land for P_t, where we have suppressed the commodity subscript. In order to circumvent the complication raised earlier, suppose that he would assume ownership at the *origin* of the tth elementary time interval, thereby entitling him to sell now the services of that unit of land for the duration of the tth interval. Assuming a unit length for the elementary interval, he would receive the rental price, r_t. Further, suppose that he plans to sell the land for P_{t+1}, thereby relinquishing ownership at the end of the tth interval. It should be stressed that he would pay P_t *now* and receive r_t and P_{t+1} *now*, that is, they are prices as of the present instant. The profit for this 'productive activity' is given by

$$P_{t+1} + r_t - P_t$$

In a *general equilibrium*, this activity, which involves constant returns to scale, must yield a zero profit: if profit were positive, the desire to acquire ownership of land would be unbounded, whereas, if it were negative, no-one would wish to own the land. Consequently, in equilibrium

$$r_t = P_t - P_{t+1} \tag{1}$$

that is, the rent for the tth interval must equal the fall in the ownership price from date t to date $t+1$.

We noted earlier that the finite time horizon of the Arrow-Debreu model causes some disquiet. This is simply illustrated using our example of land. Assuming that the time horizon of the model comprises T dates, it follows from (1) that in equilibrium

$$P_t = \sum_{\tau = t}^{T} r_\tau \; (+ \; P_{T+1})$$

where P_{T+1} is in brackets because beyond date T 'all economic activity either ceases or is outside the scope of the analysis'. Without some value imputed to P_{T+1}, the ownership prices of the land are indeterminate. Implicitly, the Arrow-Debreu model assumes that land at the end of the time horizon has no value, that is, $P_{T+1} = 0$. To attach a *meaningful* (zero or non-zero) terminal value would require analysing time periods which are 'outside the scope of the analysis'.

This example also highlights a much more significant point. Whereas several commentators on the Arrow-Debreu model have observed that there cannot logically be a justification for a market in share-holdings, most seem to have overlooked the fact that, in equilibrium, there would be no rationale for markets for transfers of ownership of land. Markets for the services of land would be sufficient, since the initial owner could obtain at the present instant the rents for the services of the land for the entire time horizon. Transfers of ownership would, to use Walras' phrase, be 'theoretically without rational motive'. To the extent that transfers of ownership can and do take place, the resulting pattern of ownership of land would be indeterminate. Transfers in the ownership of machines, trucks, houses and cars would likewise be 'theoretically without rational motive'.

A natural question is whether Walras' condition of a uniform rate of net income on capital goods has any meaning in an Arrow-Debreu economy. Although the *Theory of Value* does not do so, many expositions of the Arrow-Debreu model define a system of own rates of interest.[10] The own rate of interest for the land in question between dates t and $t+1$ would be defined as

$$\theta_{t,\, t+1} = \frac{P_t - P_{t+1}}{P_{t+1}}$$

It follows from (1) that *in equilibrium*

$$\theta_{t,\, t+1} = \frac{r_t}{P_{t+1}}$$

It is tempting to interpret r_t/P_{t+1} as a 'rate of return' on the owner-ship of a unit of land over the period in question.

A familiar proposition is that the own rates of interest between two dates for any two different goods or services need not be equal in equilibrium: $\theta_{j,t,t+1}$ is equal to $\theta_{k,t,t+1}$ only if

$$\frac{P_{j,t}}{P_{k,t}} = \frac{P_{j,t+1}}{P_{k,t+1}}$$

that is, only if equilibrium relative prices are unchanged between the two dates. It follows that there would be uniformity in the 'rates of return' on different types of land and capital goods for the same period only for special time profiles for rental payments. It might seem that the main lesson to be drawn from this is that the Arrow-Debreu model is more general than Walras' analysis, in that the former allows for changing relative prices over time. However, the significant implication is a different one, namely, that *it is not meaningful to think in terms of rates of return at all in the context of the Arrow-Debreu economy.* This follows not from the 'generality' of the model but from the assumption that *all* transactions take place at the present instant. Meaningful asset equilibrium conditions − involving uniformity in appropriately defined rates of return − can be established for models which allow for changes in relative prices over time but *only* for those models with spot markets at each date, since, in such models, ownership of a durable good is a way of transferring wealth over time. In contrast, in the Arrow-Debreu model, the notion of transferring wealth over time has no real meaning. Confronted by a disequilibrium set of prices, an agent might perceive an opportunity to increase his wealth by, say, buying, leasing and re-selling land of a particular type. As we have seen, this would not be a real opportunity, since all other interested parties would perceive the same opportunity. However, the point at issue here is that, since *all* payments would be made 'now', the decision whether to buy the land can be separated entirely from the decision whether to buy some other type of land or capital good. *An agent does not take decisions about the 'forms' in which to hold his wealth.*

Evaluation of the Arrow-Debreu model

We have argued that the Arrow-Debreu model accommodates only the feeblest of representations of the effects of the past. We have also seen that the treatment of the future is patently disquieting. As Arrow and Hahn so aptly put it, the assumption that there exists a complete set of markets 'telescopes' the future into the present (1971, p. 33). This places a considerable strain on the arbitrarily chosen present instant! The present instant of the Arrow-Debreu model cannot seriously be likened to the ever-changing present in which real people live. The Arrow-Debreu model offers no more than a pretence of taking into account what Jaques called the time of intention. The model offers no real insights into the complex relationships between memory, perception, expectation and desire.

Walras conceived of general equilibrium as a centre of gravity, that is, as a state towards which the economy would tend over time, albeit a target which would be constantly moving. His conception of general equilibrium was inseparable from his conceptions of both price and quantity adjustment processes. Notwithstanding the artificiality of the notion of tickets, his *tâtonnement* was designed to provide insights into *real* adjustment processes over time. In contrast, in the Arrow-Debreu model, general equilibrium cannot meaningfully be thought of as a centre of gravity. Debreu does not allude to any adjustment process when defining equilibrium. He does not consider the issue of stability. Since the present instant has no duration, no time is even allowed for the determination of equilibrium prices. Indeed, as Malinvaud observed, it is difficult to know how stability should be defined when 'time must ... enter both the definition of equilibrium and the process of convergence towards equilibrium' (1960-61, p. 152). A model in which markets are open only at the present instant and in which, to use Hicks' words, 'everything is fixed up in advance for a considerable period ahead' cannot provide even the first step in understanding the behaviour of real economies over time.

What *is* the justification for a model which postulates the existence of markets which everyone knows do not exist in real economies? The exponents of the model, we may assume, do not believe that it 'explains' the prices of commodities resulting from the interaction of agents in real economies.[11] Recently they have stressed the *negative* role of the model. However, one has to be careful with this type of argument. Thus the 'fundamental theorem of the theory of value' provides conditions which are *sufficient* to ensure that a general equilibrium exists. Violation of the conditions – and we know that, in reality, they are violated – does not imply that a general equilibrium does not exist. Similarly the theory identifies conditions which are *sufficient* to ensure that a general equilibrium is Pareto efficient. Violation of the conditions does not imply that, if a general equilibrium exists, it is inefficient. In any event, are we really to suppose that claims – however extravagant – for the virtues of the free enterprise system can be undermined by a model which assumes that producers have perfect information about the implications of future technical changes? Ill-informed claims cannot be exposed by invoking a meaningless benchmark.

When Hicks alluded in *Value and Capital* to a 'pure futures economy' in which 'everything is fixed up in advance for a considerable period ahead', he could scarcely have imagined how much attention would subsequently be devoted to such an economy. Hicks expressed reservations about the value of an analysis which assumes the existence of markets which manifestly do not exist in actual economies. Moreover, as we have seen, Walras rejected Böhm-Bawerk's theory of interest because he had 'looked in vain' for the markets which would enable interest to be deduced from the difference between the value of a present good and that of a future good. It is perhaps somewhat ironical that most economic theorists, invited to expound on 'Walrasian' general equilibrium theory, would now describe the Arrow-Debreu model.

Notes

1 Unless otherwise indicated, all page references in this chapter relate to Debreu (1959).

2 Debreu also notes that, in Hicks' *Value and Capital*, commodities are differentiated temporally as well as physically. Arrow has elaborated on the relationship between 'modern' general equilibrium analysis and the analysis of *Value and Capital*, claiming that 'the general aims and structure of general equilibrium theory have remained those already set forth by Hicks, and the subsequent development would have been impossible and indeed meaningless except on his foundations' (1974, p. 260). Beyond noting that Hicks treats the same good or service at different dates as economically different commmodities, Arrow's references are to the 'static' section of *Value and Capital*, not to Hicks' notion of a process in time.

3 In discussing uncertainty, we do not use Debreu's terminology, nor aspire to his precision. We simply wish to convey the essence of this interpretation.

4 Debreu indicates how date and location could be treated as continuous variables and how an infinite time horizon could be accommodated. This would involve infinite dimensional commodity spaces. Whatever the intrinsic merits of such an approach, it is certain that, had Debreu pursued it, his book would have been accessible to an even more restricted number of economists. To insist that time be treated as a continuous variable simply on the grounds that it really is continuous would, as Koopmans argued, be 'a point of pedantic purism' (1957, p. 106). Indeed, although economists typically take for granted that time itself is continuous, they do not know that it is. Philosophers debate whether time is continuous, simply dense or even discrete. It is worth noting that, in their tendency to periodise time, economists are typically out-of-step with physical scientists. Indeed, the philosopher Newton-Smith argues that the main reason people believe time to be continuous is that the best physical theories involve a continuous representation of time: 'That is, our belief in the continuity of time does not arise from any argument relating to infinite divisibility, it arises from our projecting onto the world the richness that is present in the mathematical system which we have found to date to be essential to the construction of viable physical theories' (1980, p. 118).

5 The implicit assumption that the electrician would be *in a position* to work every third minute of the day is disconcerting. We explore the relationship between time and location later.

6 The commodity specification of a truck includes model, mileage, location, etc. The commodity specification of 'use of a truck' also includes the conditions under which it is used. The quantity of the service of a truck, like the service of an electrician, is expressed in terms of time.

7 These complications relating to durable goods do not arise with Malinvaud's temporal framework, discussed briefly in Appendix 3, since durable goods are 'delivered' at the junctions between periods and they provide services during the periods.

8 The implicit assumption that all resources are initially owned by consumers is disconcerting – it is not easily reconciled with Debreu's suggestion that an individual who owns a house plays two roles, namely, that of *producer* who leases its service to himself as *consumer*.

9 Koopmans has stated: 'In any "long-run problems", that is, problems in which no fixed factors of production are recognised, one would require that every production set contain the origin, representing a state without inputs or outputs' (1957, p. 24).

10 Debreu defines just *one* interest rate between any two dates at a given

location: the interest rate from t_1 to t_2 at location s is defined in terms of 'units of value'.

11 According to Arrow: 'In my own thinking, the model of general equilibrium under uncertainty is as much a normative ideal as an empirical description. It is the way the actual world differs from the criteria of the model which suggests social policy to improve the efficiency with which risk bearing is allocated' (1974, p. 268).

8

Shackle

Many economists would impatiently reject or deride the preoccupations I have suggested to you. But I believe them to be important (*G.T.-S.E.*, pp. 17–18).

While Marshall, Walras, Lindahl and Hicks all started from the individual decision maker to derive implications for the properties of the economic system, it remains true that the weight of their attention lay with the economy rather than with the individual. We turn now, however, to two authors, Shackle and Lachmann, who both maintain – albeit with perhaps different emphases – that greater attention needs to be given to individual decision making and that the result of such deeper scrutiny is to modify significantly one's view of markets and the economic system.

With respect to Shackle, the subject of the present chapter, we shall be concerned with those aspects of his thought which appear to be most immediately connected with the role of time in economics. We shall not be concerned with his ideas on probability, possibility, potential surprise, etc., even though they are, of course, intimately related in Shackle's vision to the matters which will be considered here. Our discussion will be based on the following eight works by Shackle: *Time in Economics*, 1958 (*T.E.*); *Decision, Order and Time in Human Affairs*, 1961 (*D.O.T.*); *General Thought – Schemes and the Economist*, 1964 (*G.T.-S.E.*); *A Scheme of Economic Theory*, 1965 (*S.E.T.*); *The Nature of Economic Thought. Selected Papers 1955–1964*, 1966 (*N.E.T.*); *Epistemics and Economics. A critique of economic doctrines*, 1972 (*E.E.*); *An Economic Querist*, 1973 (*E.Q.*); *Imagination and the Nature of Choice*, 1979 (*I.N.C.*). These are not, of course, Shackle's only books – not to mention his other writings – but they will certainly suffice to direct us to Shackle's radically subjectivist views of time, of expectations and of decisions in the context of individual action and of some of the consequent implications for economics.

Economic time

Rather than our having a single, clear cut conception of time, we have, in Shackle's view, a whole 'skein of time-ideas', such as earlier and later, duration, remoteness, high and low speed processes, cause and effect (*S.E.T.*, p. 1). And varying presuppositions about time and about its implications for knowledge constitute, he asserts, the fundamental difference between alternative economic theories (*N.E.T.*, p. 17). Nor are only fine shades of difference involved here for, according to Shackle, 'In order to achieve demonstrative proof, the economic theoretician must reject time. In order to reflect the human predicament, he must consider time as the fact above all facts, conditioning every thought, act and meaning' (*E.E.*, p. 255); our view of time, then, may affect dramatically what we take to be the scope and limits of economic theory. As will be considered further below, realism and rigour are, in Shackle's judgement, irreconcilable in economics.

Shackle insists that the abstract, mathematical concept of time as a homogeneous 'space' is not the concept of time appropriate to an understanding of human thought, decision and action: 'The momentary time in which thought occurs is in arresting contrast with the endless extension of time which thought can be about' (*D.O.T.*, p. 14). In particular, 'in the experience of human individuals each of these moments is in a certain sense *solitary*. There is for us a *moment-in-being*, which is the locus of every actual sense-experience, every thought, feeling, decision and action' (*T.E.*, p. 13). Since these sense-experiences, etc. are events, the moment-in-being is not a mere instant, not a mere 'point' in the time of the physicist: 'The present moment, or the moment-in-being, must accordingly be thought of as a brief interval or finite element, not a mere point, yet it is also something whose very essence and also whose existence involves its continuous movement and continuous evolution' (*T.E.*, p. 14). (A number of commentators have detected an affinity between Shackle's ideas and those of Bergson and of Whitehead but since Shackle does not refer to these authors we shall not pursue the matter here.) The question 'where are the boundaries?' of a given 'moment-in-being' is dismissed as not being a real question (*T.E.*, pp. 13–14). Of far greater concern to Shackle is that, within the moment-in-being, memory and expectation can survey the past and the future: 'Expectation and memory are part of the essence of the moment-in-being, they are in it and of it' (*T.E.*, p. 16). Yet it is crucial to Shackle's entire analysis of choice, decision and action that the co-presence, within a moment-in-being, of thoughts relating to various times in the past and in the future *does not* permit the comparison of the *actuality* of separate moments-in-being; it permits only the comparison of *present* thoughts about those separate moments. As will be seen below, 'this consideration must lead us', in Shackle's judgement, 'to an altogether different view from the conventional one about what is the motive and purpose of decisions' (*T.E.*, p. 16).

The nature of decision

What then is Shackle's conception of the nature of decision and choice? It is that the alternatives between which choice is made are *present imaginings* of alternative future sequels to action; choice is not made between those alternative future sequels themselves. And the purpose of decision is to achieve a particular current mental state. The purpose to which decision and action are directed 'will be concerned with the feelings which the individual derives *now* from his decision, from mentally committing himself to an action-scheme, *now* within the same moment-in-being in which the decision is taken. If such a purpose consists in maximising the intensity of enjoyment, this will be an enjoyment by *anticipation*' (*T.E.*, p. 19).

As for the objects of choice, Shackle writes: 'Decision is choice, but choice amongst what? Not among actual experiences depending upon stimuli from without or our own motor responses, for when you are actually experiencing or physically doing something, it is too late to reject it in favour of something else. Choice is amongst imagined experiences' (*G.T.-S.E.*, p. 12). Shackle asks us, in effect, what choice can be among *other than* present thoughts, given that the past cannot be changed and that the future does not yet exist. (Many alternatives for the future are, indeed, mutually exclusive and thus cannot (logically) all exist.)

How many imagined experiences will there be in the list of alternatives between which choice is made? It is central to Shackle's view of decision-making that there is no answer to this question; 'the "possible" consequences of an act are *not listable*' (*N.E.T.*, p. 75).

No-one, not even the agent, can predict in advance what the range of choice will be in a future decision context (*T.E.*, p. 22).

But can he perhaps make a list of all possible consequences of each rival available act, and thus call to his aid all the apparatus of the theory of distributive probability? Even in a fundamentally random universe, statistics might rescue him. But not in a universe of ultimately creative thought. If a thought can contain an element undeducible from any record of the thinkers' past no matter how perfect, by any logical process no matter how powerful, then in principle no list can ever be made which can be known to be complete, of the distinct outcomes which a decision-maker might invent or imagine for any action-course open to him (*G.T.-S.E.*, pp. 12–13).

Indeed, it is only this capacity of the agent to create the (non-closed) choice set that allows 'decision' to have its full sense of a 'cut' between the past and the future (see further below). Using the term 'inspiration' to refer to that source of decision which is not already implicit in the past, Shackle writes that, 'It is in the creation of the range of imagined outcomes of an available immediate act that inspiration can be supposed to enter the process of history' (*D.O.T.*, p. 7) and elsewhere he makes the stronger claim that it is only inspiration with respect to imagined outcomes that permits 'decision' (*N.E.T.*, p. 80). Decision, then, in Shackle's picture of it is more than mere response; it involves novelty for 'Decision, when it is the real and living act emerging into our own private consciousness, seems to us to come in some degree *ex nihilo*' (*G.T.-S.E.*, p. 12). The act of decision is not, for Shackle, a pure act of intellect but involves also an aspect of commitment. Decision effects a transition from contemplation of alternative action-schemes to mental commitment to one of them (*T.E.*, p. 20) – 'what is the essence of the act of choice ...? Its vital nature is commitment. Choice is a resolve ... Choice erects a structure of intentions' (*I.N.C.*, p. 15).

If a decision 'is a cut between past and future', an innovation, then decision-making is incompatible with cosmic, all-embracing determinism (*D.O.T.*, p. 3). Conversely, however, decision would be pointless in a universe of complete chaos, of unbounded uncertainty (*D.O.T.*, pp. 4–5). And decision would be empty in a world of perfect foresight (*D.O.T.*, p. 4). 'Decision, therefore, is choice in face of bounded uncertainty' (*D.O.T.*, p. 5). And it is the nature of decision itself which is partially responsible for uncertainty. 'If decision means, what our ways of speech suggest, a *source* of new strands in the texture of events, then if there are to be decisions in the future we cannot know their consequences now' (*E.Q.*, p. 62). Hence decision-makers can never be sure of the consequences of their actions (*I.N.C.*, p. viii) and can thus never be certain what means to adopt to bring about a given desired end (*N.E.T.*, p. 72). They must realise, too, that the actual sequels to their actions may not even have featured in the lists of alternative outcomes which they considered when making their decisions (*I.N.C.*, pp. 41–2).

Imagination and expectations

As we have seen, Shackle maintains that the outcomes relevant to a choice are *all imagined* outcomes, imagined *now* by the chooser and that this is 'at the root of our argument' (*D.O.T.*, pp. 9-10). It need hardly be emphasised, then, that there is a strongly subjective cast to Shackle's arguments. It is all the more important therefore to make it clear that Shackle does not suggest that the relevant 'imaginings' are completely unconstrained. On the contrary, he is insistent that the imaginings relevant to decision must be constrained by what the agent believes to be possible, where this includes 'possible in the relevant time span' (*D.O.T.*, p. 11). And his explicit definition of expectation indeed has the idea of constraint built into it: 'Imagination constrained to congruity with what seems in some degree possible we shall call *expectation*' (*D.O.T.*, p. 13). Of course, even the qualification 'what seems in some degree possible' is still pointing to a subjective constraint on expectation; what does Shackle take to be the influences on that constraint?

Future time is a void which, essentially, we can fill only with imagination. This is not to say that we can fill it with pure unconstrained and wanton fantasy. Men are protected by a *practical conscience*, which bids them conceive only such sequels to their present action as are congruous with the way they have seen the world to work, and to envisage for given future dates only such situations (states of affairs) as there is time for the world to attain from its present situation, by transformations which seem possible in speed and extent (*E.Q.*, p. 62).

Experience, of course, is central to 'practical conscience': 'Experience *suggests what can* come to pass', even though it cannot show what *will* come to pass (*I.N.C.*, p. 59). It thus contributes to ease the problem that 'If choice is to be the pursuit of desires and ambitions, the chooser must have in mind some notions of *what can follow what*. He must view the world as a pattern of natural barriers rather than of narrow and prescribed tracks. What *can* take place, he must suppose, is bounded but not prescribed' (*I.N.C.*, p. 20: Shackle makes it clear that both human and non-human 'natural barriers' are involved here). Shackle also makes clear the role of the past in stating that, 'the content of each moment is partly, or perhaps overwhelmingly, an inheritance from previous moments' (*D.O.T.*, p. 38). It is thus understandable both that he can write, 'But even in the human world thoughts and decisions can be *partly* explained. The individual is pressed upon by circumstances visible to others as well as himself' (*D.O.T.*, p. 273) and that he should complain (courteously) that some of his critics have paid insufficient attention to his references to the importance of *memory* (*D.O.T.*, pp. 39–40).

Habits and stereotypical modes of thought are also invoked by Shackle as factors constraining the leaps of expectation. 'There are important contexts, such as the economic one, where it seems that a large part of conduct is given little effort of true decision, being instead a passive response to circumstances' (*D.O.T.*, p. 31). He even suggests at one point that, 'Imagination itself, the characteristic and most supremely human faculty, is perhaps no more than the composition of mosaics with *tesserae* that experience, personal and ancestral, has supplied' (*G.T.-S.E.*, p. 5). And if imagination may work on given 'materials', much thinking and practice can be based on stereotypes:

I want to suggest to you the notion of the stereotype. The ordinary business of living from hour to hour involves countless repetitions of a great number of diverse kinds of drill. By a drill I mean a settled procedure ... In each such drill we have a sequence of operations and a more-or-less confidently expected result. Without these drills and our unquestioning reliance on their efficiency we could never keep up with the ceaseless and relentless demands of life... There is an orderliness in our surroundings which we rely on, only needing to understand a fairly small part of the whole process which gives effect to our wishes. Each of us builds the unique structure of his or her personal existence out of countless stereotyped patterns of action (*G.T.-S.E.*, p. 18).

Shackle gives full recognition then to the roles of experience, of memory, of habits of thought and practice, etc. in bounding the imagined, in restricting it to 'The Imagined, deemed Possible' (the title of *I.N.C.*, Chapter 6). And yet, and yet. He insists that, 'No matter how complex the influences that bear on these thoughts' of an agent, these thoughts themselves are crucial (*E.E.*, p. 256). 'And expectation,' he writes, 'is a vast span resting on relatively slight abutments in the visible present', even the perception of present 'facts' being subjectively coloured (*E.E.*, p. 428). If this is so, it is not that surprising that 'Expectations are *kaleidic*' (*E.E.*, p. 183; 'kaleidic' is not in the *O.E.D.* or its *Supplement* but Shackle is fond of it) and that, because expectation is so difficult to analyse in a reasoned way, economists have been led 'to treat the *state of expectations* as a fixed configuration' (*E.E.*, p. 179). Shackle insists, it would seem, both that there are many constraining pressures on thought and imagination and that expectations are, nevertheless, unpredictable, undeducible from the past and easily changed in dramatic fashion.

Rationality, logic and time

Call to mind any good textbook presentation of the piece of theorising in which a consumer maximises a given utility function subject to a given (full) budget constraint, or in which a producer maximises profit subject to given prices and a production function, and then consider Shackle's statement: 'Conventional economics is not about choice, but about acting according to necessity. Economic man obeys the *dictates* of reason, follows the *logic of choice*. To call his conduct choice is surely a misuse of words' (*D.O.T.*, p. 272). For Shackle, decision and choice involve an essential element of *non-necessity*, while the dictates of rationality, by contrast, impose themselves inexorably, with *necessity*, so that choice (in its full meaning) pulls in a different direction from rationality.

Decision, when it is the real and living act emerging into our own private consciousness, seems to us to come in some degree *ex nihilo*. Yet we look upon ourselves as rational, as trying to respond to circumstances, to do our best with the situation presented to us, to make what we can of the materials given to us. How can these two attitudes, these two meanings ascribed to human action, be mutually reconciled? (*G.T.-S.E.*, p. 12).

The answer to this question turns, in Shackle's view, on time and its implications for rationality.

We consider first Shackle's approach in *Time and Economics* (1958) and *Decision, Order and Time* (1961). In both works, Shackle considers an example involving four different times, $t_0 < t_1 < t_2 < t_3$, where t_0 is 'now'. At t_0 a certain action is thought worthwhile; it gives, now, a pleasant image of t_1 at the cost of an unpleasant image of t_3. At t_2, only the unpleasant image is still to come and hence the action in question may, at t_2, be regretted (unless the pleasant memory of t_1 is strong enough to prevent this) (*T.E.*, pp. 17–18; *D.O.T.*, p. 18). If a given action-scheme can be the 'most preferred' at t_0 yet be regretted at t_2, which of these two perspectives on that action-scheme is the correct one? 'My contention', Shackle writes, 'is that this question is meaningless' (*T.E.*, p. 18); t_0 *and* t_2 *can never be 'in being' together* and thus 'The attempt to compare the individual's *actual* feelings at t_0 with his *actual* feelings at t_2 is for him impossible and does not make sense' (*T.E.*, pp. 18–19). This has, for Shackle, a striking implication: it 'destroys the distinction between rational and irrational conduct' and there can never be grounds for saying that the wrong choice was made (*T.E.*, p. 20).

It might have begun to seem as if Shackle is determined completely to expunge rationality from the concepts of economic theory. But this is not the case – recall, from the beginning of this section, Shackle's own question how *ex nihilo* decision and rational behaviour can 'be mutually reconciled'. His position is that conduct 'will be non-arbitrary; if you like, that it will be rational' (*T.E.* p. 27) *with respect to given expectations*. Thus 'decision is rational in that [the decision-maker] will necessarily choose that act whose imagined possibilities ... afford him the most desired total experience by anticipation' (*D.O.T.*, p. 272). Shackle does not here abandon rationality, understood as adopting the best means to the end; but he does abandon 'the postulate that the available ends are given' (*D.O.T.*, p. 273) because the ends between which choice is made are, for Shackle, thoughts, the imaginative creations of the chooser, which are un-given and undeducible from the past. Thus 'Non-determinism is as much the employer of reason as determinism. It recognizes, however, the question: Whence are the ideas that we reason about?' (*I.N.C.*, p. 57). For Shackle, there is freedom in the creation of the imagined alternative outcomes, reason in the making of a choice between those imagined outcomes (*N.E.T.*, p. ix).

When we turn to Shackle's later work, particularly *Epistemics and Economics* (1972), we find a perhaps more demanding conception of rationality and, correspondingly, a greater readiness on Shackle's part to minimise the role of rationality in economic decision making.

Rational choice, choice which can *demonstrate* its own attainment of maximum objectively possible advantage, must be fully informed choice ... The paradox of rationality is that it must concern itself with choosing amongst things fully known; but in the world of time, only *this* is fully known which is already beyond the reach of choice, having already become actual and thus knowable. Rational choice, it seems, must be confined to *timeless* matters (*E.E.*, pp. 245–6).

The meaning which Shackle here attributes to rationality – *i.e.*, demonstrability of superiority – is, of course, crucial to the validity of his conclusion and he insists on it on several occasions (*E.E.*, pp. 84, 229–30; *E.Q.*, p. 37). Given this meaning of rationality, time is inimical to rationality, for the passage of time implies present unknowledge and hence the impossibility of current demonstrative proof that any given course of action will best meet current aims. 'How can choice be based on foreknowledge of what that choice is called on to create?' (*I.N.C.*, p. 58), Shackle asks rhetorically. Since the actual consequences of my choice now will depend on the unknown – and indeed unknowable – future decisions of others, I can never be *certain* that I have adopted the best means to the achievement of my ends (*N.E.T.*, p. 72); I can never *demonstrate* the superiority of my choice; I can never (in this sense) act rationally.

It is not surprising, therefore, to find that Shackle repeatedly associates rationality with timelessness. 'Fully rational action can occur only in a momentary or timeless system, because the lapse of time allows choice of actions to be made at dates which follow or precede one another, and which therefore cannot be brought into the scheme of general exchange of commitments' (*N.E.T.*, p. 20; this could be read as a remark on the Arrow-Debreu construction). We may present a few more examples to give the flavour of Shackle's insistence on the rationality-timelessness link: 'If there is a fundamental conflict between the appeal to rationality and the consideration of the consequence of time as it imprisons us in actuality, the theoretician is confronted with a stark choice. He can reject rationality or time' (*E.E.*, sixth page of the unpaginated Preface). 'Rationality cannot span a temporal succession of situations' (*E.E.*, p. 84). 'Thus if economics is to be the pure logic of choice, the dismissal of time was necessary' because 'Time is what brings *new* knowledge ... Time is alien to reason' (*E.E.*, p. 151). 'We are saying, then, that in a non-timeless world, a world of earlier and later, there can be no pre-reconciliation of choice, therefore no fully rational choice, therefore no rigorous analysis of conduct as reasoned response to fully-known circumstances' (*E.E.*, p. 265).

What is one to make of Shackle's near rejection of rationality in *E.E.*? It is to be recalled that 'rationality' is a protean concept and that Shackle has here only rejected rationality *qua* choice which is *demonstrably* maximising. Given that he is correct to assert that, in the world of real time, one can never know all the consequences of one's action, his rejection of rationality so *defined* would simply seem to be inevitable. Whether that definition was ever an interesting definition of rationality could, of course, be questioned.

Time preference and time horizons

We have already noted Shackle's insistence that a decision-maker at time t_0 is *not* involved in comparing an actual experience at t_1 with an actual experience at t_2 ($t_0 < t_1 < t_2$) but in comparing the t_0 perceptions of the imagined t_1 and t_2 experiences. While, like most authors, Shackle accepts that future remoteness may lead to discounting on the grounds of reduced present confidence in the possibility of an imagined event's actual occurrence, he casts some doubt on the notion of *pure* time preference.

It is sometimes suggested that imagined enjoyments, takings-place imagined and thus 'enjoyed beforehand', by anticipation, are keener in their effect in 'the present' if their supposed date of occurrence is near rather than far. But why should this be so? All such *enjoyment by anticipation* is the fruit of imagination, not, directly, of reports from the field. All are located by the individual's thought in time-to-come. What relevance has the calendar-date of such location on the keeness or effectiveness of the anticipative experience? (*I.N.C.*, pp. 32–3).

Moreover, 'the skein of imagined sequels which the chooser conceives for any contemplated course of action will include sequels which are counter-desired, besides some which are desired. "Impatience" seems applicable only to the sequels which are desired' (*I.N.C.*, pp. 33–4). More positively, Shackle asks why, at t_0, an event expected at t_3 should be less valued than an event expected at t_1, when we take into account that the anticipation at t_0 *includes* the pleasure of anticipation at t_2, etc. ($t_0 < t_1 < t_2 < t_3$)? (*T.E.*, pp. 32–3).

Why might a decision-making agent ignore all dates beyond some particular one? Shackle suggests two kinds of reason. The first is that this will be done if it makes no difference to the agent's present feelings whether it is done or not (*D.O.T.*, p. 223). The second is that, beyond a certain date, the constraints on imagined sequels are too weak to permit the formation of *expectations* (*ibid*). (It will be recalled that, for Shackle, expectation is the imagined, deemed possible, so that if 'everything seems possible', expectation formation becomes otiose). A perhaps different emphasis is given by Shackle in a later work, in which he suggests that, for sufficiently remote future dates, the imagined possible sequels to alternative present actions will become so entangled, even fused, that any idea of current choice of action with respect to those remote dates becomes empty: the closest time beyond which this consideration has force constitutes a natural time-horizon for the decision maker (*I.N.C.*, p. 31). And there is also the more immediately pressing fact that the closer is the time-horizon used, the more imagined alternative sequels can be taken into account (*ibid.*), not to mention the brute fact that 'the whole business of choice is necessarily subject to a deadline' (*I.N.C.*, p. 32).

Markets

Even as sympathetic a critic of Shackle's work as Ludwig Lachmann felt able to complain that, 'The object of his study is the mental processes of an individual who has to take a decision in the face of an uncertain future. His theory is modelled on the equilibrium of the isolated individual (Robinson Crusoe) and stops there. It tells us nothing about market processes and nothing about the exchange and transmission of knowledge' (1978 [1956], p. 27, referring to Shackle's *Expectations in Economics*, 1949). Even in Shackle's later writings, it is perhaps fair to say, market processes are hardly the focus of attention. The following chapter, on Lachmann, will be much more concerned with the radical subjectivist view of the market process, so it may suffice here to refer to Shackle's interest both in speculative markets and in the role of convention in price formation. (Noting, as we do so, how the speculation/convention contrast at the level of the market parallels that between genuine decision and stereotyped behaviour at the level of the individual).

One particular aspect of the tension between rationality and time to which Shackle frequently refers is the phenomenon of speculative behaviour. 'The market cannot solve the problem of expectation. The only price it can distil, for a storable non-perishable good, is one which divides the potential holders of that good into two camps, those who think its price will rise and those who think its price will fall' (*E.E.*, p. 83); in the nature of the case, the agents in the two camps cannot all be correctly informed about the future and cannot all be in a position to *demonstrate* the correctness of the market stance they are adopting. 'The observed existence of speculative markets where temporary price-stability is nevertheless established, proves that expectation-forming of a non-logical kind occurs. The rational ideal cannot apply to speculative markets and cannot include them' (*E.E.*, p. 159). More generally, no activity which turns on taking advantage of other agents' lack of knowledge can be fitted into a fully rational analysis (*E.E.*, p. 93) and the existence of any *durable asset* points to the future, hence to un-knowledge and hence to the destruction of the fully rational ideal (*E.E.*, p. 235).

Shackle, then, sees the speculative market as not being amenable to a conventional rational action analysis. And he does not regard the speculative market as an exceptional or special case. On the contrary, he writes, '*all markets*, save those for ephemeral goods of instant consumption, are *speculative*' (*I.N.C.*, p. 64) and in their analysis 'we are at once involved in *time as the field of expectation*' (*E.E.*, p. 266). For any storable goods, future values must affect current values − but the former are unknown and hence the relevant current markets must be speculative ones, in which prices are held momentarily constant only by the *differences* of view as between the agents involved (*E.E.*, p. 412). Consequently bond prices and interest rates, for example, are '*inherently restless*' variables, since no state of opinion, of agents' views, can both imply constancy of bond prices and interest rates and be confirmed by such constancy (*E.E.*, p. 201). More generally, *any* speculative market price which is being held constant over time, by the balance between those who expect a price rise and those who expect a price fall, will *ipso facto* invalidate the expectations of some market agents, whose changes in stance will then lead the erstwhile constant price to change.

At the same time, Shackle insists that convention often plays an important role in price formation. By contrast with the personal valuations which various agents place upon goods and services, valuations springing from those agents' individual purposes and imagined future alternatives, 'the prices adopted on a market for the sake of exchange are conventions. They are convenient working agreements which enable the business of life to be carried on …. The market's near-miracle of engendering apparently unanimously agreed prices shows unknowledge over-ridden and trampled down by the sheer necessity of getting on with the business of living' (*I.N.C.*, pp. 64–5). Indeed, Shackle refers more generally to 'the vital part played in economic affairs by *convention*' in the context of a discussion of money and of Keynes's Chapter 17 of the *General Theory* (*E.E.*, p. 219). In the absence of objective, predictable and agreed anchorages for the formation of prices, interest rates, etc., conventions may perhaps provide substitute 'foundations'.

If Shackle has relatively little to say about market processes, he has much to say concerning the wider implications of the radical subjectivist view of time, expectation and decision for economics, both with respect to its general approach and ambitions and with respect to some of its more specific theories and forms of analysis: it is to such wider implications that we now turn.

Physicists' time and Laplacean mechanical determination

In the classical dynamics of the physicist, time is merely and purely a mathematical variable ... The solution of the differential equation, if it can be found, is complete in an instantaneous and timeless sense. This *timelessness* of the solutions of problems in classical physical dynamics makes an extraordinary contrast with the problems of how events arise in economics. For it abolishes the distinction between past and future. The physicist has, within the stated limits of his problem, complete, perfect and indubitable *knowledge* of where his particle will be at any instant; the very nature of human consciousness, of human experience of life, depends absolutely and essentially upon *ignorance* of the future, upon its non-actuality, upon the necessity to live in one moment at a time (*T.E.*, pp. 23–4).

Shackle, therefore, is not happy with what he sees as the growing influence of 'Newtonian' thinking within economics, doubting that life is like this (*T.E.*, p. 24). In his view, the creation of *essential novelty*, involved in human decision, is simply incompatible with intertemporal dynamics (*T.E.*, p. 26) and 'the question whether human affairs are amenable to be described by means of a differential equation' must surely be answered negatively in the presence of imagination and of changing knowledge (*E.E.*, pp. 282–3).

It is not surprising, then, that Shackle not only criticises general equilibrium theory for its essential timelessness and extravagant assumptions about knowledge; he is critical too of 'mechanical' trade cycle models. 'For the unreality of perfect all-pervasive relevant knowledge [in the equilibrium scheme of thought], we have substituted [in business cycle models] the artificiality of mechanism, behaviour which can be described without any mention of thought, choice, decision. Whether it adopts an equilibrium model or a cyclical one, economic theory seems resolved to treat economic conduct as mere response' (*G.T.-S.E.*, p. 11). Whereas mechanism binds different dates together, decision cuts them apart (*N.E.T.*, p. 24), intro ducing novelty and undeducibility, for in human affairs it is 'memory, insight, expectation, intention' which link variables at 't' to those at 't + 1' (*E.E.*, p. 58), so that there is not a purely mechanical linkage between them. Thus Shackle insists on the distinction 'between mechanical time and expectational time, or perhaps better, between time of mechanism and time of uncertainty' (*S.E.T.*, p. 187), suggesting that the *ex ante/ex post* language helps to release us from the mechanical conception of time (*E.E.*, fourth page of the unpaginated Preface) and arguing that Keynes's conception of economic analysis is 'Nearly at the polar extreme from' the mechanical, determinist model.

In Shackle's judgement, his emphases on origination, decision, novelty, changing knowledge, etc. 'are alien not only to Laplace's conception of the physical universe and his explicit inclusion in it of human affairs, but also to the modern economist's procedures in explaining the nature of "business" and much of human activity' (*I.N.C.*, p. 55). A 'science hopes to be able to analyse completely any situation which comes within its scope ... But what becomes, in this case, of a human capacity, if we believe in it, for unpredictable thoughts? What becomes of imagination, invention, social evolution? Economics, it seems, can try to be a science like chemistry, or it can try to explain the life of human beings, but not both' (*G.T.-S.E.*, p. 14).

Decisionism

'If all causes are themselves determinately and precisely caused, we are in a complete determinist universe where nothing can happen differently from what it does' (*G.T.-S.E*, p. 8). By contrast, 'we are regarding the world, in its state at any moment, as an incomplete system, one whose immediately future behaviour depends on the way in which data or impulses not deducible in character or quantity from the past of the system, are going to be fed into it *ex nihilo* by human agency' (*ibid.*). Thus even if an observer could be given *full* present information about every agent, including agents' current decisions, he could only infer the immediate general consequences; he could not foresee the further evolution of the system.

If there is to be foreknowledge of [time-to-come], in any sense, that must depend on recognizing the antecedents of that content and ascribing to them the power to determine it. *Beginning* is an assertion that such power may be sometimes absent. In finding a locus for *beginnings* in some kinds of thought, we are proposing to treat these kinds of thoughts as exempt from determinism and thus from foreknowledge. If there are beginnings, there is no complete inferential knowledge of the content of time-to-come (*I.N.C.*, pp. 54–5).

Given Shackle's stance, it will be clear that 'profound consequences follow for our view of the nature of economics' (*T.E.*, p. 23) but he nowhere attempts, to our knowledge, to support his election of 'decisionism' rather than 'determinism' by any sort of 'proof' of non-determinism. To note this is not, of course, to show that Shackle would have been better advised to attempt such a 'proof'; his choice of starting point may perhaps have been a shrewd one. Nor does he ever dwell at length, so far as we know, on the philosophical theme of 'free-will', although he does remark that, in the context of his picture of decision, free-will does *not* mean that choice can be arbitrarily made from a given choice set: it means, rather, that the choice set is not given but is created in imagination (*T.E.*, p. 27).

If decision involves an *ex nihilo* element, not deducible from the past, then the way is open to the presence of novelty. Shackle argues, for example, that, 'The most dramatic and spectacular secret of success [in a contest] is novelty, and novelty is that which an infallible algorithm must, by definition, exclude' (*E.E.*, p. 426) – a remark with obvious implications for theories of competition, of bargaining, of games, etc. He notes, too, that it is not only the *counter*-expected which can cause surprise to agents – novelty, the *unexpected*, can do so as well (*I.N.C.*, p. 88) and since *no* sweeping theory of how agents respond to 'disappointments' can be found (*E.Q.*, pp. 40-1), and since at least some surprises will be disappointments, it follows that novelty renders full predictability impossible. More generally, Shackle associates the existence of novelty with the non-existence of complete knowledge: 'If the Scheme of Things has unending stores of essentially new things to show us ... then we can construct no model of that Scheme of Things' (*E.E.*, p. 26).

'If there is non-empty decision in our sense, there is no objective future ... the future is not there to be discovered, but must be created' (*D.O.T.*, pp. 15 and 16). In insisting that the future is not 'out there to be discovered', Shackle is suggesting neither that nothing can be said about it, nor that it can be freely, consciously chosen. We have to suppose 'that *in some sense* [the future] will be faithful to the past. The essence of our difficulty, as analysts or as enterprisers, is to say what the mode of that faithfulness is, in what ways and degrees it will be qualified or subverted by *novelty*' (*E.E.*, p. 279). As for freely choosing the future, Shackle writes, 'Do men, then, choose their own history? Plainly no man can do so, since by the nature of non-illusory choice he cannot know what will be the sequel of any act of his. Yet if choice is non-illusory, history is created by men's choices' (*I.N.C.*, p. 53). Agents cannot make the future which they intend but nevertheless agents create the future which will actually emerge.

Prediction, explanation and description

In Chapter 31 of *Epistemics and Economics*, Shackle questions the view that explanation and prediction are simply two sides of the same coin. And while scientific prediction is conditional, Shackle doubts whether the economist can ever list the relevant conditions in a way which is both compatible with economic theory *and* sufficiently realistic and comprehensive (*E.E.*, p. 345). Explanation, he suggests, is less difficult than prediction and can draw on recognised stereotypes (*E.E.*, p. 346). 'The symmetry of prediction and explanation is true only in an abstract world, where the data on which reason is to work are complete and certain for both purposes' (*E.E.*, p. 349). The activity of prediction involves showing that from $x_{t-n}, ..., x_{t-1}, x_t$ it *must* follow that $x_{t+1}, x_{t+2}, ...$ take particular values, whereas, Shackle suggests, that explanation need only show that x_t could reasonably have followed from $x_{t-n}, ..., x_{t-1}$ (*E.E.*, p. 350): thus explanation is a less demanding task than is prediction, in Shackle's view. One *could*, of course, interpret explanation in a more demanding way — as demanding, indeed, as Shackle's interpretation of prediction. But a historian's explanation, for example, would not often claim that certain events were the only possible sequel to those put forward as their explanation. History can be seen as a *loose texture* in which there are certainly physical and mental constraints on what can happen but in which it is not *determined* what *must* happen,

there being space for origination *ex nihilo* and for novelty (*E.E.*,
p. 351).

Since genuine decision and choice involve for Shackle an *ex nihilo*,
creative element, undeducible from the past, it will hardly be surprising to find that he regards decision as inimical to prediction. 'Yet
if decision involves essential novelty, prediction of human conduct
is logically impossible' (*T.E.*, p. 21). Thus even if an observer could
be given *full* current information about every agent, he could only
infer the most immediate general consequences; he could not 'foresee
the further evolution of the system. For he could not predict what
would be the next *decisions*' (*T.E.*, pp. 25–6). It is not only decisions
that are (logically) non-predictable; so are inventions. 'A scientific
discovery, yet to be made, cannot be specified in advance' (*I.N.C.*,
p. 122). Shackle sees little scope then for prediction in economics. Yet,
as was implied just above, he does relax this view slightly in accepting that prediction may be possible in the sufficiently short term.
Things might change slowly enough at the aggregate level to allow
'a short-term predictive dynamics of the economy as a whole' (*T.E.*,
pp. 27–8). A stricter view is embodied in the following passage:

A scientific prediction starts with *if*. Now to suggest the future course of
human events can only resemble scientific prediction if the described events
are to arise out of a known configuration of desires, beliefs, intentions and
resources, and such knowledge, if it can ever be possessed by anyone, can
at the utmost refer only to the present. Prediction of human events can be
scientific only if it refers to the immediate future (*G.T.-S.E.*, p. 16).

Nor is it clear what 'the immediate future' means for this purpose,
Shackle insists. For while conditional prediction is possible up to (and
only up to) the first date at which a further decision occurs (*D.O.T.*,
p. 23), this has little content, since we *do not know when* a new
decision will be made (*D.O.T.*, p. 24; see also *N.E.T.*, p. 83 where it
is said that, because of future decisions, it cannot be said *for how
long* ceteris paribus will hold good). A less strict possibility, which
ignores the effects of decisions rather than ruling out decisions, is also
recognised by Shackle: the fact of *inertia*, and hence of lags in the
consequences of novelty, may permit a limited possibility of prediction
(*D.O.T.*, pp. 25, 31–2). But it is clear, nonetheless, where Shackle's
emphasis lies in the matter of prediction in economics – '*predicted
man* is less than human, *predicting man* is more than human' (*T.E.*,
p. 105).

What can and should economists do if prediction, other than of the most limited kind, is beyond them? In Shackle's judgement, 'a descriptive, as distinct from a predictive, analytical scheme can have value' (*D.O.T.*, p. 23). A subjective, descriptive dynamics of the mind of the individual agent may be possible and useful, even if an objective, aggregate and predictive dynamics is not (*T.E.*, p. 29). Although we cannot predict, cannot construct a self-sufficient dynamics, Shackle suggests, we can still study the ceteris paribus dynamics of given expectations, of given rules for changing expectations, etc. (*T.E.*, pp. 67–8). The 'theory of fallible expectation is *necessarily, essentially* embryonic, for we can describe what is expected, what is planned, at some present moment, but not what experience and time's new knowledge will do to those hopes' (*E.E.*, fifth page of the unpaginated Preface). Indeed it may be, in Shackle's view, that the human sciences can not do much more than catalogue, than engage in taxonomic clarification; the economist should perhaps be content to be a Fox, knowing many little things, not aiming to be a Hedgehog who knows one big thing (*E.E.*, pp. 29–30). For Shackle, then, the 'purpose and proper duty' of economic theory is descriptive, to describe what can happen (*D.O.T.*, p. 274), for 'We cannot tell, any better now than yesterday, what *will* happen. We can only hope to judge, with some presumption of skill and a fair basis of experience, what can happen, at best and at worst, if we do this or if we do that' (*N.E.T.*, p. 135). It is for these reasons that, in the penultimate sentence of *Epistemics and Economics*, Shackle urges us 'to improve economic theory as an insight-tool, as a means of understanding, and also to persuade ourselves not to insist too confidently on its powers as a *foresight-tool*' (*E.E.*, p. 448).

Having seen what Shackle takes to be some of the sweeping implications of radical subjectivism for the general nature and scope of economics, we turn now to its possible implications for a number of more specific aspects of economic analysis; there is, of course, no suggestion that the following set of considerations is exhaustive of those implications.

General equilibrium theory

While not dismissive of general equilibrium theory (see below), Shackle certainly interprets it as a severely limited construction.

The whole brilliant, incisive and all-inclusive neo-classical theory of value, brought to perfection by Walras and Pareto, Wicksteed and Wicksell about the turn of the present century, depended on the astounding assumption that people know everything relevant to their choices. The question what this knowledge must consist of and how it is to be obtained is cut out by an Alexandrine sword-stroke of superb efficiency: the notion of general equilibrium (*G.T.-S.E*, p. 15).

'But general equilibrium with all its splendour and incomparable intellectual efficiency, reducing everything to the logic of maximization, only describes a momentary world. The world of change, evolution and invention is quite beyond its scope' (*G.T.-S.E*, p. 16). Shackle is even more explicit when he writes that, 'the Walras-Pareto type of general static equilibrium system in its modern form ... leaves out: *Time* and everything that belongs to time: expectation and uncertainty; change and growth; ambition, hope and fear; discovery, invention and innovation; novelty and news. *Money* and everything that goes with it ...' (*T.E.*, p. 93). Thus, 'the Rational General Equilibrium owed its encompassing completeness, exactness and certitude to its neglect of all that is essentially implied by *time*. The rational, sure and pre-reconciled world is timeless' (*E.E.*, third page of the unpaginated Preface).

Static versus stationary analysis

Yet if the static general equilibrium analysis leaves something to be desired, it is still, in Shackle's judgement, greatly to be preferred to stationary state analysis. While general equilibrium theory is described as 'brilliant', etc., Shackle suggests that the stationary state 'is a pointless declension from the purity of argument of the timeless system' (*E.E.*, p. 238). Why is this? In the stationary state, 'Not only physical endowments and tastes, but also *beliefs*, knowledge, expectations, might in general be supposed to be carried from one interval to another' (*S.E.T.*, p. 19) and to be not only constant but to have the same effects in each interval; there is no learning, forgetting or imagining (*S.E.T.*, p. 20). Thus, strangely enough, the strictly *static* system, in which time is abolished, provides a better basis for 'a time-conscious theory' (*T.E.*, p. 95) than does the multi-period stationary state construction. We cannot study imagination, anticipation, etc. − with their seeds of change, development and evolution − in the stationary state but we can do so in a static model (*T.E.*, p. 95).

Nor are stationary states a useful construction for the purpose of studying transition by a comparative method, if they are intended to ensure that only external causes provoke the transition; unless a purely hand-to-mouth, equipment-less economy is studied, transition would always leave internal disturbances, ripples in the equipment adjustment process (*E.E.*, p. 270). It is perhaps better, in any case, not to try to describe the process of transition but rather to regard it as disorderly (*E.E.*, p. 271). Shackle also holds it against stationary state analysis that it involves the assumption of *perfect foresight*, which is self-contradictory in any other context (*T.E.*, p. 95). (It can hardly be expected, of course, that Shackle would wish to embrace 'the meaningless and self-destructive assumption of "perfect foresight"' (*E.E.*, p. 265) – which is, he suggests, 'simply another name for timelessness' (*E.E.*, p. 165) – since 'perfect foresight would render decision *empty*' (*D.O.T.*, p. 4). 'For the idea that two or more persons, with rival or conflicting interests, can in general have perfect foresight is self-contradictory, unless we assume a complete determinism. But to assume determinism is to abolish the reality of the act of choice' (*S.E.T.*, p. 14)).

Money, Keynes's theory and period analysis

For Shackle, the role of money is inseparable from lack of confidence in present beliefs. 'A money-using economy is one which acknowledges the permanent insufficiency of the data for rational choice. For money is the means by which choice can be deferred until a later and better-informed time' (*E.E.*, p. 160). And that is why money is difficult to include in a general equilibrium analysis. 'Money is the means of deferring choice and in the timeless system there is no date to which choice can be deferred, nor is there any prospect of subsequent improvement of knowledge as a reason for electing to defer it' (*E.E.*, p. 235). The most interesting theories, for Shackle, will thus be those in which money plays a genuine role as, for example, in Keynes's *General Theory*.

In Shackle's reading of the *General Theory*, 'Keynes's meaning was the precariousness and fragility of expectations ... His method or formal frame was an equilibrium' (*N.E.T.*, p. 28): Keynes thus combined 'the formal analysis of equilibria and the entire repudiation of their ostensible meaning' (*S.E.T.*, p. 46). Keynes's equilibrium presentation of unstable expectations Shackle describes as a '*kaleido-static*' method (*S.E.T.*, p. 5), in which the effects of given expectations are allowed time to work through and then one imagines a veritable cascade of events following an upset in expectations (*E.E.*, p. 435). 'The kaleidic method shows the struggle and frustration of reason in face of those uncertainties which are part of the scheme of things ... In doing this it plainly surpasses the value-construct in realism' (*E.E.*, p. 437). The equilibria considered in this method of analysis are not optima in any sense 'but merely positions which do not contain within their structure an immediate source of movement' (*ibid*). In Shackle's interpretation, the logic of Keynes's position is that 'it is logically inconceivable for business to be rational' (*E.E.*, p. 163), even if this logic, albeit implicit in Chapter 12 of the *General Theory*, did not become explicit until 1937, in the famous *Quarterly Journal of Economics* article. Shackle describes Keynes's rejection of the possibility of rationality as 'this position of nihilism' (*E.E.*, p. 160) and argues that in macro-economics since Keynes, 'The aspect of disintegration, of purely negative and nihilistic resignation, has been successfully cut out of the new body of doctrine' (*E.E.*, p. 430) – the use of 'successfully' here does not, presumably, convey any sense of approval!

According to Shackle, Keynes distrusted both 'periods' and precise 'time-lags' in economic theorising (*E.E.*, pp. 434–5) and he 'preferred to leave calendar divisions alone' in both the *Treatise on Money* and the *General Theory* (*E.E.*, pp. 441). As Shackle himself asks in support of Keynes, can life be forced into neat periods, with everything 'happening' at their junctions? (*E.E.*, p. 434). The distinction between *ex ante* (figments) and *ex post* (records) was a brilliant innovation on Myrdal's part, Shackle accepts, 'Yet the Myrdalian scheme has its own problems. It is plain that there are many competing, and somewhat incompatible, criteria for the length of the Myrdalian period. Is it not essentially a mere moment of time?' (*E.E.*, p. 440). Thus the period method is 'a highly unreal construction' and the only way to defend its use 'is to ask what better method can we find?' (*E.Q.*, p. 40).

The role of models

If the just-mentioned defence of period analysis is a weak one, it is still a defence. Shackle is *not* a complete iconoclast, dismissive of all economic theory, or even of all economic theory not centred on decision, changing beliefs, the role of money, etc. We noted above that Shackle refers to the 'brilliant, incisive and all-inclusive neo-classical theory of value' and to the 'splendour and incomparable intellectual efficiency' of general equilibrium models. These phrases are not tongue-in-cheek deflations of such theory. Immediately after listing the limitations of the Walras-Pareto system, Shackle at once presents a *defence* of that system, praising the way in which it draws economic *interdependence* to the centre of our attention (*T.E.*, p. 93). And a later critique of rational, timeless theory is also followed immediately by an affirmation of the *value* of such static theory (*E.E.*, p. 246). More generally, Shackle makes the point that while one can be certain about the logical validity of formal constructs, one can never be certain about the 'other' reality — if any! — which they represent: it would be a mistake to suppose that any one formal construct is '*the* right' one (*I.N.C.*, p. 148). It is thus not surprising that after discussing a number of quite different kinds of economic theory, Shackle should conclude, 'If models of all the types we have dissected are necessary or useful (and we think they are) we have to be content to use them one at a time' (*S.E.T.*, p. 195). Shackle does not dismiss static value theories, or mechanical cycle theories, etc, out of hand but insists on their limited, partial natures. Can these various different economic models be smoothly combined into a grander, more inclusive one? No, says Shackle, they cannot, because different models start from mutually incompatible premises, so that an amalgam of models would be internally incoherent. Does this reduce us to engaging in purely 'descriptive historiography? We think not' (*S.E.T.*, p. 195). The correct procedure, Shackle recommends, is to engage in a *non*-logical blending of models (*S.E.T.*, p. 196); he sets out no recipe for such blending.

However such joint use of different models is to be effected, Shackle does not 'believe in the practicability or efficiency of a general model of economic society, embracing all its important aspects' (*S.E.T.*, p. x). This is not surprising, given Shackle's view that, 'Economic affairs are not self-contained or insulated, they cannot have a self-sufficient explanation' (*E.E.*, p. 240). Moreover, the rigorous proof of theorems has little role in economics outside value theory, in Shackle's judgement, because a 'rigorous proof is necessarily about abstractions. Proof exists in thought, and can be composed only of thought-entities designed for its purpose' (*E.E.*, pp. 343 and 342). Economists should thus accept the example given by Marshall, 'who made clear by his bold practice that economics is an *essentially* imprecise subject' (*E.E.*, pp. 262).

Some concluding comments

Few readers will disagree that Shackle's ideas and emphases are different from those found in most writings of economic theorists; they are, indeed, sufficiently different – and sufficiently insistent – that they may even provoke, in some quarters and on some occasions, immoderate and unmeasured reactions, reactions which impede a clear-sighted assessment of Shackle's contribution. Setting aside, then, such responses as 'Shackle is just a complete nihilist with respect to economic theory', we now consider briefly some potentially more serious criticisms of that contribution.

From the famous 1959 *Metroeconomica* symposium on Shackle's work, we may first note Åkerman's fear that, in *Time and Economics* at least, Shackle offers no causal analysis of the environmental and institutional factors 'which form and restrict the plans' of the individual decision-maker and that he 'eliminates all connections between this individual's mind and his own experiences as well as the experiences and actions of other individuals' (1959, p. 4). For Shackle, Åkerman reiterates, 'experience does not influence the decision-maker' (p. 5). But just two pages later Åkerman himself quotes Shackle as referring (in *Time and Economics*, pp. 80-81) to entrepreneurs taking account of experience! Åkerman's problem here perhaps illustrates a general difficulty in arriving at a measured assessment of Shackle's views. Prompted, it may be, by the radical nature of his objections to much economic theorising, Shackle's writing often lays an overwhelming stress on subjectivism, on the possibility of uncaused imaginings, etc. and, correspondingly, often says little about other considerations. But it is always dangerous to slip from the observation that an author does not assert proposition ... to the suggestion that the author denies proposition ...; it is especially dangerous when confronted by a writer who, like Shackle, is overwhelmingly concerned to emphasise certain particular aspects of a complex matter. As it happens, we have seen above that – whatever Shackle's emphases may be – his writings do contain perfectly explicit discussions of the relevance of experience, of memory, of the individual's judgement of what is possible, of habits, of stereotyped modes of thought, and even of social conventions. Shackle certainly does not stress the role of experience, etc. but, equally certainly, he does not deny it. While it is true that uncaused imaginings, creative novelty, etc. do 'drive a wedge between behaviour and circumstances' (Coddington, 1982, p. 486) and no less true that, 'if the wedge were to become comprehensive [theorists stressing such phenomena] would be left with no theory at all, all behaviour would appear equally capricious and unintelligible' (*ibid.*), it is not obviously the case that Shackle's 'wedge' really is comprehensive. He does assert that not every economically relevant decision can be deduced from information about the past and current situations. He does not assert that such information has no bearing on individuals' decisions and he does not assert that such information has no bearing on 'our' attempts to understand why those decisions were taken or even, in restricted circumstances, to make limited, cautious attempts to predict some such decisions. Setting the record straight in this way does not, of course, amount to answering such questions as: How prevalent does Shackle take uncaused, innovative decision-making to be in practice? For which agents does he take his account of decision and choice to be most appropriate? We are not in a position to answer these questions: let us, rather, ask a question on Shackle's behalf – 'Is the economic theorist entitled to suppose that all decisions are deducible from the past and present situations? or even that, if there exist non-deducible decisions, at least they have only negligible economic consequences?' If we are not so entitled then Shackle's message is highly important and it would be futile to seek to shrug it off by complaining (even if correctly) that that message is delivered with a one-sided emphasis.

We have ourselves suggested above that it is not easy to be sure quite what Shackle has to say about rationality – even if one can be reasonably sure that its status is lower in Shackle's picture of economic life than it is in many more orthodox pictures. This is not unrelated to criticisms of Shackle's earlier work made, independently, by both Keirstead and Lachmann in the *Metroeconomica* symposium already referred to. Keirstead objects that, while Shackle allows the individual to have thoughts about both the past and the future, 'One cannot find any admission of the identity of the past, present and future self' and argues both that there is such an identity and that it is crucial for decision making and for predictability (1959, p. 47). Here again one may observe that not finding 'any admission of ...' is not equivalent to finding 'a denial of ...'. Similarly, after citing

Locke to the effect that 'madmen and fools are the only freemen', Keirstead has to acknowledge that, 'Professor Shackle, in all fairness, is fully aware of this, and he never says or intimates that decisions are not taken in the light of experience' (p. 48). Keirstead, then, is more careful than Åckerman, but he insists that there is more knowledge available and more calculation carried out than Shackle admits (p. 49). Lachmann too was worried by Shackle's treatment of the individual: after writing that 'We can, and occasionally do, learn from experience ... the human mind is continuous' (1959, p. 66), Lachmann suggests that Shackle on occasion has come dangerously close to denying this (p. 67). This he finds disturbing, since some degree of such continuity is necessary for the very meaningfulness of the *ex ante / ex post* distinction, of the idea of plans, of the testing and revision of plans, etc. (p. 66). These latter claims are well-founded but we are not aware that Shackle has ever actually denied some continuity to the human mind; more importantly, there would seem to be no need to make any such denial in order to justify Shackle's most characteristic concerns and emphases.

It is undoubtedly an implication of Shackle's arguments that economists ought to be far more modest in their claims than some economists have sometimes been. It would be question-begging, however, to dismiss those arguments as 'nihilistic'; they can properly be brushed-aside only once they have been shown to be false. Until such a demonstration has been provided, it would be more fitting to acknowledge that Shackle has made us far more aware than have some economic theorists of the immense difficulties which time poses for economics.

9

Lachmann

As soon as we permit time to elapse, we must permit knowledge to change, and knowledge cannot be regarded as a function of anything else (1977 [1959], p. 92; 1976(b), p. 127).

For over forty years, Ludwig Lachmann has been a relentless critic of 'formalism' and, in particular, of the 'neo-classical paradigm'. According to Lachmann: 'The vice of formalism is precisely this, that various phenomena which have no substance in common are pressed into the same conceptual form and then treated as identical' (1977 [1971], p. 189). The alternative paradigm offered by Lachmann is that of radical subjectivism. He frequently cites Hayek's claim that 'it is probably no exaggeration to say that every important advance in economic theory during the last hundred years was a further step in the consistent application of subjectivism' (1955, p. 31).

This chapter focuses on Lachmann's conception of the 'market process'. His image of the market is that of 'a continuous process without beginning or end, propelled by the interaction between the forces of equilibrium and the forces of change' (1976(a), p. 61). Lachmann's distinctive contribution has been to emphasise the importance of knowledge: 'The market process is the outward manifestation of an unending stream of knowledge' (1976(b), p. 127). He has consistently argued that the outcome of the market process is necessarily indeterminate. More recently, he has argued that economists must even revise their conception of the market process as at least potentially terminating in a state of long-run general equilibrium.

Lachmann is always generous in acknowledging his intellectual debts, in particular, the inspiration which he has derived from Menger, Weber, Mises, Hayek and Shackle. He is also modest about his own contributions. Thus, when in 'From Mises to Shackle: An Essay on Austrian Economics and the Kaleidic Society' he credits Shackle with 'more or less single-handedly' extending the scope of subjectivism to encompass expectations, he mentions only in a footnote his own 1943 article 'The Role of Expectations in Economics as a Social Science' and does not mention at all his own *Capital and its Structure*, first published in 1956.

Lachmann should not be regarded as being representative of the modern Austrian school. Some members of the school, at least, would seem to regard him as an extreme exponent of Austrianism. Lachmann *is* extreme. He has consistently argued that, whereas economists can formulate systematic generalisations which can enhance our understanding of the past and the present, they *cannot* predict the future. It is instructive to examine the reasons which have led him to adopt this position. Surely most serious economists must, at some time, have reflected on the sorts of issues which are always at the forefront in the writings of Lachmann and Shackle. If this and the previous chapter provoke some economists to reflect more deeply – or for the first time – on these difficulties, they will have served their purpose.

Lachmann and Shackle

Like Shackle, Lachmann is a subjectivist *par excellence*. Both emphasise not the 'doings' of individuals but their *thoughts*. Thus Shackle conceives of the individual as choosing between imagined alternatives, the purpose of decision being to achieve a good current state of mind. When Lachmann asserts that the role of the economic scientist is to explain economic phenomena in terms of individual acts, he means *acts of the mind*. Both stress purposefulness. For Shackle, decision involves a mental commitment on the part of the individual. According to Lachmann, rational conduct – as opposed to 'mere behaviour' – requires that an individual try to 'chart the path leading to the achievement of his purpose in the topography of his mind' (1977 [1943], p. 69). Furthermore, both emphatically reject any idea of a mechanical relationship between past events and expectations of the future – the past, though irrevocable, has to be *interpreted* and the future, being unknowable, can only be *imagined*.

Lachmann, like Shackle, believes that the infinitely divisible, uniformly flowing and purely quantitative time of classical mechanics is inappropriate for the study of human action. However, when reflecting on Shackle's *Time in Economics*, Lachmann was clearly troubled by Shackle's conception of the moment-in-being as solitary and self-contained and, in particular, by his insistence that it is impossible to compare different moments in time: 'But if we were to take Professor Shackle's thesis literally, there could be no testing the success of plans, no plan revision, no comparison between *ex ante* and *ex post*. In fact planned action would make no sense whatever' (1977 [1959], p. 84). As we saw in the last chapter, Lachmann suggested that, 'on occasion', Shackle comes 'perilously close' to denying the continuity of mind. Lachmann claimed:

It seems to us that while his thesis applies to human ends, of which we are unable to postulate any continuous existence in time, it does not apply to our knowledge of the adequacy of means to ends .... We can, and occasionally do, learn from experience. Whatever may be discontinuous in us, the human mind is continuous. The acts of the mind of which our conscious life consists, follow each other ceaselessly. Bergson and Husserl have shown that the content of our consciousness is best regarded as a continuous stream of thought and experience (1977 [1959], p. 84).

Both Shackle's moment-in-being and Lachmann's continuous stream of thought have an affinity with Bergson's conception of time. Shackle's moment-in-being is certainly reminiscent of Bergson's notion of 'the real concrete live present'. According to Bergson:

The essence of time is that it goes by; and we call the present the instant at which it goes by. The real, concrete live present necessarily occupies a duration. The duration lived by our consciousness is a duration with its own determined rhythms, a duration very different from the time of the physicist, which can store up, in a given interval, as great a number of phenomena as we please .... In our duration – the duration which our consciousness perceives – a given interval can only contain a limited number of phenomena of which we are aware (1911, p. 176).

For Bergson, the time of classical mechanics is not 'real time' but merely a mental diagram. The notion of an empty and homogeneous frame, filled *après coup* by concrete events, is an illusion, albeit one which is necessary for daily life. When Bergson insists that real time is 'radically continuous', he does *not* have in mind mathematical continuity. The essence of real time is that it passes; real time is flux; 'continuity' and 'becoming' are indissolubly joined. Bergsonian *durée* and Heraclitean flux are aspects of what Jaques calls the time of intention. What Lachmann's observations on *Time in Economics* indicated is that, notwithstanding the similarities between the approaches of Shackle and Lachmann, there are subtle differences between their *emphases*. Whereas Shackle stresses the *breaks* between the past and the future, Lachmann emphasises the *continuity* between the past and the future. Whereas Shackle focuses on the solitary and self-contained moment-in-time, Lachmann highlights the passage of time *per se*.

Individual actions and plans

For Lachmann, purposefulness is exemplified in plans: 'Action is thought .... Action is guided by plans .... In each plan means and ends are riveted by choice' (1976(a), p. 57). All economic phenomena are intelligible only as the result of planned action:

If we say that we wish to 'explain' an action, what we mean is not merely that we wish to know its purpose, but also that we wish to see the plan behind the action. Plan, a product of the mind, *is* both the common denominator of all human action and its mental pattern, and it is by reducing 'action' to 'plan' that we 'understand' the actions of individuals. Plan is the *tertium comparationis* between our mind and the mind of the person who acts (1977 [1943], p. 69).

In formulating a plan, an individual draws on his 'knowledge'. An individual's knowledge – being 'a compound of thoughts an individual is able to call upon in preparing and planning action at a given point in time' (1986, p. 49) – is derived from his *interpretations* of his own previous experiences and from sifting through other information for 'particles' which might be useful to him.[1] Using his knowledge, an individual must *diagnose* the situation in which he must act:

How is this done? We analyse the situation, as we see it, in terms of *forces* to which we attribute various degrees of strength. We disregard what we believe to be *minor forces* and state our expectations in terms of the result we expect the operation of the *major forces* to have. Which forces we regard as major or minor is of course a matter of judgement. Here the subjective element of interpretation is seen at work. In general, we shall be inclined to treat forces working at random as minor forces, since we know nothing about their origin and direction, and are therefore anyhow unable to predict the result of their operation. We treat as major forces those about whose origin and direction we think we know something. This means that in assessing the significance of price changes observed in the past for future changes we shall tend to neglect those we believe to have been due to random causes, and confine our attention to those we believe due to more 'permanent' causes (1978 [1956], pp. 23–4).

For Lachmann, the *subjective* element in interpretation and diagnosis is crucial, since it implies that the formation of expectations is *not* one of 'mere lagged response':

Expectations, it is true, are largely a response to events experienced in the past, but the *modus operandi* of the response is not the same in all cases even of the same experience. This experience before being transformed into expectations, has, so to speak, to pass through a 'filter' in the human mind, and the undefinable character of the process makes the outcome of it unpredictable (1977 [1943], p. 67).

Lachmann thus shares Shackle's conviction that 'predicted man is less than human', his reference to a 'filter' in the human mind being consistent with Shackle's *ex nihilo* element in decision. Nevertheless, as we have suggested, there are differences in their emphases. Thus Lachmann stresses the *continuity* of the process whereby, with the passage of time, an individual revises his expectations of the future in the light of changes in his knowledge:

Each expectation does not stand by itself but is the cumulative result of a series of former expectations which have been revised in the light of later experience, and these past revisions are the source of whatever present knowledge we have. On the other hand, our present expectation, to be revised later on as experience accrues, is not only the basis of the action plan but also a source of more perfect future knowledge. The formation of expectations is thus a continuous process, an element of the larger process of the transmission of knowledge (1978 [1956], p. 23).

A further contrast with Shackle is that Lachmann emphasises individual rationality: 'If the aim of our inquiry is to enable us to understand why men act in the way they do, we shall of course have to assume that their action, by and large, though not necessarily in each individual case, conforms to a universal, and thus recognizable pattern, that is, that of rational action' (1986, p. 115). Needless to say, for Lachmann, 'rational action' does not connote action which is demonstrably superior in some 'objective' sense. Nor, he insists, is he using the term in the 'textbook' sense of maximisation of some function. Instead, he is using the term in the 'traditional' sense of 'bringing reason and experience interpreted by reason to bear on one's circumstances' (1986, p. 115).

Lachmann further insists that the notion of *individual* equilibrium is indispensable: 'It is simply tantamount to *rational action*' (1976(b), p. 131). In arguing that individual equilibrium has 'a clear meaning and real significance', he has asserted: 'Men really aim at bringing their various actions into consistency. Here a tendency toward equilibrium is not only a necessary concept of praxeology, but also a fact of experience. It is part of the logic inherent in human action' (1977 [1971], p. 189). This claim that individuals *aim* at bringing their various actions into consistency connotes Hayek's conception of individual equilibrium, one which *explicitly* involves the passage of time. Thus, in also arguing that the concept of equilibrium has a clear meaning when applied to the actions of a single individual, Hayek claimed that 'since equilibrium is a relationship between actions, and since the actions of one person must necessarily take place successively in time, it is obvious that the passage of time is essential to give the concept of equilibrium any meaning' (1937, p. 36). This, it should be noted, involves what Jaques called the time of succession; it entails 'ideas of before and after, earlier and later', a conceptualisation of time which an individual must have when planning for the future.

For Lachmann, as for Hayek, an individual's plan at any point in time embodies the individual's desire to ensure that the actions which he intends to undertake at different times during some future period are consistent with each other (and possibly with actions which he has already undertaken). Whereas, at the time a plan is formulated, it will be *perceived* to be internally consistent by the individual, at least if he has brought reason to bear on his circumstances, the plan may need to be revised with the passage of time as internal inconsistencies become apparent to the individual, as unexpected obstacles arise and as new opportunities emerge – in short, as the individual's knowledge changes.[2] Being a ever-changing compound of *thoughts*, knowledge is an elusive concept. Since interpretation, diagnosis and expectations formation are, by their very nature, subjective acts of the mind, it follows inexorably that, in general, individuals learn different lessons from the same experiences, that they perceive and diagnose the same 'situation' differently and that their expectations diverge.

The market as a process

The inspiration for Lachmann's conception of the market process comes from Mises. In *Human Action*, Mises asserted:

The market is not a place, a thing, or a collective entity. The market is a process, actuated by the interplay of the actions of the various individuals cooperating under the division of labour. The forces determining the – continually changing – state of the market are the value judgements of these individuals and their actions as directed by these value judgements .... The market process is entirely a resultant of human actions. Every market phenomenon can be traced back to definite choices of the members of the market society .... The market is the focal point to which the activities of the individuals converge. It is the centre from which the activities of the individuals radiate (1949, pp. 258–9).

For Lachmann, a fundamental question for any society involving the division of labour is how individuals, who rely on using the resources of others and on satisfying the wants of others, acquire the requisite knowledge. This knowledge is generated and transmitted by a continuous process of interaction between individuals. Since, for Lachmann, it is the *thoughts* of individuals, as embodied in their plans, which are paramount, the market process involves interaction between the *minds* of individuals. *This is the larger continuous process of which the individual continuous processes of interpretation, diagnosis and expectations formation are but elements.*

Is it possible to determine the outcomes of market processes? Indeed, what is meant by an 'outcome' of a market process? The natural interpretation would seem to be a 'state of rest' – or 'equilibrium' – for the process. Many years ago, Lachmann himself explained, in the simplest possible terms, the rationale for employing an equilibrium method: 'The common sense case for the equilibrium method is that if we wish to survey a constellation of diverse forces, the easiest method of doing so is to perform the mental experiment of imagining that state of affairs which would be reached when all these forces have unfolded all their implications' (1978 [1956], p. 138). But what would be a state of rest for the sort of process which Lachmann envisages? Consider one of Lachmann's more specific statements on the nature of equilibrium:

The market process is kept in permanent motion, and equilibrating forces are being checked, by the occurrence of unexpected change and the inconsistency of human plans. Both are necessary, but neither is a sufficient condition. Without the recurrence of the first, i.e. in a stationary world, it is indeed likely that plans would gradually become consistent as men come to learn more and more about their environment including one another's plans. Without the inconsistency of plans prompted by divergent expectations, on the other hand, it is at least possible that all individuals would respond to exogenous changes in such a manner that general equilibrium can really be established (1977 [1971], p. 190).

This statement is not entirely transparent, partly perhaps because it involves conditions for *not* being in, or *not* achieving, a state of rest. In particular, at one point, Lachmann seems to suppose that non-recurrence of unexpected change is synonymous with a 'stationary world'. This would appear to rule out, as a logical possibility, *expected* changes in the environment. Ruling this out cannot be justified by invoking Lachmann's claim elsewhere that the future is unknowable, since it is logically *conceivable* that individuals' (common) expectations of future changes in the environment might be correct. Perhaps Lachmann is implicitly invoking the argument of Hayek that 'change' can only be defined in relation to individuals' expectations, so that 'expected change' would be a contradiction in terms. According to Hayek:

In fact it seems hardly possible to attach any definite meaning to the much used concept of a change in the (objective) data unless we distinguish between external developments in conformity with, and those different from, general expectations, and define as a 'change' any divergence of the actual from the expected development, irrespective of whether it means a 'change' in some absolute sense. Surely if the alternations of the seasons suddenly ceased and the weather remained constant from a certain day onward, this would represent a change of data in our sense, that is a change relative to expectations, although in an absolute sense it would not represent a change but rather an absence of change (1937, p. 40).

But, if he does have in mind Hayek's argument, it is not clear what is meant by Lachmann's claim that, if plans were consistent, it is conceivable that general equilibrium could be established even with exogenous changes, since this could be interpreted as implying that there *can* be changes in the environment which are expected.

For a clearer idea of what would constitute an equilibrium, it is worth again looking to Hayek. Referring to 'plans determined upon simultaneously but independently by a number of persons', Hayek states:

In the first instance, in order that all these plans can be carried out, it is necessary for them to be based on the expectation of the same set of external events, since, if different people were to base their plans on conflicting expectations, no set of external events could make the execution of all these plans possible. And, secondly, in a society based on exchange their plans will to a considerable extent refer to actions which require corresponding actions on the part of other individuals. This means that the plans of different individuals must in a special sense be compatible if it is to be even conceivable that they will be able to carry all of them out. Or, to put the same thing in different words, since some of the 'data' on which any one person will base his plans will be the expectation that other people will act in a particular way, it is essential for the compatibility of the different plans that the plans of the one contain exactly those actions which form the data for the plans of the other (1937, pp. 37–8).

Thus, for a market process to be in a state of rest, the plans of individuals must be compatible with one another *and* with what will happen to the 'environment'.

Lachmann has consistently insisted that it *is* not possible to determine the 'outcomes' of market processes. As we have seen, he asserts that the process of expectations formation for a single individual – for a single mind – is inherently indeterminate. It is scarcely surprising then that, as an exponent of methodological individualism, he insists that market processes cannot have determinate outcomes: *if the thoughts of individuals are unpredictable, the outcomes of processes of interaction between those thoughts will likewise be unpredictable.* He argues:

No market process has a determinate outcome .... The outcomes of market processes depend on what happens at their various stages and on the order in which events happen. This means in particular that antecedents will influence subsequent events *in so far as acting men attribute significance to them* and that therefore the order in which events happen matters .... At any moment the actor's mind takes its orientation from (but does not permit its acts to be dictated by) surrounding facts as seen from its own perspective, and in the light of this assessment decides on action, making and carrying out plans marked by the distinction between means and ends. This perspective applies to the future as imagined, as well as to the past as known. Interaction as reflected in market events is always interaction between individual plans. Each stage of the market process reflects a mode of interaction (1986, pp. 4–5).

For Lachmann, a fundamental obstacle to determining the outcome of a market process – and, more generally, to providing a *formal* portrayal of such a process – lies in the very nature of knowledge:

The pattern of knowledge is continuously changing in society, a process hard to describe. Knowledge defies all attempts to treat it as a 'datum' or an object identifiable in time and space .... Now knowledge, whether costly or free, may prove valuable to one and useless to another, owing to the complementarity of new and old knowledge and the diversity of human interests. Hence it is impossible to gauge the range of application of some bit of knowledge until it is obsolete. But we can never be certain that knowledge is obsolete since the future is unknown. All useful knowledge probably tends to be diffused, but in being applied for various purposes it may also change character, hence the difficulty of *identifying* it.

Knowledge then is an elusive concept wholly refractory to neoclassical methods. It cannot be quantified, has no location in space, and defies insertion into any complex of functional relationships. Though it varies in time, it is no variable, either dependent or independent. *As soon as we permit time to elapse, we must permit knowledge to change, and knowledge cannot be regarded as a function of anything else* (1976(b), pp. 127–8).

In *The Market as an Economic Process*, Lachmann has again emphasised that time and knowledge are inextricably linked: 'Time cannot elapse without the state of knowledge changing. The successive stages of market processes do not reflect the effect of a sequence of events on successive individual actions, but that of a sequence of interpretations of past and future upon them. Successive stages of market processes thus reflect nothing so much as successive modes of re-orientation as the mind of the actor fits means to ends in ever new forms prompted by new forms of knowledge and imagination' (1986, pp. 4–5).

Restless markets

Lachmann is prepared to concede that a market process in an individual market – an *'intra-market* process' – may *actually* converge on an equilibrium position. However, he cautions:

We have to bear in mind, though, that this is a short-period, partial, stock-and-flow equilibrium. While in this position the market clears, it does not denote a 'state of rest'. That it is partial means that the market is temporarily isolated against influences emanating from other markets. That demand for stock and supply from stock play a part means that our period, whatever length we give it, is not really what Sir John Hicks calls an 'isolated period' and the 'static method', Marshall's method, is, strictly speaking, not applicable, since the holding of stocks must be prompted by expectations of future events. As these expectations and the desired stock magnitudes governed by them necessarily change over time, so does our equilibrium position. The market process, having led to one equilibrium position, will sooner or later have to start again. Here as elsewhere, the notion of time is a major source of our difficulties (1986, pp. 7–8).

The volatility of a market will depend on the proximity of traders, on whether or not there are intermediaries but, above all, on the *nature* of the commodities traded:

In general, the more durable the goods traded in a market, the more important are expectations for it. In capital goods markets and those for durable consumer goods they matter more than in those for simple consumer goods. In a modern market economy, in which there are markets for permanent assets, such as shares in capital combinations which outlast the individual capital goods forming part of them, expectations matter more in these markets than in those for single capital goods, first or second-hand. Here expectations matter not only because such capital combinations are regarded as sources of income streams extending into an infinite future, but also for another reason often not fully appreciated: while flows of consumer goods end at the consumption stage and stocks of them usually bear some relation to the rate of flow, all permanent assets that have ever been created are, in principle, at least potentially 'in the market' (1986, p. 18).

Lachmann's contrast between, at one extreme, the markets for 'simple' consumer goods – he cites cauliflowers and potatoes – and, at the other extreme, the Stock Exchange highlights both his own short-term perspective and his preoccupation with speculation, hedging and arbitraging rather than with production. It is noteworthy that, when suggesting that there is little scope for expectational ingenuity in the market for potatoes, he does not acknowledge the uncertainty facing farmers when they plan what future quantities to produce. Nevertheless, there is surely some basis for Lachmann's claim that 'neoclassical orthodoxy has, to this day, failed to grasp the consequences of the volatility of asset markets' (1986, p. 42). Lachmann stresses what Walras acknowledged but could not accommodate in his general equilibrium model, namely, that transactions on the Stock Exchange reflect *differences* in expectations. Lachmann insists that 'however minute the proportion of total assets traded each day, the price changes resulting are of far reaching importance in a market economy. They affect all asset holders and their creditors by bestowing capital gains and inflicting capital losses. In such a society the mode of distribution of wealth is changing by the hour – hardly a "datum"' (1986, p. 18).

Never-ending processes

Lachmann does have a short-term perspective. He has argued: 'It is possible to take the classical view that all economic theory has to say necessarily refers to the long run. Or we might agree with Keynes when he says that in the long run we are all dead. It is hard to see how one can hold both opinions at the same time' (1986 [1984], p. 164). Lachmann believes that economists cannot legitimately say anything about the 'long run'. He is not prepared to concede that an *individual* market might actually achieve a long run equilibrium – it could not be insulated, for a sufficient length of time, from the effects of *inter-market* processes.

What about the economic system as a whole? Lachmann has often been scathing of general equilibrium theorists and of Walras in particular, sometimes seeming to hold him personally responsible for the Arrow-Debreu economy! And yet, whereas Lachmann clearly could never share Walras' enthusiasm for formal analysis, much of Lachmann's description of the market process is consonant with Lesson 35 of the *Elements*. Recall how Walras insisted that, in reality, because the processes of adjustment operate slowly, the continuous market is forever chasing, *but never reaching*, a moving target. In similar vein, Lachmann has argued:

In a kaleidic society the equilibrating forces, operating slowly, especially where much of the capital equipment is durable and specific, are always overtaken by unexpected change before they have done their work, and the results of their operation disrupted before they can bear fruit. Restless asset markets, redistributing wealth every day by engendering capital gains and losses, are just one instance, though in a market economy an important one, of the forces of change thwarting the equilibrating forces. Equilibrium of the economic system as a whole will never be reached. Marshallian markets for individual goods may for a time find their respective equilibria. The economic system never does (1976(a), p. 60).

The similarity between Walras' continuous market and Lachmann's market process is more than superficial – and yet it is not complete. For Walras, the obstacle to the attainment of equilibrium is not simply the recurrence of 'autonomous' changes in the data; the 'endogenous' changes resulting from the accumulation of capital goods could preclude the economy reaching equilibrium. It is perhaps tempting to characterise Lachmann as also arguing that the attainment of equilibrium is frustrated not simply by the recurrence of 'autonomous' changes but also by 'endogenous' changes, such as redistributions in wealth.

But Lachmann would object to such a characterisation. He argues that, for his process, the distinction between external forces and the internal market mechanism is 'essentially misleading'. Moreover, he denies that the process must at least be 'pointing' in the 'direction' of equilibrium:

In the first place, though a process may have a direction at each point in time, it may change direction over time. The direction the process follows need not be the same throughout. Second, and more important, two kinds of process have to be distinguished here. The first is a limited process, in the course of which we witness the successive modes of interaction of a set of given forces, given initially and limited in number. Such a process may terminate or go on forever; whatever happens depends entirely on the nature of the (given) set of forces. The system may be subjected to random shocks from external sources, which it may take some time to absorb, such absorption interfering with the interaction of the forces. The second variety of the process is the very opposite of the first. No initial set of forces delimits the boundaries of events. Any force from anywhere may at any time affect our process, and forces that impinged on it yesterday may suddenly vanish from the scene. There is no end or final point of rest in sight. Need I assert that history is a process of the second, not of the first, variety? (1976(b), pp. 130-1).

In insisting that the market process is inherently never-ending, Lachmann has explicitly distanced himself from both Hayek and Mises:

Professor Hayek and Mises both espouse the market process, but do not ignore equilibrium as its final stage. The former, whose early work was clearly under the influence of the general equilibrium model, at one time appeared to regard a strong tendency towards general equilibrium as a real phenomenon of the market economy. Mises, calling the Austrians 'logical' and neoclassicals 'mathematical' economists, wrote: 'Both the logical and mathematical economists, assert that human action ultimately aims at the establishment of such a state of equilibrium and would reach it if all further changes in data were to cease.'

It is this view of the market process as at least potentially terminating in a state of long-run general equilibrium that now appears to require revision (1976(a), p. 60).

What does Lachmann's most recent conception of the market process amount to? He is clearly denying, as he has done for many years, that economists can determine what the 'outcome' of a market process will be. It also seems that he has repudiated the view, expressed in 1971, that in a 'stationary world' it is 'indeed likely' that the plans of individuals would come to be consistent with each other. He is not simply claiming that, given a network of inter-related markets, one cannot be sure that equilibrating forces will prevail; he is now insisting that they will *never* prevail: 'What emerges from our reflections is an image of the market as a particular kind of process, a continuous process without beginning or end, propelled by the interaction between the forces of equilibrium and the forces of change' (1976(b), p. 61). Obvious though it may be, it must be stressed that this vision of the market process relies on a notion of equilibrium: equilibrating and disequilibrating forces can *only* be defined in relation to the characteristics of an equilibrium state. Thus those economists who claim that economic analysis should involve processes with no reference whatsoever to any notion of equilibrium *cannot* invoke Lachmann's market process.

In *The Market as an Economic Process*, Lachmann could be construed as looking for some 'logical' justification for his contention that market processes are inherently never-ending. Thus, in arguing that price changes which are equilibrating in one market *necessarily* have disequilibrating implications for other markets, he claims: 'The root of our difficulty lies in this: in a market ... all co-ordinating activity must engender some disco-ordination of existing relations' (1986, p. 11). This argument is reminiscent of the claim that the hare will never catch the tortoise – precisely the sort of paradox which Bergson sought to refute. *If* Lachmann is looking for some *logical* justification for his conception of the market process as never-ending, he is surely engaged in an inherently mis-conceived endeavour.

Explanation and prediction

Lachmann's philosophy is well captured in the words of Sören Kierkegaard: 'We live forwards but we can only understand backwards'. Thus Lachmann has insisted: 'Economists should, in our view, openly admit that they are unable to make positive predictions about the world' (1977 [1959], p. 89). This conviction, which follows inexorably from his belief that the outcomes of market processes are inherently indeterminate, has posed a dilemma for some of his Austrian colleagues. This dilemma has been highlighted, with creditable candour, by Kirzner in 'On the Method of Austrian Economics'. He cites Lachmann: 'Economics has two tasks. The first is to make the world intelligible in terms of human action and the pursuit of plans. The second is to trace the unintended consequences of such action' (1977 [1973], p. 261). Kirzner also identifies two basic Austrian tenets: 'First, there is the insight that *human action is purposeful*, and, second, there is the insight that *there is an indeterminacy and unpredictability inherent in human preferences, human expectations and human knowledge*' (1976, p. 42). As Kirzner acknowledges, the dilemma is that the second tenet is inconsistent with the requirement that economic explanations trace the unintended consequences of human action: 'It seems therefore that the future progress of the Austrian school in applying its basic methodological tenets requires some decision about the extent to which the second tenet about the inconstancy of human purposes and knowledge can be upheld as a general proposition' (1976, p. 50). Whatever his Austrian colleagues may decide, Lachmann, we may be sure, will never relinquish his conviction that there is an indeterminacy inherent in human action and in human interaction. In *The Market as an Economic Process*, he states:

It is true that to trace the undesigned consequences of economic action has for a long time been regarded as one of the tasks of economic theory, if not its only task. But it has also been recognized for what is by now a fairly long time that, strictly speaking, this can be achieved only under fairly stringent *ceteris paribus* conditions, where expectations figure prominently among the *cetera* that have to remain *paria* for the duration of our enquiry. It is hard to see how expectations, fed by the continuous stream of the news, can remain constant for any significant stretch of time (1986, p. 115).

This has been a constant theme of Lachmann's writings − time cannot pass without modifying knowledge and this, in turn, means that expectations cannot satisfactorily be treated as data. This is reminiscent of Bergson's claim that memory − without which there can be no consciousness − inexorably 'swells' with the passage of time.

Lachmann, it should be emphasised, does not regard his views as nihilistic. He believes that economists can legitimately make *negative* predictions. Thus if economists observe a government trying to

achieve mutually incompatible objectives, they *can* predict that it will
fail: 'To uncover such inconsistencies and to warn the public that what
the politicians propose to do cannot be done, is, in all countries,
perhaps the most important public duty of economists in our time'
(1977 [1950], p. 171).[3] But, for Lachmann, the *real* role of the
economist is to render the world *intelligible*. Of his conception of the
market process, he argues: 'A model in which individual plans, each
consistent in itself, never have time to become consistent with each
other before new change supervenes has its uses for elucidating some
striking features of our world' (1976(a), p. 61). More generally, he
believes that economists can enhance understanding of the past and
present: 'The main social function of the economist is to provide the
historian and the student of contemporary events with an arsenal of
schemes of interpretation' (1959, p. 89). Lachmann also argues that
the social sciences, whilst inferior to the natural sciences in terms of
the ability to predict and control, are superior to them in one crucial
respect. Thus, the social sciences can provide an intelligible account
of the social world in terms of *human choice*:

We shall never know why a rose smells as it does, but I can see no insurmount-
able objection to our knowing why a perfume, say Chanel No. 5, smells as
it does. In the second case we can ask the creators what they had in mind;
in the first case we cannot. In the social sciences the quest for final causes
is a meaningful enterprise, and in this lies their superiority (1977 [1950],
p. 171).

Some concluding comments

Austrian economists sometimes seem to be so anxious to stress
purposefulness that they convey the impression that individuals, on
the basis of *definite* expectations, decide *precisely* what they intend
to do. Often they refer to the Hayekian notion of the compatibility
of plans without − even in general terms − elucidating the nature
of those plans. 'Plan' sometimes seems to be an almost mystical
concept which apparently needs no further elaboration. They pay far
less attention than Shackle to habits and stereotypical modes of
thought.

Lachmann, of course, is not a typical Austrian. Indeed, he has
criticised his Austrian colleagues for paying insufficient attention to
the subjective nature of expectations. Yet Lachmann does seem
reluctant to explore the diversity of individual plans.

In this respect, the contrast with Lindahl's 1939 essay is marked. Lindahl tells us much more about the diverse nature of plans than does Lachmann. Recall that Lindahl differentiates between plans which determine uniquely the intended actions and those which simply specify the planned actions between limits; he distinguishes between plans according to the degree to which individuals deliberately leave themselves leeway to modify their plans; and he differentiates between those planned actions which are conditioned and those which are unconditioned. Further progress in Austrian economics may well involve systematically exploring, along Lindahlian lines, the diverse types of individual plans.

Although we have not been able to do justice to this in the present chapter, Lachmann's *The Market as an Economic Process* does seek to highlight the diverse types of institutional arrangements in different markets.[4] It is interesting to note that, in discussing the coexistence of fixprice and flexprice markets, he claims that 'all market transactions consist of sequences of acts of offer and acceptance' (1986, p. 131). This is clearly reminiscent of Lindahl's 1939 essay. Lachmann would, of course, repudiate Lindahl's conception of the aim of economic theory and, in particular, he would deny that it is legitimate, for purposes of prediction or control, to construct models designed to explain economic developments as a result of certain given conditions prevailing at the beginning of the period studied. The contrast between Lindahl and Lachmann in this respect, however, should perhaps not be exaggerated. Recall that Lindahl observed in his 1929 essay that 'the development of human nature is regulated not by mechanical but by organic laws, that give rise to new impulses and new acts breaking away from the stationary tendency' (p. 331); and that he asserted in his 1939 essay: 'The study of economics is largely concerned with human actions or the result of human actions. Leaving aside the question whether man can exercise free-will or not, it is of course not possible to determine the causes of his behaviour in the same way as those of the events of the external world' (1939, p. 35).

What is distinctive about the treatment of time by Shackle and Lachmann? In contrast to the other authors we have considered, the distinctive feature is their emphasis on what Jaques called the time of *intention*. Both Shackle and Lachmann focus on purposive behaviour. Both are concerned with the interaction between memory, perception, expectation and desire − and, indeed, with the complexity of that interaction. Nevertheless, it should be noted that − in contrast

to Bergson and in contrast to some critics of mainstream economics
– neither Shackle nor Lachmann insists that he is concerned with
'real time'. Bertrand Russell accused Bergson of failing to realise that,
in explaining his notion of duration and in thereby seeking to justify
his notion of 'real time', he 'is unconsciously assuming the ordinary
mathematical time; without this, his statements are unmeaning' (1946,
p. 834). Moreover, Jaques insists: 'There is no "real" time as against
some other time' (1982, p. 38). He argues that the time of intention
is just one of the dimensions of time and that the notion of time as
points along a string needs to be supplemented – *not* supplanted –
by the continuous flux of Heraclitus. Neither Russell's accusation nor
Jaques' insistence implies criticism of Shackle and Lachmann.

Lachmann's arguments, like those of Shackle, should not be
dismissed out of hand. In stressing the subjective nature of 'knowledge' and, in particular, in emphasising the formidable difficulties
in representing formally the ways in which the knowledge of individuals changes, Lachmann is highlighting an issue which has troubled
many economists. As we will see, mainstream economists have in
recent years been increasingly prepared to acknowledge openly these
difficulties.

Notes

1 In *The Market as an Economic Process*, Lachmann uses the term 'information' in a very specific way to mean 'the tradeable material embodiment
  of a flow of messages' (1986, p. 49).
2 Lachmann has claimed: 'Action controlled by one mind is, as Mises
  showed, necessarily consistent' (1976(b), p. 131). We take this to mean that
  the plan underlying the action is *perceived* by the individual at the time to
  be consistent. It is then consistent with Lachmann's earlier acknowledgement that a plan may fail because it is 'faulty from the beginning because
  of lack of consistency between its various elements' (1943, p. 69).
3 Lachmann does not explain how, if it is truly impossible to predict the
  effects of actions, it can be *known* that objectives are mutually incompatible.
4 Lachmann does seem to have mellowed somewhat towards Walras. In
  particular, in *The Market as an Economic Process*, he refers to the letter
  from Keynes to Hicks which we mentioned in Chapter 3 (1986, pp. 40-1).
  Lachmann will never mellow towards Pareto! He could never accept
  Pareto's claim: 'The individual can disappear, provided that he leaves
  us a photograph of his tastes' (1971, p. 120).

10

Concepts of equilibrium

All I have tried to do has been to find the way back to the common-sense meaning of our analysis, of which, I am afraid, we are apt to lose sight as our analysis becomes more elaborate. You may even feel that most of what I have said has been common-place. But from time to time it is probably necessary to detach oneself from the technicalities of the argument and to ask quite naively what it is all about (Hayek, 1937, p. 54).

Since 1937, economic analyses have become ever more elaborate and ever more technical. It has thus become particularly appropriate, once again, 'to detach oneself from the technicalities of the argument and to ask quite naively what it is all about'. Drawing on the previous chapters, we must focus on the fundamental question of how to analyse economies 'moving through time'. With the possible exception of Debreu, all our authors can be construed as wrestling with this question.

Notwithstanding differences in their analyses, Marshall, Walras, Lindahl, Hicks and Debreu all invoked methods of analysis involving *some* notion of equilibrium. Recall Lachmann's rationale for employing an equilibrium method: 'The common sense case for the equilibrium method is that if we wish to survey a constellation of diverse forces, the easiest method of doing so is to perform the mental experiment of imagining that state of affairs which would be reached when all these forces have unfolded all their implications' (1978, [1956], p. 138). Thus equilibrium is an 'imaginary' state in which the diverse forces under consideration are at rest. Jevons' justification for studying equilibria was more specific, involving a particular analogy:

It is much more easy to determine the point at which a pendulum will come to rest than to calculate the velocity at which it will move when displaced from that point of rest. Just so, it is far more easy to lay down the conditions under which trade is completed and interchange ceases, than to attempt to ascertain at what rate trade will go on when equilibrium is not attained (1970 [1871], p. 138).

Edgeworth offered a similar rationale but expressed more dramatically:

> To illustrate the economical problem of exchange, the maze of many dealers contracting and competing with each other, it is possible to imagine a mechanism of many parts where the law of motion, which particular part moves off with which, is not precisely given – with symbols, arbitrary functions, representing not merely *not numerical knowledge* but *ignorance* – where, though the mode of motion towards equilibrium is indeterminate, the position of equilibrium is mathematically determined (1881, p. 4).

A crucial question is, of course, precisely whether, in analysing an economic system, one *can* determine 'the position of equilibrium' *without* considering 'the mode of motion'. Looking at the matter in another way, is the mechanical analogy of a pendulum appropriate for analysing an economic system? Or is Walras' lake – which is 'agitated by the wind, where the water is incessantly seeking its level without ever reaching it', and which is, 'at times, stirred to its very depths by a storm' – a more appropriate analogy? Or is the most appropriate analogy that of Marshall's stone hanging from a string held by a moving hand and dangling 'in the troubled waters of a mill-race, whose stream was at one time allowed to flow freely, and at another partially cut off'? To pursue these questions, we must first contrast and evaluate some of the equilibrium notions encountered in the earlier chapters. We will then examine the legitimacy of comparative statics. This inevitably raises dynamic issues. We will consider the formidable difficulties in analysing dynamic processes of adjustment in the next chapter.

Stationary states

> Thinkst thou existence doth depend on time
> It doth; but actions are our epochs: mine
> Have made my days and nights imperishable,
> Endless, and all alike, as sands on the shore.   (Byron)

Can the analysis of stationary states be justified? As we have seen, Hicks claimed that the stationary state 'is, in the end, nothing but an evasion' and Shackle described it as 'a pointless declension from the purity of argument of the timeless system'. In contrast, Georgescu-Roegen has argued that criticisms of analyses of stationary states often reflect a narrow perspective: 'From the dawn of man's economic evolution to this day only the present interlude constitutes an exception to the rule that human society has advanced at such a slow speed that the change becomes visible only in the perspective of centuries or even millenia' (1971, p.228). But can the analysis of stationary states be justified if one is interested solely in the 'present interlude'?

The one persuasive argument is that, as Lindahl stressed, imagining the circumstances under which an economy is unchanging over time can give insights into change.[1] However, unless the nature of the analysis − of the 'mental experiment' − is properly understood, the analysis of stationary states is potentially dangerous. In particular, if one enters an economy at some arbitrary point in time, it *cannot*, in general, be supposed that the economy could immediately become stationary. What would be the obstacles to an economy immediately becoming stationary? As Lindahl recognised, for an economy to be stationary implicitly imposes restrictions on its past behaviour. Thus whether an economy could immediately *become* stationary would depend on its past behaviour. Pigou emphasised this in *The Economics of Stationary States*:

At first sight, it might be supposed that, so far as *a priori* considerations go, a stationary state might have *any* structure whatever; that to any actual state a freezing process could − in theory − be applied, in such wise that it would be turned into a stationary state and held so permanently. This is not so. A state cannot be frozen into stationariness unless at the time the freezing takes place it has a definite structure. The reason is that a stationary state must be stationary, not in one respect only, but in all respects; while it is only with certain structures that the several required kinds of stationariness are compatible with one another (1935, p.16)

As Pigou noted, stationarity requires not only a constant total population but also a constant age-distribution, since variations in the age-distribution of the population would, in general, 'entail change both in its power as an instrument of production and in the direction of its choice among different objects of consumption' (1935, p.16). A population will have the requisite age-structure 'provided that, at the time when freezing is attempted, the birth-rate and the death-rate at every age have already remained constant for a period as long as the life of the oldest living person, but not otherwise' (1935, p. 17). Similar considerations apply to capital equipment.[2] Moreover, even if the economy's initial total quantities of each type of resource are compatible with stationarity, the *immobility* of many types of capital equipment could preclude the immediate attainment of stationarity. Thus, if we enter an economy at some arbitrary point in time, it would, in general, take time – indeed, possibly a *very* long time – to achieve population and capital structures compatible with stationarity.

Furthermore, even if there are no 'physical' obstacles to the immediate attainment of stationarity, it *cannot* be supposed that prices compatible with stationarity would be immediately established. In particular, whereas it may be legitimate to perform the mental experiment of visualising a state in which, as a result of a process of *learning*, individuals' expectations that prices will remain the same are correct, it would be a different matter to seek to justify the immediate attainment of stationarity by endowing individuals with perfect foresight *ab initio*. As Pigou observed, 'knowledge percolates slowly, and, having percolated, only slowly overcomes the inertia of habit' (1935, p. 4). It should also be stressed that, whereas it may be relatively straight-forward to stipulate 'physical' requirements for stationarity, knowledge and beliefs raise more delicate issues. Recall that Lindahl argued that stationarity does not logically imply perfect foresight, that is, individuals could continue, wrongly, to expect certain changes. One would, perhaps, not need to be an extreme devotee of rational expectations to believe that, while a logical possibility, it would be unlikely that such a state would persist for ever more. Nevertheless, Lindahl's claim should caution against thinking that one can readily identify conditions which are absolutely necessary for economies to be stationary.

We have insisted that it is not, in general, legitimate to suppose that a stationary state could be established immediately. But there is a further caveat. For reasons which we will consider later, it would not, in general, be legitimate to interpret the analysis as identifying the state which *would* eventually be attained. Properly interpreted, the analysis of stationarity at best involves visualising the *characteristics* of a state which *might* be achieved at some time in the future when all the diverse forces – including the processes whereby knowledge is acquired and disseminated – have 'unfolded all their implications'.

Pigou justified his analysis of stationary states as an introductory stage towards understanding real conditions: 'It provides a taking-off place, but little more; a first stage only, which needs extensive supplement. The building is much more than the foundation. But, none the less, to take pains over the foundation is not to waste time' (1935, p. 264). In his 1929 essay, Lindahl also regarded the understanding of stationarity as a stage in the development of a more realistic theory. However, as we have seen, in his 1939 essay, Lindahl repudiated this view and insisted that there are 'considerable disadvantages' to starting with the analysis of stationary states. The central difficulty is that of making the transition to taking seriously the *time of intention*, that is, to addressing meaningfully the nature of purposeful behaviour in the face of uncertainty. This surely explains Hicks' and Shackle's forthright condemnations of the analysis of stationary economies.

Rhythmical changes

>   Keeping time,
> Keeping the rhythm in their dancing
> As in their living in the living seasons
> The time of the seasons and the constellations
> The time of milking and the time of harvest
> The time of the coupling of man and woman
> And that of beasts. Feet rising and falling.
> Eating and drinking. Dung and death.   (T. S. Eliot)

Are there any circumstances in which one might make sense of the idea of an economy being in a 'full' equilibrium which involves 'change'? We can visualise cases of equilibria which entail regular, rhythmical daily, weekly, monthly, and 'seasonal' changes – changes with concomitant implications for prices. Indeed, as Hayek asserted in 1928, in an article which is often credited with introducing (a year before Lindahl) the notion of intertemporal equilibrium and with drawing the analogy between time and space, we cannot realistically visualise an economy *not* subject to such changes:

From the outset there can be no doubt that, even in a stationary economy, in which the same processes are repeated in the same order, the same goods will not necessarily realize the same prices at every point in time. Rather, under certain conditions, their prices will be different at different points in time, and such price changes *must* recur if the economy is to regularly reproduce itself. The reason is that regular self-reproduction of the economy is not at all synonymous with continuity in the flow of the individual processes within it. In fact, under given external conditions, this will never be so .... Not merely external circumstances such as changes in the time of day and the season of the year, and the particular technical characteristics of many production processes, but also the natural variations in human needs, ensure that even a self-replacing economy cannot present the same picture at every moment in time .... In precisely the same way as, in static theory, the difference in the price of a particular good at different locations due to transport costs and the like must be regarded as the precondition for the existence of an equilibrium, the disparity between the prices of the same goods at different points in time in a self-reproducing economy is a necessary precondition for that self-reproduction to take place (1984 [1928], pp. 72–3).

For Hayek, such intertemporal variations in the prices of technically equivalent goods are only explicable in terms of an equilibrium analysis, that is, an analysis of the conditions under which individuals would have no incentive to alter their modes of behaviour.

It is scarcely possible to deny that the explanation of the different prices realized by a good or service at different times of the day still falls within the sphere of static theory, yet simultaneously it can equally scarcely be doubted that, from an economic viewpoint, the same services which are produced on one occasion during the day and on another occasion at night must be regarded as different goods .... And the resulting gradation of prices is explicable only within the context of equilibrium, in which the decisions made by every economic subject are such that he achieves the ends he seeks.

Basically the same can be said of those gradations of prices which emerge in the course of the change of the seasons. For them, too, it is easy to show that the difference between the prices of technically equivalent goods at different seasons fulfils a definite function, and, whenever a condition of equilibrium does not exist, it is advantageous for the individual participants in the market to continuously change their decisions, and thus call forth changes in the gradation of prices in the direction of equilibrium .... In this context as well, all that has to be shown is that a quite definite gradation of these prices is a necessary precondition for a continuance of the regular repetition of the economic processes currently taking place to just the same extent as it is with simultaneously existing prices (1984 [1928], pp. 85–6).

As we have seen, Hayek subsequently argued that what constitutes a 'change' should be defined in relation to expectations, so that an economy with regular and perfectly predictable seasonal forces should be regarded as 'changeless' (Hayek, 1937). Thus we can invoke a broader conception of 'stationarity', one which would involve the regular repetition of possibly quite complex patterns of quantity and price movements.

The importance of various 'rhythms' was highlighted by Sorokin in *Sociocultural Causality, Space and Time*, published in 1943 but apparently ignored by economists. In contrast to Hayek, Sorokin emphasised the importance of time units which have 'social' rather than 'natural' origins. Sorokin contrasted what he termed 'sociocultural time' with the 'continuous, infinitely divisible, uniformly flowing, purely quantitative time of classical mechanics':

Factually, our living time does not flow evenly, is discontinuous, and is cut into various qualitative links of different value. The first form of this qualitative division is given by our *week*. Mathematical or cosmic time flows evenly, and no weeks are given in it. Our time is broken into weeks and week links. We live by the week; we are paid and hired by the week; we compute time by weeks; many fairs and markets take place once in a week; we walk and exercise or rest so many times a week. In brief, our life has a weekly rhythm. More than that: within a week, the days have a different physiognomy, structure, and tempo of activities. Sunday especially stands alone, being quite different from the weekdays as regards activities, occupations, sleep, recreation, meals, social enjoyments, dress, reading, even radio programs and newspapers .... A week of any kind is a purely sociocultural creation, reflecting the rhythm of sociocultural life but not the revolution of the moon, sun, or other natural phenomena. Most human societies have some kind of week, and their very difference between weeks is evidence of their independence from astronomical phenomena. There are 'weeks' consisting of three, four, five, six, seven, eight, nine, sixteen, and more days .... The constant feature of virtually all these weeks of varying lengths is that they were always found to have been originally associated with the market .... Like other weeks, our week is not a natural time period but a reflection of the social rhythm of our life. It functions in hundreds of forms as an indivisible unit of time, with its Sunday and weekdays. Imagine for a moment that the week suddenly disappeared. What a havoc would be created in our time organization, in our behaviour, in the co-ordination and synchronization of collective activities and social life, and especially in our time apprehension (1943, pp. 190–3).

A further qualitative time unit is the month: 'Months do not exist in evenly flowing cosmic or purely quantitative time, especially such curious months as ours .... Like the week, a month is an indivisible unit of sociocultural time. We live by months and have hundreds of monthly rhythms in our social processes. We use them as the point of reference in our time orientation and time apprehension' (1943, pp. 193–4). Yet another time unit is the year: 'The rhythm of social life is cut in yearly links. There are annual sociocultural rhythms. The point is, not that the mathematical length of these rhythms is equal to so many mathematical seconds or hours, but that the rhythms of annual duration are one unbreakable unity corresponding to the annual rhythm of social life' (1943, pp. 194–5). Even 'seasons' are sociocultural notions which do not simply reflect natural forces.

The contrast between sociocultural time and the time of classical mechanics is of crucial significance:

in our modern society, side by side with quantitative time (which itself is in a degree a social convention), there exists a full-blooded sociocultural time as a convention, with all its 'earmarks': it is qualitative; it is not infinitely divisible; its units are different from purely quantitative units; it does not flow on evenly as a mere quantity; it is determined by social conditions, and reflects the rhythms and pulsations of the social life of a given group .... If we try to replace sociocultural time by a purely quantitative time, time becomes devitalized. *It loses its reality, and we find ourselves in an exceedingly difficult position in our efforts to orient ourselves in the time process, to find out 'where we are' and where are the other social phenomena on 'the bridge of time' ....* The knowledge of the main kinds of sociocultural rhythms – no matter whether periodical or not – is by itself a very important knowledge concerning the sociocultural phenomena. Stripped of their specific qualities, all rhythms and punctuations would disappear, and the whole sociocultural life would turn into a kind of gray flowing fog in which nothing would appear distinct. From the standpoint of science, there is a decided disadvantage in replacing a living reality by its dead and imperfect diagram (1943, pp. 197–201).

Sorokin's conception of sociocultural time – in particular, the notion of time units which, while divisible mathematically, are indivisible socioculturally – has implications for the appropriate specification of commodities and the nature of contracts:

We rent a room by the day or week or month or year. Perhaps we do not stay a whole day, but only thirteen hours and twenty-five minutes; yet we pay for a day. The same is true in regard to a week, month and other sociocultural durations agreed upon and unbreakable for the sociocultural purposes involved. We are hired by the hour, by the day, by the week, semester, and so on. If the worker works only fifty-six minutes or sixty-three minutes, he is paid for the one hour agreed upon. The same is true for other sociocultural units; they function as unbreakable, no matter whether the actual duration of the services is a little longer or shorter (1943, p. 201).

It would be misleading to liken the week of *Value and Capital* to Sorokin's week, since Hicks' (elastic) week was an artificial construct, invoked for reasons of analytical tractability. However, Sorokin's notion of sociocultural time could – indeed, should – be assimilated within the general dynamic theory of Lindahl's 1939 essay, with its deliberate emphasis on discontinuities, since individuals and bodies do formulate plans in terms of the sociocultural time units highlighted by Sorokin. In this context, we must challenge an argument of O'Driscoll and Rizzo. They contrasted Bergsonian 'real time' with 'Newtonian time'. Although their main theme was the importance of the former, they claimed: 'The concept of time directly incorporated in plans is Newtonian. The planner can imagine units of time that are isolated, empty, and as small as convenient. These homogeneous units can then be filled with specific activities' (1985, p. 62). In reality, however, planners typically think in terms of indivisible qualitative time units.

But the point at issue here is that, in all societies, there are 'rhythms', albeit highly complex ones, which may be amenable to the sort of equilibrium analysis which could be justified by Lachmann's common-sense argument. The sort of rhythms highlighted by Hayek and Sorokin have been little explored by economic theorists, at least in any systematic way.[3] Naturally our earlier strictures regarding the analysis of stationary states in the narrow sense would apply with equal, if not greater, force to the analysis of economies which are stationary in this broader sense. There should be no suggestion that such states could be established immediately. In particular, to the extent that individuals' expectations are correct, this would be because they have *learned* to predict the implications of the rhythmical changes. Are Hayek's daily and seasonal variations in prices and Sorokin's rhythms explicable *only* in terms of some form of equilibrium analysis? It would be interesting to know what 'mental experiments' those economists who insist that economic analysis must involve 'processes' and never any notion of equilibrium would use to study them.

Walras' equilibrium

> Time present and time past
> Are both perhaps present in time future,
> And time future contained in time past.

> If all time is eternally present
> All time is unredeemable.   (T.S. Eliot)

Walras analysed equilibrium from a *point de vue statique*. He entered his economy at an arbitrary point in time; insisted that the inherited resources might be any quantities whatever; assumed explicitly that the governing conditions would remain constant over a certain ensuing period of time of limited duration; and examined the conditions under which prices would be stationary over that period. His purpose was not to characterise a thorough-going stationary state; he was concerned with a 'progressive' economy. To maintain the fiction of a period over which the economy would be imagined to be stationary, he assumed that capital goods produced during the period would not themselves provide services until some subsequent period.

What obstacles would there be to the 'immediate' attainment of Walras' equilibrium state? Would there be any physical obstacles? The answer to this question depends on how strictly one interprets his formal conditions for equilibrium. We have seen that the inherited stocks of resources – which, we repeat, Walras insisted may be any quantities whatever – may well be incompatible with an equilibrium involving positive outputs of all capital goods proper and thus with a uniform rate of return on the 'supply prices' of all capital goods. If so, one could at most visualise an equilibrium being established immediately which would involve a uniform rate of return on the *ownership* of all capital goods but a uniform rate of return on supply price *only* for those capital goods actually produced over the period in question.

It should be recalled that Walras swept aside other physical obstacles to the attainment of equilibrium. Contrary to his model, the services of the capital goods in existence at any point in time are not, in reality, perfectly and instantaneously mobile between different entrepreneurs in the same and different lines of activity, the services of, say, machines frequently being 'reallocated' between producers as a result of some producers acquiring newly-produced machines and others not replacing machines which wear out. Thus, from a temporal perspective, there is a tension between the zero profit condition for equilibrium – at least as conceived of by Walras – and the assumption that new capital goods play no part in production until subsequent periods.

Walras was, of course, aware that there would be informational obstacles to the immediate attainment of equilibrium. This is precisely why he conceived of the 'fiction' of an hypothetical phase of preliminary *tâtonnement* involving tickets. But the real tension in Walras' analysis is between, on the one hand, the way he entered an economy at a particular point in time and, on the other, his failure to take account of the uncertainty facing individuals. In his theory of capital formation, Walras fudged the issue by supposing that decisions to acquire new capital goods would be based solely on current prices. As we suggested, his theory of capital formation could *at best* be salvaged by explicitly supposing that, in taking decisions, capitalists invoke current rates of net income as a rule of thumb in the face of uncertainty.

Intertemporal equilibrium

> For was, and is, and will be, are but is;
> And all creation is one act at once,
> The birth of light: but we that are not all,
> As parts, can see but parts, now this, now that,
> And live, perforce, from thought to thought, and make
> One act a phantom of succession: thus
> Our weakness somehow shapes the shadow, Time.   (Tennyson)

Whereas Walras sought to characterise equilibrium over a limited period of time, both Lindahl, in his 1929 essay, and Debreu visualised an equilibrium being established immediately which would relate to a time horizon encompassing many periods. Both an equilibrium for Lindahl's dynamic economy with perfect foresight and an equilibrium for the Arrow-Debreu economy would, in modern terminology, be described as 'intertemporal equilibria'. Both can be interpreted as involving 'simultaneous' equilibrium in all the periods encompassed by the analysis, with market demands and supplies in any period depending, in general, on prices in all periods, and with everything effectively being determined at the beginning of the time-horizon of the analysis.

Neither analysis requires the repetition characteristic of stationarity in its narrow or broad senses. Both allow for quantities and relative prices to change over the time horizon of the analysis. Neither requires restrictions on the inherited stocks of capital goods. Rather, the inherited stocks of capital goods restrict what is possible and thereby influence the nature of the equilibrium. Since the analyses do not require that a particular composition of the capital stock be achieved for equilibrium to be established, there are no physical obstacles to an intertemporal equilibrium being established immediately. Rather the obstacle is one of *knowledge*. Lindahl and Debreu sought to circumvent this problem in different ways. To see why neither way provides a satisfactory basis for understanding the behaviour of actual economies over time, we need simply recall briefly salient features of their analyses.

Lindahl's 'dynamic economy with perfect foresight' involved assuming that, at the beginning of the first period, all individuals know and can solve all the conditions determining prices for *all* relevant future periods, so that they can base their actions on the equilibrium prices. We saw that Lindahl, himself, was rightly disturbed by the tension between, on the one hand, assuming that individuals know what prices will turn out to be when they decide on their actions and, on the other, insisting that prices are the result of those actions. Furthermore, we saw that the assumption that individuals 'know' all future prices – heroic though it may be – would not be sufficient to pre-reconcile plans.

In the Arrow-Debreu economy, plans are pre-reconciled by the supposed existence at the present instant of a full complement of futures markets and of contingent commodity markets. According to Dasgupta and Heal: 'Dated commodities are a very intuitive notion' (1979, p. 100). Certainly, differentiating between commodities according to 'date' is a natural procedure: any analysis which distinguishes between different time periods must implicitly or explicitly differentiate between the same physical commodity in different periods. However, what is *not* natural is to assume that there exist 'now' markets for all future commodities – and, at the same time, that such markets did not exist in the past! Still less was Debreu entitled to claim that the assumption that markets exist for all contingent commodities 'is a natural extension of the usual assumption that markets exist for all the certain commodities' (1959, p. 102, n. 2).

Lindahl's economy trivialises the problem of knowledge, and its relation to time, by endowing individuals with perfect foresight *ab initio* (as opposed to treating perfect foresight as a property of equilibrium). The Arrow-Debreu economy trivialises the problem of knowledge, and its relation to time, by postulating the existence of a complete set of markets. If one insists on considering an economy at some arbitrary point in time, one cannot meaningfully think of a 'full' equilibrium being established immediately. Furthermore, it is meaningless to conceive of an economy *ever* getting into a state in which individuals have perfect foresight of the sorts of future changes which both Lindahl and Debreu envisaged. For example, in both Chapter 4 and Chapter 7, we expressed our scepticism about the possible usefulness of assuming that producers know perfectly the 'implications' of future technological changes but not the 'nature' of those changes. It is difficult to see how such an assumption could be described as instructive, whether for positive or normative purposes. The crux of the matter is surely that it is meaningless to attempt to embrace, within the notion of equilibrium, changes which are *inherently* unpredictable. Such misconceived attempts simply bring equilibrium analysis into disrepute.[4]

Temporary equilibrium

> The positive and negative ways through time
> Embrace and encourage each other
> In a brief moment of intersection. (W. H. Auden)

If one enters an economy at some arbitrary point in time − and eschews patently unrealistic views of the situations in which individuals find themselves − one is led, perhaps inevitably, to thinking in terms of a temporary equilibrium, in which equilibrium in the current markets depends on individuals' expectations of future prices. Competitive equilibrium might be defined, before the markets even open, as a set of prices at which the desired transactions of individuals would be compatible with one another (or, to accommodate demand and supply correspondences, as a set of prices *and* individual transactions such that excess demands on all markets would be zero and such that for no agent would there be a set of preferred transactions at those prices given the constraints on his choice). Alternatively, equilibrium might be defined as a state of rest for the trading process. Whether these would amount to the same thing would, as we have seen, depend on the nature of the trading process.

There need be no physical obstacles to a temporary equilibrium being established immediately, since the individual period may be thought of as sufficiently 'short' that the supplies of produced commodities are limited to the 'stocks on hand' as a result of previous production. The real obstacle to the immediate attainment of temporary equilibrium is again one of knowledge, since it cannot reasonably be supposed that the transactors would immediately 'hit upon' an equilibrium set of prices. Hicks, having invoked his 'Monday' precisely to allow the process of trading to take time, did not attempt to analyse that process but, instead, rather undermined the rationale for his Monday by making the questionable assumption of 'an easy passage to temporary equilibrium' (1946 [1939], p. 123).

As we have seen, Hicks assumed that individuals' expectations of future prices could be represented as single-valued, thereby enabling him to invoke 'static' theories of individual behaviour. In principle, of course, analyses of temporary equilibrium could accommodate all sorts of expectations, including cases where expectations depend on current prices and cases where they do not. If the flexibility of the notion of temporary equilibrium is its strength, it is also, in a sense, its weakness: a state which *merely* involves 'supplies equal demands' cannot offer the insights into the *relationships* between prices sought by authors such as Marshall and Walras.

Comparative statics

Now, *here*, you see, it takes all the running you can do, to stay in the same place. If you want to get somewhere else, you must run at least twice as fast (Lewis Carroll).

Few economists, of course, have been content with understanding the conditions under which an economic system, or an individual market, would be in equilibrium. Most economists have sought to make predictions, whether of a qualitative or quantitative nature, typically using the method of 'comparative statics'. What does this method entail? It clearly involves comparing the equilibrium states corresponding to different governing conditions, with the purpose of identifying the impact of the assumed changes in those conditions. But what is the temporal interpretation placed on such analyses? Few economists have been forthcoming on this.

Winston has characterised the method of comparative statics as involving two *separated* time units − 'with indefinite separation for pure comparative statics' (1982, p. 14) − the implicit assumption being that the equilibrium which prevails in the first period would also prevail in the second period were it not for the assumed change in the governing conditions. A simple example of comparative statics which would accord with Winston's characterisation would be where the economy is assumed to be in a stationary state in some initial period; where some change takes place in the governing conditions; and where the analysis seeks to identify the new stationary state which would (might?) be established after some suitable period of transition. However, not all economists have shared Winston's conception of comparative statics as necessarily involving two separate time periods. For example, one might seek to compare the stationary states which, for different governing conditions, an economy would (might?) eventually achieve in the *same* future period, without requiring that the economy already be in a stationary state. In other words, rather than comparing two 'actual' states at different times, one would be comparing two hypothetical states, only one of which could become 'actual' for the time period under consideration. As another example, Hicks conception of comparative statics in *Value and Capital* involved a comparison between alternative hypothetical temporary equilibrium states for the *same* time period, that is, for the current week.

It is scarcely possible to exaggerate the significance for theoretical and applied economics of whether or not the method of comparative statics is legitimate. In his recent book, *Disequilibrium Foundations of Equilibrium Economics*, Franklin Fisher has claimed:

The view that equilibria are the points of interest must logically rest on two underlying properties about the dynamics of what happens out of equilibrium. First, the system must be *stable*; that is, it must converge to some equilibrium. Second, such convergence must take place relatively quickly. If the predictions of comparative statics are to be interesting in a world in which conditions change, convergence to equilibrium must be sufficiently rapid that the system, reacting to a given parameter shift, gets close to the predicted new equilibrium before parameters shift once more (1983, p. 3).

Similarly, Kuenne has noted that 'we are most justified in using a comparative statics approach when we can make just these assumptions: that an equilibrium is stable, the approach to it rapid, the path strongly damped' (1963, p. 462). We must consider whether these requirements are likely to be met.

Consider first an example which would correspond to Winston's characterisation of comparative statics. Consider an economy which is in a thorough-going stationary state. Suppose that, at some particular point in time, there is an autonomous change in the governing conditions, say, a change in technical knowledge. Suppose that we formulate and solve a system of 'static' equations based on the new governing conditions. Assume, for the sake of argument, that there is just one set of endogenous variables which, given the new conditions, would be compatible with stationarity. We know that, in general, such a state could not be established instantaneously. Would it nevertheless be legitimate to interpret the solution as the stationary state which *would* be achieved given sufficient time for the various necessary adjustments to take place?

There are various reasons why it would not necessarily be legitimate to do so. First, before a new equilibrium could be reached, there might be further autonomous changes in the governing conditions. Pigou was emphatic that, *in reality*, since 'the run needed to pass from the stationary state proper to one set of governing conditions to that proper to another set is a very long one' and since the governing conditions 'change frequently and widely', fresh disturbances would inevitably frustrate the attainment of a new stationary state.[5] In a sentence which might well have been quoted *ad nauseam* if Keynes had written it, Pigou asserted: 'Transition rules always; stationariness never; the long-run never comes' (1935, p. 264). Second, even if there were no further autonomous changes in the governing conditions, the economy might never attain full equilibrium, however long was allowed for the processes of adjustment. Pigou also acknowledged this: 'The swings of the economic pendulum are as likely to grow in amplitude as to diminish .... The fact that an equilibrium position is *attainable*, which, if attained, would satisfy all parties, *may* ensure that that position will in fact be attained. On the other hand, there *may* come about a perpetual oscillation backwards and forwards round that position' (1935, p. 14).

Finally, even if a position of equilibrium would eventually be reached, it might well be dependent on the process of transition and thus not be that given by the solution of the 'static' equations. A specific illustration may be helpful. Not only the classical economists but also Marshall, Walras and Pigou emphasised the dependence of population changes on standards of living. For the classical economists, the relationship was encapsulated in the notion of the 'natural wage', that is, the wage at which population would be constant. The natural wage was not, of course, some irreducible biological subsistence but was taken to depend on customs and habits. If we were to formulate and solve a system of static equations, we would have to take *some* natural wage as part of the 'data'. But what level should be chosen? We would presumably take the natural wage prevailing in the initial stationary state. However, the natural wage might well change over time in response to the subsequent behaviour of the economy. More generally, the dilemma is that, whereas formulating a system of static equations requires a sharp distinction between exogenous and endogenous variables, some variables are exogenous at each particular point in time but endogenous from a longer-term perspective and thus potentially dependent on the process of transition itself. Consequently, even if an equilibrium would eventually be reached, it might well be path-dependent. As Lindahl observed in 1929, introducing some change into a stationary economy will give rise to a dynamic process, 'concerning which nothing definite can be said without more specific assumptions as to anticipations and planning' (p. 311).

What credence could be attached to comparative static predictions derived from Walras' static general equilibrium model? Consider first whether Winston's characterisation of comparative statics as involving two *separate* time periods would be meaningful in the case of Walras' model. Thus, supposing that an economy is in equilibrium in some initial period and supposing further that some change takes place in, say, the technological coefficients for producing some commodity, would it be legitimate, even in principle, to substitute the new coefficients into the static equations and interpret the solution as the equilibrium corresponding to some future period? In fact, this would not be meaningful. The reason is that, even if there were no further autonomous changes in the governing conditions, there would be *endogenous* changes over time in the conditions determining equilibrium, since the production of capital goods in the initial period − and, indeed, in each intervening period − would change the economy's stocks of capital goods.

Interpreting the comparative statics exercise as involving a comparison of hypothetical states for the *same* period, that is, for the 'current' period, raises other tensions. As we have seen, Walras' assumption that newly produced capital goods play no part in production until a subsequent period suggests that the period under consideration needs to be thought of as 'short' − and, indeed, if our interpretation of his theory of circulating capital is correct, as '*very* short'. In the limit, we could think in terms of a continuous representation of time and interpret the solution to the static model as a 'momentary' solution implied by the governing conditions at a point in time. However, the shorter the period, the more disconcerting the supposition that the equilibrium conditions would be attained. Indeed, with the continuous time interpretation, there would not be any time for any adjustment processes to take place.

Recall Fisher's requirement for comparative static propositions to be interesting, namely, that 'in a world in which conditions change, convergence to equilibrium must be sufficiently rapid that the system, reacting to a given parameter shift, gets close to the predicted new equilibrium before parameters shift once more'. Certainly, Walras himself would not have claimed that this requirement would be satisfied. As we have seen, he was emphatic that, *in reality*, an economy will forever be chasing, but never reaching, a moving target. He stressed that the processes of adjustment – in particular, the diversion of productive services from unprofitable to profitable enterprises – operate, at best, slowly and that, in the meantime, autonomous and endogenous changes in the conditions determining equilibrium would have occurred. Walras clearly believed that, although equilibrium is never achieved, understanding the conditions for equilibrium is valuable, in particular, for understanding, controlling and preventing those 'sudden and general disturbances' which periodically throw the market into 'violent confusion' (1954, p. 381). Nevertheless, Walras' description of the 'continuous market' – as dynamic a vision as that of any Austrian – surely suggests that he would not have been prepared to attach as much credence to predictions based on comparative static propositions derived from general equilibrium models as many of his successors seem to have done.

What confidence might one have in comparative static propositions derived from Hicks' temporary equilibrium model? Hicks' model provides yet another example of a recurrent theme of this chapter: given that time *is* allowed for all the operative forces 'to unfold all their implications', there is a crucial difference between, on the one hand, the claim that an equilibirum analysis is identifying the state which *would* be established and, on the other, the much more modest claim that the analysis is describing the *characteristics* which an equilibrium would possess, *if* one were to be reached. Again there are various reasons why it might be inappropriate to claim that the solution to a set of equations based on the pertinent data before the markets open constitutes the state which would result from the operation of the process of adjustment. There may be more than one solution consistent with the data. More significantly, the process of interaction between the agents would almost certainly render the initial data obsolete, such interaction typically changing the knowledge and beliefs of individuals. If attaching credence to comparative static propositions is not to be purely a matter of faith, it is necessary to demonstrate not simply that the processes concerned would converge on an equilibrium but also that the resulting equilibrium would not be path-dependent. Justifying comparative statics – whether for stationary states or temporary equilibria – must involve dynamic analysis.

Notes

1 Indeed, Georgescu-Roegen has argued: 'The study of growth must begin with the study of the stationary state and develop up from this basis if it is to be a well-planned scientific enterprise. The view – expressed quite often, albeit sotto voce rather than solemnly – that the concept of the stationary state constitutes only a textbook cumber is therefore inept. Actually, the reverse is true: ordinarily, writers do not pay enough attention to clarifying the concept' (1971, p. 228).

2 The reader may feel that we have said relatively little in the previous chapters about the precise circumstances under which an economy would be stationary. We simply note that, in *The Economics of Stationary States*, Pigou wrote some 300 pages on this matter! A study of that book will quickly disabuse any reader who thinks that examining conditions for stationarity is a trivial undertaking. It is perhaps also worth stressing that – in contrast to, say, Meade's *The Stationary Economy*, which is essentially atemporal – Pigou's analysis does involve time in an essential way. It is also interesting to note that the introduction to Pigou's work contains a spirited defence of subjectivism.

3 The 'time-specific' analysis of Winston (1982) involves an attempt to capture the effects of certain regular, rhythmical changes, such as systematic variations during the day in the demand for electricity.

4 We should perhaps recall that Lindahl regarded his dynamic economy with perfect foresight as but a stage in the development of a more realistic theory.

5 To put matters in some sort of calendar perspective, it might, as Pigou noted, take thirty years for the full effects of a given wage increase on population to be manifested. It might, of course, take a great deal longer for an economy to attain both a wage *and* a population structure actually compatible with stationarity.

11

Some recent developments

In all the traditional philosophies and religions of the world, time is regarded as the enemy and the deceiver, the prison and the torture chamber (Aldous Huxley).

Recent attempts to analyse rigorously the behaviour of economies over time have typically focused *either* on the question of market adjustment *or* on the question of capital accumulation and growth. As we have seen, these are the two aspects in which Hicks' 'process in time' was deficient. We should make it clear from the outset that the main purpose of this chapter is not to survey all the various models which have been advanced but rather to highlight certain fundamental issues which arise in any serious attempt to understand the behaviour of economies over time. As in the last chapter, we are, as far as possible, eschewing technicalities and 'asking quite naively what it is all about'.

It is convenient to consider first the dynamic issues raised by capital accumulation. To provide a focus for our discussion, we will consider in the next section Burmeister's *Capital Theory and Dynamics*, a work which draws on a wide range of recent analyses and which is generally more forthcoming than most as to the limitations of these analyses. In the following section, we will take up the question of market adjustment. Of the works we have considered so far, only the *Elements* attempted to analyse processes whereby market equilibria are achieved. A relevant question is whether subsequent research has led to any real insights into such processes. Again to provide a focus for our discussion, we will examine the 'general model' offered by Franklin Fisher in *Disequilibrium Foundations of Equilibrium Economics*. Finally, we will examine certain selected works of Frank Hahn. His inaugural lecture, 'On the Notion of Equilibrium', is particularly illuminating for our purposes, since its theme is 'to make precise the limits of economic analysis'. It is striking that much recent work has more in common with Lindahl's 1939 essay – and, indeed, with Lachmann's conception of market processes – than it does with the Arrow-Debreu economy.

Equilibrium dynamics

> A bicycle certainly, but not *the* bicycle.
> I am familiar with forty-two impressions left by tyres (Sherlock Holmes).

Although Burmeister acknowledges, in the opening sentence of *Capital Theory and Dynamics*, that in reality uncertainty is pervasive, most of the book ignores uncertainty and focuses on what he calls the 'pure role of time'. He presents a sequence of models, starting with the case where there is just one commodity and culminating in multi-sector models with heterogeneous capital goods and 'money'. He initially considers an Arrow-Debreu economy in which all contracts are signed at the present instant, denoted by $t = 0$. However, he argues that this must be rejected 'if our objective is to better understand the operation of real-world economies, for obviously economic transactions are continually occurring' (p. 228). Accordingly, Burmeister considers models of economies in which, at each point in time or for each elementary period, there is a limited number of competitive markets. He assumes that these markets always clear 'instantaneously'. Burmeister describes this method as 'equilibrium dynamics', where 'the focus of attention is on the time path of an evolving economy always in momentary (static) full-employment equilibrium' (p. 38).

Burmeister sometimes represents time continuously and sometimes discretely; he sometimes assumes infinite time horizons and sometimes finite time horizons. Although we cannot get drawn into considering in detail the respective merits of his different temporal specifications, it is worth recalling that, whether one chooses a finite time horizon or an infinite time horizon, there are grounds for disquiet. Thus, at one point, Burmeister notes that 'it will only take a finite time for our sun to burn out, a fact that vividly illustrates why no one can possibly believe that the model specification will remain appropriate for infinite time' (p. 95). But then, in a note to the same sentence, he claims: 'Since there is no natural time horizon, at least in models without uncertainty, and since there are no economically natural terminal valuations at any finite stopping time, it is logical to avoid these difficulties by postulating an infinite-time horizon' (p. 295, n. 32). He might perhaps have stressed that a compelling reason for his frequent choice of an infinite time horizon is that, in his descriptive models, his main preoccupation is with dynamic stability, which he defines as convergence on a rest point as t tends to infinity![1]

What are the questions which Burmeister asks of his various models? Consider, first, momentary competitive general equilibrium. There are two questions pertinent to *each* point over the time horizon, *including* t = o. First, does there exist a momentary general equilibrium? Second, is such a momentary general equilibrium unique? The question of stability would be meaningless in relation to momentary equilibria, since market clearing prices are assumed to be established 'instantaneously'; there is nothing resembling Hicks' Monday to allow time for market clearing prices to be identified. Suppose that there *does* exist a unique momentary equilibrium at *each* point in time. Given the initial conditions, that is, given the economy's resource endowments at t = 0, the evolution of the system over time would be determined: the model would then be termed 'causal'. For a model to be causal, it is, of course, not sufficient that there be a unique set of market clearing prices at each point in time; there must be a unique set of momentary equilibrium market prices *and quantities* at each point in time.

Consider now whether an economy would achieve a 'dynamic rest point', that is, a steady-state equilibrium involving certain per capita stocks of capital goods which, once attained, would persist over time. There are three questions which can be asked. First, does there exist a dynamic rest point? Second, is such a dynamic rest point unique? Third, what are the stability properties of such dynamic rest points? It should be stressed that Burmeister is not asking, say, 'Is there a unique steady-state equilibrium on which the economy would converge *given the initial conditions*?' but rather, 'Is there a unique steady-state equilibrium on which the economy would converge *whatever the initial conditions?*'.

One of the main themes of Burmeister's book – arguably *the* theme – is to highlight the complications which abound once one leaves the one-commodity economy. Burmeister notes that, even in a model with a single pure consumption good, a single pure capital good and no 'money' (so that the only asset is the capital good), there may be multiple steady-state equilibria. Moreover, the system may be 'non-causal', that is, there may not exist a unique momentary equilibrium at each point in time. Indeed, there may not exist a unique momentary equilibrium at t = 0, so that, given the initial stock of capital, 'the system does not even know where to start' (p. 81). Furthermore, the system may exhibit cyclic motion around an unstable steady-state equilibrium.

The introduction of more than one asset complicates matters considerably – even though Burmeister generally simplifies drastically the associated portfolio-choice problems by assuming that every economic agent has 'perfect myopic foresight', that is, each individual knows not only current prices but also the current rate of change of each price. He demonstrates that, even though the system may be causal *once the initial prices are known*, there will not be a unique set of prices at t = 0 consistent with momentary equilibrium, so that the time path for the system cannot be uniquely determined. Furthermore, given that there are heterogeneous capital goods, the so-called 'Hahn problem' arises: if a steady-state equilibrium exists, it may well be a saddle-point, such that the system converges on the steady-state if *and only if* the initial position is on the stable arm of the saddle-point (or, what is termed, more generally, the convergent manifold of the dynamic system). Since the assumption of perfect myopic foresight is consistent with more than one set of momentary equilibrium prices at t = 0, it *cannot* ensure that the initial position will be on the stable arm. Except by chance, the system will follow an 'errant' time path.[2]

According to Burmeister, the problem of dynamic instability would be 'solved' if there were a complete set of Arrow-Debreu markets at t = 0. The legitimacy of this contention is, however, not as self-evident as Burmeister (and others) make it out to be. It is true that the errant time paths of momentary equilibria would not constitute equilibria in an Arrow-Debreu economy. However, Burmeister's claim is based implicitly on the assumption that an Arrow-Debreu equilibrium would be achieved 'instantaneously'. But it is meaningless to assert that the problem of instability could be 'solved' by postulating a scenario in which no stability questions of any sort could even be asked!

The assumption that individuals have perfect myopic foresight is worth exploring further. Burmeister claims that there is no need to assume perfect foresight into the infinite future, that perfect myopic foresight is sufficient to eliminate uncertainty (though, as we have just seen, it is not sufficient to eliminate dynamic instability). In Chapter 4, we saw that perfect foresight is not sufficient to pre-reconcile plans given constant returns to scale, that is, the ability of individuals to determine equilibrium future prices would not ensure that individuals would (collectively) behave in a way compatible with the subsequent realisation of those prices. Why does this question not arise in Burmeister's model with perfect myopic foresight, given that he assumes that production involves constant returns to scale? The reason is that Burmeister contrives conditions under which firms can maximise profits 'myopically'.[3] This exemplifies another potential danger inherent in a continuous representation of time: drastic assumptions can easily appear to be relatively innocuous. To appreciate this, consider, by contrast, a *discrete* representation of time and suppose that the production of some commodity takes one period. The assumption that individuals have perfect myopic foresight – that they 'know' the rates of change of prices – would presumably mean that the producers of the commodity concerned 'know', in any period, what the price will be in the next period. On grounds of realism, the assumption of perfect myopic foresight is clearly even more disquieting here than with a continuous time formulation. But the point at issue here is one of logical coherence. Supposing, provisionally, that producers of the commodity concerned do 'know' what the price in the next period will be, their behaviour will not be uniquely determined under constant returns to scale; there is no mechanism to ensure that (collectively) they will produce just the 'right' amount. On this basis, one is obliged to ask what it can mean to suppose in the first place that producers 'know' what the price in the next period will be.

This problem would not be eliminated by endowing individuals with 'perfect foresight' into the infinite future. At one point, Burmeister examines 'perfect foresight competitive paths' where individuals are assumed to have perfect foresight into the infinite future. Although he claims that the notion of a perfect foresight competitive equilibrium offers a 'promising theoretical attack' on the problem of dynamic instability, he does doubt that it is an appropriate descriptive assumption (pp. 6–7). But the point at issue here is that he does not confront the question of what perfect foresight into the infinite future could *mean* if there is not a unique dynamic equilibrium time path. How could individuals 'know' what future prices will be if the model admits of more than one dynamic equilibrium path? Knowledge of what Lindahl called the 'conditions determining prices' would not enable individuals to determine future equilibrium prices uniquely. Certainly, it would be arguing in circles to justify 'perfect foresight' by supposing that there is a unique dynamic equilibrium path and then to invoke 'perfect foresight' in a demonstration that there is a unique dynamic equilibrium path. Furthermore, even if there were a unique dynamic equilibrium path and individuals could calculate it, this would not ensure that they would actually behave in a way compatible with its realisation. It would not, of course, be meaningful to suppose that the 'right' prices would be established on the grounds that, since individuals know what the 'right' prices are, they would refuse to transact at 'wrong' prices. The relevant question has to be what would be in the *self-interest* of each individual at any point in time given current prices and given that individual's beliefs about future prices. If self-interest does not determine uniquely the behaviour of each individual at each point in time, there are potential complications in any form of sequence analysis, complications which should be confronted.

What implications can we draw from Burmeister's models? They clearly confirm our doubts about using comparative statics to short-circuit dynamic questions. For example, Burmeister's demonstration that there may be cyclic motion around an unstable equilibrium confirms Pigou's surmise that there may be 'perpetual oscillation' around an equilibrium. More generally, as Burmeister stresses, the comparison of steady-states – what he would call 'comparative dynamics' – can lead one astray if the question of *transition* from one steady-state equilibrium to another is not confronted.

Burmeister asserts, on several occasions, that the 'central difficulty' with multi-sector models is that of 'dynamic stability' or, rather, the lack of it (pp. 7, 98, 213, 261). Burmeister's main reason for being troubled by his inability to demonstrate dynamic stability seems to be that, in his view, it casts doubt on the realism of the models. He does not go so far as to assert that actual economies are dynamically stable but he does claim: 'Actual economies apparently are not featured by this dramatic type of dynamic instability, and thus we are forced to look for "more realistic" descriptive models' (p. 7). Although we do not, of course, doubt the desirability of looking for more realistic models, we must challenge the legitimacy of the inference which he draws from observations of actual economies. As far as we can tell, nothing can be deduced from the models as to *how* 'dramatic' the instability would be. Certainly, since the models do not say anything about speeds of adjustment in calendar terms, one cannot invoke observations on the 'present interlude' to draw inferences about models which relate to an infinite time horizon.[4]

One could draw a different conclusion, namely, that the 'central difficulty' is not dynamic instability *per se* but *indeterminacy*. If, given the initial resource endowments at time $t = 0$, the theorist could generate *the* time path for an economy, it would not matter for economic analysis whether that path would or would not converge on a steady-state. *The theorist could generate the path – and that would be that*! As Frisch argued, the very notion of equilibrium is not strictly necessary in a truly dynamic analysis: in a 'full' dynamic system, the dynamic relations, together with the initial conditions, would determine the complete evolution of the system (1936, pp. 100−1). On this basis, the really fundamental conclusion to be drawn from Burmeister's models would be that – even if one assumes that there are no fixed inputs, no asymmetries in information, no bankruptcies, no research and development activities, no frictions, no stochastic disturbances and so on – *the time path of an economy with heterogeneous assets cannot be determined uniquely*. In other words, one might conclude that there is no way of deriving an economically meaningful 'full' dynamic system.

The difficulty is that this is an area in which any simple conclusion is suspect. Consider further the notion of a model in which the path of the system is determined once the initial prices are given but where the model cannot determine uniquely the initial prices. The appropriate conclusion may be, not that the future behaviour of the economy is *inherently* indeterminate, but that the model is simply incomplete. Although Burmeister does not do so, consider Dasgupta and Heal's suggestion that 'presumably' the initial prices would be 'a consequence of the past history of the economy' (1979, p. 230). An objection to treating the initial prices as part of the initial conditions might be that there is no guarantee that these 'given' prices would be compatible with momentary equilibrium at $t = 0$. But, against this, it could be argued that the choice of $t = 0$ is essentially *arbitrary*, so that it would scarcely be meaningful to suppose that the economy will always be in momentary equilibrium in the future but not to suppose that it has been in momentary equilibrium in the recent past. On this basis, it could be argued that, at t = 0, the economy is already 'locked into' a determinate path and that it is perfectly legitimate to treat prices at t = 0 as part of the initial conditions. To put the point another way, if the 'given' prices at t = 0 were not compatible with momentary equilibrium, this would seriously call into question the assumption that the system will always be in momentary equilibrium in the future.

We must not leave any impression that Burmeister minimises the difficulties of dynamic theory. In his concluding chapter on uncertainty and on rational expectations, he seeks to provide some 'new clues in the search for a realistic and theoretically rigorous economic solution to the general problem of dynamic stability' (p. 282). Yet while Burmeister notes that 'slow' speeds of market adjustment may be stabilising, he stresses that the 'mere introduction of uncertainty does not resolve the saddlepoint instability problem' (pp. 282–3), that agents' choices of time horizon might well be endogenous and that the precise specification of adjustment models can significantly affect the *qualitative* behaviour of dynamic systems. And there is more. 'All of the known "solutions" to the instability problem ... *exclude the possibility of speculative booms rather than provide an economic explanation for them*' (p. 285). No doubt Shackle, Lachmann and many others would share Burmeister's concern that so much rigorous dynamic theorising of market economies excludes the phenomenon of speculation! The analysis in Burmeister's concluding chapter thus does little to soften his earlier remark: 'As our models become more complex, we find that new behaviour can arise; all too often "nearly anything can happen" is the only possible unqualified conclusion' (p. 215).

Market adjustments

> History opposes its grief to our buoyant song;
> The Good Place has not been; our star has warmed to birth
> A race of promise that has never proved its worth.   (W. H. Auden)

We must now explore the complex issue of market adjustment. As we have seen, Walras' 'dynamic' analysis of the process of *tâtonnement* was heuristic rather than rigorous. Has subsequent research resulted in any *real* insights into processes of adjustment? Notwithstanding the application of sophisticated mathematical techniques to this question, the harvest has been disappointing – at least, if one is only interested in 'positive' results. Much of the work has involved Walras' assumption that transactions do not take place at disequilibrium prices, thereby eliminating the complication of path-dependence. Indeed, whereas Walras used the term *tâtonnement* simply to describe the processes whereby markets grope to solutions through trial-and-error, the term is used in the recent literature to *mean* processes for which transactions do not take place at disequilibrium prices. But, even with this fiction, little of substance has been achieved, research on '*tâtonnement*' processes having failed to yield any meaningful necessary conditions for the local or global stability of equilibria or of processes. Moreover, the known sufficient conditions for stability involve extremely implausible restrictions on individual or aggregate demand functions. As Hahn has acknowledged:

> It must now, I fear, be admitted that the study of the Walrasian 'groping' or tâtonnement process has not been very fruitful. It was hoped that, by considering a situation so drastically simplified by the supposition of 'recontract' or no exchange, it would be possible to lay bear the essentials of the law of 'supply and demand' and that once revealed they would be found to be 'good'. What has been achieved is a collection of sufficient conditions, one might almost say anecdotes, and a demonstration by Scarf that not much more could be hoped for (1984 [1970], p. 89).[5]

There have, of course, been attempts to dispense with Walras' assumption that no trades take place at disequilibrium prices. A first stage is to allow transactions at disequilibrium prices but *not* to allow actual production and actual consumption to take place until equilibrium is established. Since no attention is paid to the time taken for adjustment, this preserves the fiction of equilibrium being established (more or less) 'immediately'. In such a scenario, as in the Arrow-Debreu economy, transactions have to be interpreted as involving trades in commitments. As Fisher has observed, the perhaps surprising discovery is that, at least for pure exchange models, the stability results for '*tâtonnement*' models essentially carry over to such 'trading' models. However, as he has also observed, since these stability results are not particularly compelling anyway, this does not take us very far (1983, p. 28). Moreover, the assumption that production and consumption do not take place until equilibrium is established is highly restrictive, since, in reality, households and firms make *irreversible* decisions which constrain their future activities. In particular, as Hahn has acknowledged, if we 'allow for the embodiment of production decisions in some durable concrete objects, the path of the system will at any time be strewn with the remnants of past mistakes' (1984 [1970], p. 90).

There is a further extremely disquieting feature of most analyses of market adjustment processes, namely that, having derived the market excess supply functions which would obtain if all individuals acted 'as if' in equilibrium, they then invoke an *ad hoc* market price adjustment equation relating price changes to such market excess supplies. As Arrow (1959) did years ago, Fisher has asked:

Whose behavior does the equation represent? It seems very plausible, to be sure, that price should adjust upward when demand exceeds supply and downward in the opposite case, but just how does this happen? ... in a world in which all participants take prices as given, who changes the price? Indeed, in the center of a subject which deals with individual behavior how does there arise a behavior equation (not an identity) based solely on aggregates? The familiar story ... of the auctioneer who adjusts prices until demand equals supply is at best an inconvenient fiction (1983, p. 21).

To be meaningful, disequilibrium processes must be analysed at the level of *individual* behaviour: it is individuals − not markets *per se* − who react to disequilibrium phenomena and they may differ in their perceptions of, and reactions to, such phenomena.

It would be inappropriate for us to attempt to survey the large literature on '*tâtonnement*' and '*non-tâtonnement*' processes. It is far more illuminating to examine the 'general model' advanced by Fisher in *Disequilibrium Foundations of Equilibrium Economics*. The importance which Fisher (rightly) attaches to the analysis of adjustment processes can scarcely be exaggerated:

The theory of value is not satisfactory without a description of the adjustment processes that are applicable to the economy and of the way in which individual agents adjust to disequilibrium. In this sense, stability analysis is of far more than merely technical interest. It is the first step in a reformulation of the theory of value (1983, p. 16).

A central feature of Fisher's approach is that he allows individual agents 'to realize that they are not in equilibrium and to act on arbitrage opportunities as they occur. This fundamentally requires that agents be permitted to do two things. First, they must recognize that prices may change. Second, they must recognize that they may not be able to complete their desired transactions' (p. 85). Individual agents, realising that the economy is not in equilibrium, are able to adjust their individual price offers and bids; it is therefore not supposed that, in a disequilibrium, there will be a uniform price for each commodity (p. 153). The essence of Fisher's approach is to examine conditions under which individuals acting on perceived arbitrage opportunities will drive the system towards an equilibrium.

Figure 11.1

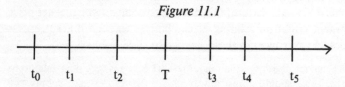

Fisher's temporal framework, and the assumed institutional arrangements, can be explained in terms of Figure 11.1. Fisher enters his economy at a particular point in time, designated by t_0. Time is represented as continuous; commodities are continuously dated; and the time-horizon is infinite. As in the Arrow-Debreu economy, there exists at the present instant a 'complete' set of markets for future commodities.[6] However, Fisher does not assume that markets clear 'instantaneously', an essential feature of his model being that not only trading but also production and consumption take place out of equilibrium. Since markets never close, there will exist at *each* point in time a complete set of markets for commodities which relate to dates which are still in the future. The optimal plan for an agent at time t – the plan will specify the *timing* of transactions, production and consumption – will depend on irreversible actions taken prior to t; on his expectations of future prices; and on his perceptions of constraints on his ability to conclude transactions. Each agent is assumed to have point expectations concerning future prices, any price expectation having three pertinent dates. Thus an agent would have an expectation held at, say, t_1 as to what the forward price will be at, say, t_2 of a unit of the physical commodity to be delivered at, say, t_3. It is the existence of these markets for future commodities which provides the opportunities for 'arbitrage'. Thus an agent may plan at t_1 to buy forward at t_2 a unit of wheat to be delivered at t_4 with the intention of making a profit by reselling that delivery commitment at t_3.

With the passage of time, an agent will, in general, continuously revise his plan in the light of his experiences. A 'momentary personal equilibrium' for an individual at t is defined as 'a state in which the agent's optimal program does not change because his plans and expectations are fulfilled' (p. 160). What constitutes an equilibrium for the system? Referring again to Figure 11.1, equilibrium for the system as a whole is attained at T if *all* agents are in momentary personal equilibrium for *all* subsequent times from T onwards (p. 160). Thus for the system to be in equilibrium the relevant expectations of all agents must be realised. For example, with respect to Figure 11.1, the point expectation held by each agent at t_3 of the forward price at t_4 for a unit of wheat to be delivered at t_5 must be correct (at least if that price is 'relevant' to the agent's plans).[7] That agents' price expectations are correct in equilibrium is true by definition. Are there any meaningful characteristics of equilibrium which can be deduced from the assumed behaviour of agents? Note first that an equilibrium may, but need not, be a 'Walrasian' equilibrium, defined as one in which there are no binding transaction constraints on any agent. A Fisherian equilibrium is consistent with perceived transaction constraints, provided that constraints prove to be no more binding than expected (p. 165). Indeed, the model offers no insights into whether, if an equilibrium is achieved, it would be 'Walrasian' or 'non-Walrasian'. Note further that an equilibrium could involve the sort of rhythmical changes which we discussed in the last chapter. Certainly, a Fisherian equilibrium need not be a steady state as in Burmeister's models. The precise relationship between Fisher's and Burmeister's notions of equilibrium is, in fact, obscure. This is partly because Burmeister and Fisher assume different institutional arrangements; partly because, for the most part, Burmeister assumes that markets always clear 'instantaneously'; and partly because it is of the essence of Fisher's model that individuals are *not* 'myopic'. But it is worth stressing that, whereas Burmeister assumes perfect myopic foresight *ab initio*, Fisher treats perfect foresight as a property of equilibrium and, indeed, as its defining characteristic.

Does a Fisherian equilibrium imply any restrictions on prices? There is certainly no requirement that the 'spot' price of, say, wheat be constant over time or even that it change in line with the rate of interest. However, it can be shown that, in equilibrium, the discounted money prices at which any *dated* commodity is bought or sold must be constant over time. Thus, in Figure 11.1, the money price at t_3 of t_5 wheat discounted back to, say, T must be equal to the money price at t_4 of t_5 wheat discounted back to T − or, equivalently, between T and t_5, the money price of t_5 wheat must change in line with the rate of interest. The reason for this is that the essence of the Fisherian adjustment process is that agents act on perceived arbitrage opportunities; a state of rest for such a process must involve no agents perceiving any opportunities for arbitrage.[8] Although the attainment of equilibrium involves the cessation of arbitrage activities, transactions continue to take place in equilibrium. Fisher emphasises the contrast with the Arrow-Debreu economy: 'We leave, as we must, the Arrow-Debreu world of prehistoric market clearing; economic activity of all sorts goes on in disequilibrium and does not cease when equilibrium is reached. Equilibrium in the present model involves continued trade at correctly foreseen prices and not the end of the economic system' (p. 213).[9]

Fisher's objective is not to demonstrate the global stability of *equilibrium*; the mere presence of multiple equilibria — which Fisher takes to be the rule — would preclude such stability. Rather, it is to prove the global stability of the *adjustment process*. An adjustment process is said to be globally stable if, for any set of initial conditions, there is a rest point to which the system converges. This does not have to be the same rest point for all initial conditions. Moreover, starting from any particular set of initial conditions, if a rest point is achieved, it will generally be path-dependent. Thus Fisher's objective is to identify conditions under which a system whereby agents act on perceived arbitrage opportunities will converge on *some* equilibrium, be it 'Walrasian' or 'non-Walrasian'. Fisher is concerned with asymptotic convergence as t tends to infinity. As he acknowledges, a proof of *asymptotic* convergence says nothing about how close to equilibrium the system will get in finite time (p. 12).

Fundamental to Fisher's demonstration of asymptotic convergence is the assumption of 'no favorable surprise'. For an economy to be *in* a Fisherian equilibrium, there clearly cannot be any surprises at all for agents, at least ones which are relevant to their plans. Furthermore, one could not reasonably expect that the arbitrage activities of rational agents who are conscious of disequilibrium would always be sufficient to drive an economy *towards* equilibrium: 'It may well be true that an economy of rational agents who understand that there is disequilibrium and act on arbitrage opportunities is driven toward equilibrium, but not if these agents continually perceive new previously unanticipated opportunities for further arbitrage' (p. 87). Referring explicitly to the works of Joseph Schumpeter, Fisher notes various different kinds of new opportunities whose unexpected arrival would 'keep the economy moving' (p. 88). These include new products, new production methods, changes in tastes, new raw material sources, improvements in enterprise organisation, improvements in marketing procedures and increased ease of raising funds or of completing transactions. Indeed, since opportunity is in the eye of the beholder, even if agents believe *wrongly* that such new opportunities will arise, this can 'keep the economy moving':

> The lesson is clear. Following Schumpeter, we cannot suppose it to be true that an economy in which new opportunities constantly arise will converge to equilibrium.... Further, it is agents' perceptions of new opportunities that matter rather than (directly) their reality. Finally, since agents plan over time, what must be ruled out is sudden optimistic revisions in agents' expectations. *There must be no favorable surprise* (p. 90).

The role of the assumption of no favourable surprise is intimately bound up with Fisher's use of Lyapounov's Second Method to demonstrate convergence. This method involves identifying a function which is monotonically decreasing through time except at rest points. The Lyapounov function used by Fisher is the sum over agents of the average target utilities or profits which the agents will ever expect along the path of the system. The assumption of no favourable surprise for every agent at every t is *sufficient* to ensure that the function does decrease over time unless an equilibrium for the system has been achieved, thereby ensuring stability of the adjustment process.[10] Clearly the significance of Fisher's contribution depends crucially on what one makes of the assumption of no favourable surprise for every agent at every point in time. It must be stressed that Fisher does not regard this assumption as at all realistic. It is important to be clear just how restrictive this assumption is. Suppose, for the sake of argument, that an economy has just been subjected to some 'exogenous' disturbance, such as an unanticipated invention. What Fisher would really like to demonstrate − the most that one could hope to demonstrate − is that, in the absence of *further exogenous* shocks, the economy would converge on an equilibrium. But the assumption of no favourable surprise does not simply rule out further favourable exogenous shocks: 'it rules out favorable surprises which arise in the course of absorption of the original shock − endogenous shocks as it were − as well as simply optimistic (possible incorrect) changes in expectations. Yet the really interesting stability question may lie in just how such "endogenous" shocks disappear' (p. 91).

In essence, Fisher's proof involves demonstrating that ruling out favourable surprises implies that *endogenous un*favourable surprises will cease asymptotically as a result of arbitrage.[11]

Fisher is generally very forthcoming as to the limitations of his model. What are some of these limitations? First, the really disconcerting feature of the assumption of no favourable surprise is that it 'is not, as it were, a natural "primitive" idea to impose on adjustment mechanisms' (p. 188). Fisher concedes that it would be highly desirable to replace the assumption of no favourable surprise by more primitive assumptions. Second, the assumption of a complete set of markets at any point in time is disquieting. Fisher, perhaps surprisingly, does not comment on just how strong this assumption is; he simply notes that 'the exploration of what happens with a system of incomplete markets is not undertaken' (p. 96). But at least Fisher does not assume that there never existed a complete set of markets prior to the present instant. Third, the number of firms is taken to be fixed and, while there is a market in existing shares, firms cannot issue *new* shares (p. 112, n. 10 and p. 125, n. 17).[12] Thus, even in Fisher's very flexible model, there is still something completely arbitrary about the temporal starting point: firms were created and shares issued *before* that starting date but such creations and issues are prohibited *after* that date, even though t runs to infinity. Fourth, Fisher assumes that, at any point in time, there is a unique optimal plan for an agent. As we have repeatedly seen, this begs fundamental questions – questions which Fisher does not address. Finally, the assumption that individuals have point expectations is highly restrictive. Fisher suggests that there would be considerable benefits from generalising the model to incorporate subjective uncertainty but he offers no more than hints as to how this might be accomplished.

Fisher claims that an achievement of his book is that he was able 'to jettison the traditional assumption that prices move in the direction of the corresponding aggregate excess demands and replace it with a very general assumption about individual price adjustment' (p. 215). He acknowledges that economists know very little about how such price adjustments take place. The frustrating feature of Fisher's book is not that he does not provide a 'realistic' story of price adjustment but that he does not provide, even by way of illustration, any *specific* story of price adjustment consistent with his 'general model'. In other words, he does not provide a story which details, *ex ante* as it were, the ways in which agents form and change perceptions of their monopoly and monopsony power and the ways in which price offers are made and accepted. This is why, even if the system converges, the model offers no insights into whether the corresponding equilibrium would be 'Walrasian' or 'non-Walrasian'. But, more fundamentally, it is not evident that one could tell a *remotely plausible* story which would be compatible with there not being endogenous favourable surprises as the economy absorbs the impact of some exogenous disturbance.

Whatever the limitations of Fisher's study, he has sought to confront directly many complications which other economists have evaded, his main achievement being that he has highlighted many of these complications in a relatively systematic way. Fisher recognises that equilibrium must be seen as the outcome of a process of learning, not as a state which could be established instantaneously. Moreover, he never attempts to embrace within his equilibrium notion changes which are inherently unpredictable.

Fisher does *not* claim that he has provided a satisfactory 're-habilitation' of equilibrium analysis generally or of comparative statics in particular:

The generality ... of our stability proof is such that we know nothing about speeds of adjustment. This means that we cannot be sure that the ability of the economy (as modeled) to absorb shocks means that it absorbs them very quickly — quickly enough that it spends most of its time between shocks near equilibrium rather than in a non-negligible adjustment process. Real economies do have new opportunities and favorable surprises do occur. The fact that, absent such effects, one obtains asymptotic convergence does not justify analyzing economies as though they were in equilibrium without a showing that convergence is rapid (p. 216).

Demonstrating the stability of an *adjustment process* cannot *per se* rehabilitate comparative statics, even if it could also be shown that the process would converge 'rapidly'. As Fisher observes: 'If comparative statics is to be useful, the adjustment process must not only be rapid and thus unimportant in terms of real time, it must also be unimportant in terms of its effects on equilibrium. In the present state of our knowledge, there is no basis for the belief that this is the case' (p. 216). The importance which Fisher attaches to these questions of adjustment speed and path-dependence can scarcely be exaggerated.[13] Thus he insists:

If disequilibrium effects are in fact unimportant we need to prove that they are. If such effects are important, then the way in which we tend to think about the theory of value needs to be revised. Interest must then center not on equilibrium itself but on disequilibrium adjustment. Different economies cannot then be studied as though their future were determined solely by tastes, technology, and initial endowments with adjustment but a transient matter (p. 217).

Those economists who, for whatever reason, construct models which assume 'instantaneous' market clearing ought to be extremely troubled by Fisher's inability to provide a compelling demonstration of even 'eventual' convergence of market adjustment processes. Since Fisher's demonstration of convergence involves the implausible assumption that there are no favourable exogenous or endogenous surprises, since we know nothing useful about speeds of convergence and since we have no reputable way of denying the presence of path-dependence, it is not surprising that Fisher concludes his stimulating book with the following words: 'The issues involved in disequilibrium analysis are too important to economics to be avoided. They must be faced head on rather than assumed away in the course of a desire to do what economists do best – analyze equilibrium without regard for the foundations on which such analysis must rest' (p. 218).

Equilibrium over time

That straight line from the first hiccup to the last gasp is a dead thing. Time is two modes. The one is an effortless perception native to us as water to the mackerel. The other is a memory, a sense of shuffle fold and coil, of that day nearer than that because more important, of that event mirroring this, or those three set apart, exceptional and out of the straight line altogether.

(William Golding)

Is there a meaningful notion of 'equilibrium over time' which is not only less demanding than requiring that an economy be in a stationary or steady state (as with Burmeister's dynamic rest point) but also less exacting than requiring that individuals' single-valued expectations are being fulfilled (as with Fisher's equilibrium)? We have seen that, in *Value and Capital*, Hicks was prepared to countenance a weaker notion of equilibrium: 'when we remember that the expectations of entrepreneurs are in fact not precise expectations of particular prices, but partake more of the character of probability distributions, then it becomes evident that the realised prices can depart to some extent from those prices expected as most probable without causing any acute sense of disequilibrium' (1939, p. 133). In *Capital and Growth*, Hicks subsequently repudiated this view, claiming that, if one wishes to say that an economy is in equilibrium over some particular period, 'there must be equilibrium at every point *within the period*, looked at both ways' (1965, p. 25). He argued that 'for period equilibrium expectations that relate within the period will have to be certain. This may seem awkward, but I think it has to be faced' (1965, p. 25, n. 1).[14] Since time goes only one way, the claim that it is necessary to 'look both ways' is perhaps not particularly compelling at first sight. At the same time, if an economy were 'staggering' through time with individuals' expectations repeatedly being wildly at variance with what actually happens, one would scarcely wish to describe the economy as being in 'equilibrium over time'.

Hahn has long been concerned with the question of what meaning can be attached to the notion of equilibrium over time given that individuals base decisions on expectations. In 'Expectations and Equilibrium', published in 1952, Hahn argued that it is 'the invariance of behaviour over a certain period which gives significance to the concept of equilibrium' (1984 [1952], p. 24). Referring to the 'Swedish disequilibrium method', that is, the method advanced by Lindahl in 1939 and discussed in Chapter 5, Hahn claimed that 'invariant behaviour' requires that the *method* by which individuals arrive at the expectations on which they base their decisions must remain constant. Thus the notion of invariant behaviour may be interpreted sufficiently broadly to accommodate, say, systematic changes in demands:

As long as the variations in demand are systematic and not random it is possible (it should be noted that we do *not* maintain that this actually happens) to learn by experience and thus to evolve a 'rule of thumb' or a mode of routine behaviour which will ensure that the output forthcoming at the planned price is exactly sold .... The existence of equilibrium through time therefore presupposes the existence of an expectation function of constant form or, what comes to the same thing, a form of routine behaviour on the part of the entrepreneur .... Equilibrium always entails the repetition of some particular experiences, although these experiences need not be simple (1984 [1952], p. 25).

Noting the contrast between 'routine behaviour' and the sorts of 'decisions' emphasised by Shackle, Hahn acknowledged that the latter cannot be accommodated within an equilibrium analysis. Hahn's notion of routine behaviour which has evolved as a result of a process of learning is, of course, entirely consistent with our earlier discussion of rhythmical changes.

Hahn's 1952 article was primarily a critique of the proliferation of dynamic models characterised by 'a great deal of formal mathematics and relatively little economics' (1984 [1952], p. 23). He was particularly critical of the failure of theorists to acknowledge that it is not legitimate to use models which implicitly assume *invariant* routine behaviour to derive propositions about the 'long run' – at least if the behaviour of the economy in the interim would involve the systematic disappointment of expectations, since the latter would, in reality, lead to the adoption of *new* routines. Hahn initially assumed that all expectations are single valued and insisted that all expectations would have to be fulfilled for there to be equilibrium. But he conceded: 'It is, however, well known that expectations are not single valued, and it may therefore be argued that no sensible meaning can be given to the statement that all expectations are fulfilled' (1984 [1952], p. 41). Like Hicks in *Value and Capital*, Hahn was prepared to countenance a weaker notion of equilibrium, one which would be consistent with multivalued expectations. Thus he suggested that 'even partial success' may be sufficient for a routine to be maintained. Nevertheless, he was insistent that 'if the actual achievement differs (over time) from a successful achievement in a systematic way, then this constitutes new "experience" and attempts will be made to change behaviour' (1984 [1952], p. 41).

In 1974, Hahn returned to these issues in his inaugural lecture, 'On the Notion of Equilibrium'. Specifically, he considered the question of whether there is some notion of equilibrium which would not require that common single-valued expectations be precisely fulfilled and which would reflect 'the sequential character of actual economies' (1984 [1974], p. 53). He further insisted that the equilibrium notion must be sequential in an 'essential' way: 'By this I mean that it should not be possible without change in content to reformulate the notion non-sequentially. This in turn requires that information processes and costs, transactions and transaction costs and also expectations and uncertainty be explicitly and essentially included in the equilibrium notion' (1984 [1974], p. 53).

Briefly, Hahn supposed that, at date t, an agent has a 'theory', which encapsulates the way in which the agent processes the history of messages received by him up to that date. The agent's 'policy', based on his theory, is a mapping from future messages to acts: it specifies for every message array at any date from t onwards an associated act for that date. Hahn proposed the following definition: 'an economy is in equilibrium when it generates messages which do not cause agents to change the theories which they hold or the policies which they pursue' (1984 [1974], p. 59). Thus, for an economy to be in equilibrium, each agent's policy and thus each agent's theory must be independent of date t, that is, he must not be 'learning'. For an agent to be 'not learning' does not preclude his acquiring information: he can still be in equilibrium, provided that new information does not lead him to change the way in which he processes information.

Hahn claimed that one of the reasons for invoking an equilibrium notion is that 'it serves to make precise the limits of economic analysis' (1984 [1974], p. 56). In particular, as in 1952, he conceded that, given the present state of knowledge, economists can only hope to describe *routine* behaviour. He asserted that 'it is, of course, precisely my contention that equilibrium actions of agents will reveal themselves in habitual behaviour.... But notice the difference between the man who says that people choose goods out of habit and the one who says people have a habitual way of translating prices and incomes into choices. The former is not very helpful' (1984 [1974], p. 59). A crucial question is: when might new information lead an agent to change his theory – and thereby his habitual behaviour? According to Hahn: 'I am at this stage not at all clear of what the precise formulation should be. So I content myself with the ill specified hypothesis that an agent abandons his theory when it is sufficiently and systematically falsified' (1984 [1974], p. 59). Furthermore, Hahn did not pretend to know what new theory the agent would adopt:

The concept of the equilibrium action of an agent here proposed is that if it is in fact the action pursued by the agent an outside observer, say the econometrician, could describe it by structurally stable equations. When the agent is learning, however, then there is a change in regime so that one would require a 'higher level' theory of the learning process. Such a theory is not available at present (1984 [1974], p. 56).

Furthermore, Hahn noted that his conception of equilibrium is such that one can only discuss the *local* stability of equilibrium:

Disturbances which in a proper sense are small and short enough will allow us to suppose that agents continue in equilibrium actions .... Indeed it is part of the case that when 'regularity of behaviour' has been translated into the

rather broad definition of 'equilibrium behaviour' which is here proposed,
we have gone as far as an economist can in the present state of knowledge
go. That is why the notion of equilibrium behaviour is of interest and
importance (1984 [1974], p. 61).

Hahn's notion of equilibrium over time is, indeed, a very general
one. It is clearly much less demanding than stationarity in even its
broadest sense; it does not require that agents have single-valued
expectations which are being realised; and, furthermore, it does not
require that the economy always be in temporary equilibrium given
the expectations which individuals do have: 'short enough and rare
enough episodes of uncleared markets would on my definition be
consistent with equilibrium' (1984 [1974], p. 60). Indeed, to appreciate
the full generality of Hahn's notion of equilibrium − which, it should
be noted, does not presuppose competitive conditions − it is instructive to consider its meaning in the context of Lindahl's 'disequilibrium
theory of price determination'. Recall that Lindahl presented a
scenario in which sellers decide on prices on the basis of their
expectations of what demands will be forthcoming over some ensuing
period. In Hahn's terminology, the price set by each seller would
constitute a 'message' to himself as well as to other relevant agents;
the quantity actually demanded at the price set by a seller would
constitute a 'message' from others to the seller. Provided that these
messages do not induce sellers to change the ways in which they
process information, the economy would be in Hahn equilibrium.
This would be consistent with sufficiently small divergences between
actual sales and planned sales − and thus with prices which are
changing over time as agents acquire new information. Whether it
is useful to define equilibrium quite so broadly is perhaps debatable.
Certainly one might still wish also to invoke more specific notions
of equilibrium. For example − given that an economy is in Hahn
equilibrium, in that the theories and policies of agents are unchanging
− one might still want to ask whether, in the absence of any exogenous disturbances, the process of price adjustment would converge
over time on, say, a set of prices which would thenceforth be
unchanging.[15]

It is worth pursuing Hahn's theme of the limits of economic
analysis further than he does himself. A crucial consideration is
whether, following, say, a 'large' disturbance, those agents who
change their theories adopt new theories 'instantaneously' or whether

formulating new theories takes time. Whereas Hahn explicitly referred in 1952 to agents 'evolving' rules of thumb or modes of routine behaviour, it is not clear in the 1974 lecture whether agents 'evolve' theories. However, his notions of an agent's 'theory' and 'policy' would seem to imply this. Recall that his conception of the equilibrium action of an agent is such that it could, in principle, be described, by an outside observer, by *structurally stable equations*. There is surely a presumption that it *would* take time for an agent, who has just abandoned a theory, to formulate a new theory which would give rise to actions which could be described in such a way.

With this in mind, suppose that we enter an economy at some arbitrary point in time denoted by t_0. At best, we could only say something about the behaviour of the economy until the next 'large' exogenous disturbance occurs. However, what we could say may be more limited than that. In Hahn's terminology, the agents' current policies – his notion of policies seems to correspond very closely with Lindahl's notion of contingent plans – might be so incompatible with each other that, even in the absence of exogenous disturbances, their current theories might be 'sufficiently and systematically falsified' in the very near future. We should perhaps anticipate the objection that it would necessarily take more than a 'very short time' for theories to be 'sufficiently and systematically falsified'. This objection would be ill-founded, since experiences in the recent past may have already led some agents to doubt their theories, so that it may not require many *additional* messages for them to abandon those theories.

Indeed, it may be that we would have nothing at all to say. Thus, if some 'large' disturbance has occurred *just prior to t_0*, agents may, at t_0, still be in the process of formulating new theories and new policies. Lacking a 'higher level' theory of the evolution of agents' theories, we would have nothing to say about the future behaviour of the economy even in the shortest of runs. In other words, past 'shocks' may be as disconcerting for economic analysis as future 'shocks'. It is scarcely profound to observe that what one might be able to say about the behaviour of an economy in the near future is likely to depend on its behaviour in the recent, and sometimes not-so-recent, past – and, indeed, it is of the essence of Hahn's approach that this will be so. And yet it would be only too easy to take for granted that, if we enter an economy at some arbitrary point in time, each agent would have *some* theory and *some* policy.

In 1987, Hahn returned again to the relationship between information and equilibrium, his central theme being that, since 'the state
of the economy which we single out as equilibrium depends on our
theory of the behaviour of agents out of equilibrium' and since 'such
a theory must turn on the information available to agents and on the
manner in which they learn from such information', it follows
inexorably that 'equilibrium will not be independent of the history
of the economy' (1987, p.321). He argued:

When we remove the auctioneer and allow actual agents to change prices it
will be clear that the agent will do so in the light of his expectations − I shall
call it theory − of the consequences of such a change. Such a theory will
be conditioned by his information. The latter will change as actual consequences are observed and theories will be updated − the agent will be learning.
If an equilibrium on my definition is reached by such a process then it will
be a state at which learning has ceased or more accurately when the relevant
information set remains what it is so that no further modification of the
agents' theory is called for and so also no further change in the agents'
optimum policy (1987, p.324).

Hahn's approach is motivated by the hope that a dynamic analysis
may circumvent the complications posed by the multiplicity of
potential equilibria yielded by a 'static' analysis:

if you start at a concrete time, with concrete initial beliefs and information
and if you let agents at each date do the best for themselves given these and
then recalculate what new information this generates and so what new
decisions, then you may hope to follow a particular path and if you are lucky
it will lead you to one out of a multitude of equilibria (1987, pp.324−5).

If a determinate equilibrium can be identified, it will, of course, be
path-dependent: the equilibrium is being identified precisely by
determining the path.

Although we cannot explore the details of the example used by
Hahn to illustrate his method, it is worth noting that it is very much
reminiscent of Lindahl's 1939 essay: firms set prices at the beginning
of any period in the light of their beliefs about the demand conditions
which they will face during that period − where these beliefs will,
of course, depend on their previous experiences.[16] It is also worth
noting that Hahn's new notion of equilibrium is much more specific
than the notion of equilibrium advanced in the inaugural lecture. In
both cases, equilibrium is characterised as an 'absence of learning'.
In the inaugural lecture, as we have seen, agents are 'not learning'

provided that new information does not lead them to change the *ways* in which they process information. In contrast, in the recent model, the question of agents changing the ways in which they process information does not arise, 'not learning' having the more mundane meaning that additional observations only confirm what agents already 'knew', so that the (given) ways in which they process information lead to the same expectations and to the same actions as before.

Hahn's analyses of economies which are 'moving through time' are to be welcomed – provided that his earlier strictures about the limits of economic analysis are kept firmly in mind. It would be regrettable if his latest approach – it may 'yield determinacy where at the moment there is none' (1987, p. 325) – were to give rise to a resurgence of a naive 'Laplacean determinism'. According to Laplace:

An intellect which at a given instant knows all the forces with which nature is animated, and the respective situations of the beings which compose it – supposing the intellect were vast enough to subject these data to analysis – would embrace in the same formula the motions of the largest bodies in the Universe and those of the slightest atoms: nothing would be uncertain for it, and the future, like the past, would be present to its eyes (1820, p. vii).

As Jaques (1982, p. 18) has noted, most of the writers who quote from this famous passage omit to mention that Laplace immediately proceeded to put this in perspective: 'All the efforts of the human spirit in search for the truth tend to enable it continuously to get closer to the understanding of which we have just conceived, *but from which it must always remain infinitely far*' (emphasis added).

Notes

1 Much of Burmeister's book is concerned with normative questions. We will concentrate exclusively on his descriptive models.
2 As Dasgupta and Heal have observed, the literature on the 'Hahn problem', which has stemmed from Hahn (1966), is 'simply huge' (p. 254).
3 Recall the Malinvaud analysis considered in Appendix 3.
4 It may be that Burmeister's reference to 'dramatic instability' alludes to the proposition that, for certain model specifications, all non-convergent paths would result in some prices becoming zero in finite time, thereby contradicting the assumptions of the model (p. 226). But, in the absence of a demonstration of *how soon* this would happen, this proposition *per se* says nothing about the appropriateness of the model for the 'present

interlude'. Certainly, as Burmeister acknowledges, the proposition cannot justify focussing only on convergent paths; this could only be justified by postulating some plausible 'mechanism' whereby the 'right' prices would be established at t = 0.

5 The reference is to Scarf (1960), which provided examples of global instability under competition.

6 In contrast to Debreu, Fisher does not distinguish different states of nature and thus does not invoke the notion of contingent commodity markets.

7 For equilibrium to be attained at T does not require that the expectations which agents held prior to T about prices after T be correct.

8 We have supposed that there are no inter-agent price differences in equilibrium. We will not consider Fisher's somewhat convoluted discussion of whether such differences would be compatible with equilibrium (pp. 165–71).

9 Since equilibrium does not involve the cessation of trading, the model allows some limited role for 'money' in equilibrium, namely, that of financing transactions. 'Money' comprises very short-term bonds, bearing the same rate of interest as all other assets in equilibrium. Thus Fisher's model does not explain why agents might hold non-interest bearing bank notes in equilibrium. Note also that Fisher imposes various rules on agents to limit 'short sales'.

10 Formally, the assumption of no favourable surprise states: There exists a $\Delta^* > 0$ such that, for every agent and every t, the programme which is optimal for that agent at t was feasible at $t - \Delta$ for every Δ such that $0 \leq \Delta \leq \Delta^*$. This assumption, though sufficient for stability, is not necessary. For example, it would be sufficient if the assumption simply held beyond a certain point in time. Moreover, there will be convergence if there are favourable surprises for some agents, provided that, at each point in time, these are outweighed by unfavourable surprises for other agents (so that the relevant sum which constitutes the Lyapounov function decreases over time).

11 Fisher acknowledges that the distinction between 'exogenous' and 'endogenous' shocks involves 'deep issues' (p. 91). However, he does not pursue them.

12 Trades in existing shares take place both because of differing price expectations and because households purchase expected dividend streams as a way of transferring liquidity across time periods.

13 We have seen that Fisher's model allows for 'irreversible' actions out of equilibrium which could affect the ensuing equilibrium (if one is achieved). But it does not follow that such actions *would* affect the resulting equilibrium. Since Fisher does not attempt to derive explicit adjustment paths, his analysis does not *directly* throw any light on the likelihood of path-dependence. Fisher, it should be noted,

does not claim that it does, but simply treats the question of path-dependence as an open one.

14 In terms of the temporal framework of *Value and Capital*, equilibrium at a 'point' in time would correspond to temporary equilibrium for some particular Monday; 'period equilibrium' would refer to equilibrium over a period of weeks and would presumably require that expectations on any Monday within the period pertaining to any other Monday within the period be correct.

15 This may be what Hahn has in mind by his cryptic claim: 'Stability will mean that for short enough periods and small enough disturbances the set of equilibria is large but that it shrinks' (p. 61).

16 As in Fisher's model, if an equilibrium is achieved, it may be 'non-Walrasian'.

12

Concluding remarks

It seemed that the next minute they would discover a solution. Yet it was clear to both of them that the end was still far, far off, and that the hardest and most complicated part was only just beginning (Anton Chekov).

The cumulative impact of our study of the diverse attempts of various economic theorists to wrestle with time is surely compelling: a recurrent theme is just how limited economic analysis really is once time is taken seriously. Recall Marshall's claim that the element of time is 'the centre of the chief difficulty of almost every economic problem'. Recall Walras' insistence that economies are *never* in equilibrium. Recall how Lindahl's 1929 essay culminated in an acknowledgement of the 'considerable difficulties' of allowing – in some way which is *not* arbitrary – for individuals to have different expectations about the future. Recall Hicks' claim, in *Value and Capital*, that we may have to face the disappointing conclusion that there is not much that can be said about the 'ulterior consequences' of changes in the data. Recall the observation that the Arrow-Debreu economy 'telescopes the future into the present'. Recall Burmeister's admission that: 'all too often "nearly anything can happen" is the only possible unqualified conclusion'. Recall Fisher's assertion that the theory of value itself is in need of reformulation to take account of disequilibrium phenomena. Recall Hahn's acknowledgement of the limits to economic analysis which result from our lack of a 'higher-level' theory of the processes of learning. In chapter after chapter, we have found that eminent economists who have directed their efforts explicitly to wrestling with time have all found the opponent impossible to master.

Obvious as it may be, it is noteworthy that no unique temporal framework has secured universal acceptance amongst economists.

This does not necessarily imply failure. Perhaps, *mutatis mutandis*, we can say of economic theorists what Long and Sedley said of the Stoics: 'Given the notorious difficulties of the concept of time, the Stoics' flexibility on the subject is to their credit. They recognized that temporal discourse is unavoidably imprecise and may legitimately vary with the context' (1987, p. 308). Economics is not like, say, hydrodynamics. Hydrodynamicists can specify systems of differential equations with confidence not only that they have included the relevant variables and parameters but also that they have specified both the forms and the numerical parameters of the equations appropriately. With modern computing techniques, even highly complex systems are amenable to numerical solution. In contrast, in economics, we are not always confident about what are the relevant exogenous and endogenous variables, let alone the relationships between them. Indeed, we seldom know the relevant objective facts. Thus, although we often *conceive* of knowing 'initial conditions', we do not, in fact, know them. In economic life, the purposes, preferences, beliefs, information and expectations of individuals are of crucial significance. We cannot truly know what these are or how they may change. Moreover, economic life involves *interaction* between individuals. Even if we did know all we wanted to know about individuals, we would not be able to overcome the indeterminacy inherent in their interaction. As Lindahl observed in his 1939 essay, 'all inexactness can be avoided by explicit *assumptions* about all these phenomena which in the real world cannot be definitely determined'. But it would be self-deception to regard propositions derived from analyses based on such assumptions as more than suggestive.

Presumably few economic theorists would be prepared to admit, as did Charles Lamb, 'nothing puzzles me more than time and space; and yet nothing troubles me less, as I never think about them'. It is extremely healthy that more and more economists seem to be acknowledging that substantive progress in economic analysis can only come from confronting the formidable difficulties associated with time. These difficulties are not confined to the 'neo-classical paradigm', whatever that is taken to be. They must be confronted in *any* method of economic analysis.

Appendix 1   Dimensions, stocks and flows

In order to think clearly about dimensional questions in relation to discrete period analysis, it is essential to draw a sharp distinction between the length of the period, on the one hand, and the numerical expression of that length, on the other. The distinction having been made, it is clear that the length of the period is quite independent of the unit in which time is measured, while, by contrast, the numerical expression of the length of the period changes with every change in the unit of time. *One* week, *seven* days, *168* hours, ... etc. are different numerical expressions of the same length of period. To say that any physical magnitude – e.g., acceleration, or energy – has a time dimension is not to say anything at all mysterious; it is simply to say that the numerical expression of that fixed magnitude changes as the unit of time changes.

In a continuous-time economic analysis, one distinguishes readily between stock variables, such as the money supply or the number of houses, and flow variables, such as the rate of increase of the money supply or the output of houses: the former two variables have no time dimension, while each of the latter two variables has a time dimension. This, combined with the fact that the volume of steel output over some given period has no time dimension, enables one to say, correctly, that that steel output has the *same* dimensions as a *stock* of steel. Yet many economists appear to feel a strong desire to refer to the steel output over some period of time as a flow quantity; a tension thus seems to arise between their intuitive idea of a flow and the conceptually sound dimensional statement. Patinkin may well be right to suggest (1972, p. 5) that this apparent tension is an illusion, in that the economists' common idea of a 'flow' is not really that of a magnitude with a time dimension but rather that of a quantity which varies with the length of the period. (With the actual length of the period, that is, not merely with the varying numerical expression of a fixed length.)

The above remarks may help to clarify certain dimensional and terminological matters in the context of period analysis. The length of the period does, of course, have a time dimension but the volume of steel produced during a finite period does not; it has the same *dimensions* as a stock of steel. (By contrast, of course, the 'average rate of steel output' – namely, that constant output rate which would, over the period, produce the given period volume of steel output – does have a time dimension). At the same time, it may well be unhelpful to refer to the volume of steel produced during a finite period either as a stock or as a flow since, in either case, misleading associations may be inferred by the reader. The best solution is perhaps to follow Baumol's eminently sensible suggestion and to 'talk of the *amount* (used, produced, sold, etc.) during a *period* of time' (1970 [1951], p. 127). We thus refer to *stocks* at period junctions and to *amounts* produced, etc. during periods. In the discrete period context, it is never necessary to mention flows, rates of flow, etc. and it is always potentially confusing to do so.

Appendix 2 Alternative interpretations of the Arrow-Debreu model

We must consider briefly alternative temporal interpretations for the Arrow-Debreu model. According to Koopmans:

> The simplest interpretation in this regard is that of a stationary state, in which all choices are made once and for all, in terms of rates of flow that are to remain constant for an indefinite period of time. In a way this interpretation raises the least difficulties, because its abstract character is obvious to all and thus serves to silence detailed objections on grounds of realism. The great value of this interpretation lies in its combination of simplicity with relevance to the more fundamental problems of the economic organization of society that have been and will be with us for a long time (1957, p. 60).

This is a surprisingly naive suggestion for Koopmans to make. Presumably the claim that the abstract character of such an interpretation is 'obvious to all' means that everyone knows that actual economies are not stationary. Granting that, the fundamental problem is that the exact nature of the abstraction is far from being obvious.

The notion that 'all choices are made once and for all' suggests that, as in the Debreu interpretation, the economy is being considered at some (arbitrarily chosen) moment in time. The only difference might appear to be that, with this interpretation, the agents' choices involve 'rates of flow that are to remain constant for an indefinite period of time'. But this begs a crucial question: what resources are to be treated as historically given at the moment of time in question? Recall that Debreu assumes that all the land, buildings, equipment and inventories of goods existing at the present instant and available to the agents are a legacy of the past. However, these historically given resources will not, in general, be compatible with the economy being, or immediately becoming, stationary. For example, the stocks of capital goods may not have the requisite age structure. Even if stationarity is conceivable on the basis of the *a priori* given resources, unless the choices of the agents are artificially constrained, they will not, in general, be consistent with maintaining the equipment and inventories at their initial levels. In short, it is incoherent to assume *a priori* given stocks of capital goods in an analysis of a stationary economy. If the set of *a priori* given resources is construed as referring only to primary resources, conceiving of a once and for all determination at a point in time of the economy's capital would surely conceal, rather than illuminate, many of 'the more fundamental problems of the economic organization of society'.

Yet another interpretation has been placed on the Arrow-Debreu model. This interpretation does not postulate the existence of a complete set of markets but assumes, instead, that there exist 'spot' markets in each elementary time period and institutions which permit agents to transfer wealth freely over time and across states of nature. The assumption that all agents face the same prices has now to be interpreted as meaning that they all have the same point expectations of future prices. Furthermore, these price expectations are assumed to be realised *ex post*. Given these assumptions, it is claimed, the formal analysis is the same as for the case where a complete set of markets does exist.

That this interpretation has gained credence surely highlights the extent to which economists so often fail to think seriously in sequential terms. Suppose that the production of some particular commodity involves constant returns to scale, where the use of inputs at date 1 results in outputs at date 2 (and so on). Consider an inter-temporal equilibrium as conceived under this interpretation of the Arrow-Debreu model. Even if we suppose that there is a unique set of prices consistent with equilibrium – prices which would, in particular, imply zero (expected) profits for producers of the commodity concerned – and further that there is a unique date 2 *industry* output of the commodity consistent with inter-temporal equilibrium, the date 2 outputs for *individual* producers would not be determined uniquely: any quantity, produced at minimum cost, would yield zero (expected) profit. Even if each producer knows the spot prices of inputs and bases his decision on a point expectation of the date 2 product price which accords with what the price would be if all producers were collectively just to produce the equilibrium industry output, *there is no mechanism which would ensure that the equilibrium date 2 industry output would be produced.*[1]

Note

1 It is worth stressing that market demand and supply *correspondences* – rather than single-valued functions – would be the rule rather than the exception. Consider coffee at a stipulated location on a particular day. Suppose that, to accommodate the preferences of some particular agent, the analysis discriminates between, on the one hand, coffee delivered from 9.00 a.m. to 9.10 a.m. and, on the other hand, coffee delivered from 9.10 a.m. to 9.20 a.m.. An individual who is indifferent as to when he receives coffee between 9.00 a.m. and 9.20 a.m. cannot have single-valued demands at all prices.

Appendix 3   Malinvaud's *Lectures on Microeconomic Theory*

We have noted, in our discussion of the Arrow-Debreu model, that Debreu's use of the 'date' as an elementary interval of time of finite length, combined with the fact that, by definition, commodities cannot be distinguished within a 'date', has a number of disturbing implications. (Recall our discussions of the electrician's time, of the precise instant at which ownership of a truck (or a piece of land) is acquired, of storage and transportation activities, of the lecturer's time.) It may therefore be of interest to point out that *some*, at least, of those disturbing implications disappear if one represents the timing of economic activities in a different way – even when many other aspects and emphases of the analysis are left unchanged. To this end, we here consider, *very* briefly, some aspects of Edmond Malinvaud's *Lectures on Microeconomic Theory*.[1]

In his first chapter, on the 'conceptual framework' of microeconomic theory, Malinvaud adopts, in effect, Debreu's definition of a commodity. In particular, he distinguishes commodities by location, so that, 'Transport of the product from the first place to the second is then a productive activity with the first good as input and the second as output' (p. 7). Similarly, commodities are distinguished by date and Malinvaud notes that, if the number of commodities is to remain finite, 'we must adopt a discrete representation of time and put a limiting terminal date to the future' (p. 7). (Analogous points are made with respect to commodity qualities, p. 6, and locations, p. 7.) 'Under certain additional assumptions, the theories with which we shall be concerned can be generalised to the case where time is represented by an unlimited sequence of periods .... However, the generalisation is not straightforward and often leads to weaker results' (p. 7). Malinvaud makes it clear that, in the theory presented, 'consumption, production and price are determined simultaneously for all periods' (p. 8). Differences in quality and location being set aside, it follows that, 'The price p_{qt} is that price which must be paid now (at the moment considered) to obtain delivery at time t of a unit of the product q. It is therefore a "forward price"' (p. 8). Malinvaud himself then suggests that

To assume the existence of forward prices for all dates and all products, as we do here for a time economy, is clearly more restrictive and perhaps much less realistic than to assume the existence of actual prices for all products in an economy without time .... Doubts may be expressed as to the relevance of some possible temporal interpretations of our theories. But such doubts do not destroy its usefulness, though they sometimes restrict its field of application (p. 8).

Malinvaud's Chapter 10, 'Intertemporal economies', is divided into two sections, labelled '(A) A date for each commodity' and '(B) Production specific to each period'. While we shall be more concerned here with the latter, we must first notice a few points from Section (A) which, in effect, presents a (simpler) version of Debreu's theory.

With respect to the consumer, Malinvaud draws attention to the assumptions that the consumer:

(i) has knowledge of all discounted prices (for all dates and all goods) as well as knowledge of all his future needs;
(ii) has the possibility of making forward contracts, that is, of buying or selling forward, for any date, quantities of products or services which he may wish to acquire or dispose of (p. 236)

After suggesting that (ii) may be replaced by the assumption that future prices are known and that the consumer may lend or borrow any quantity of *numéraire* at the appropriate interest rates, 'subject only to the constraint that he must balance his operations over all the T dates' (*ibid.*), Malinvaud concludes that 'This theory therefore ignores uncertainty on future needs and prices, as well as possible stricter limitations on individuals' borrowing facilities than is required by their solvency over all the T periods considered' (p. 236).[2] With respect to the firm, Malinvaud writes:

The physical capital existing in the economy at date 1 is often treated as a primary resource available at that date. The part of this capital that is used by the *j*th firm must therefore appear among its inputs at date 1. Conversely, the capital equipment of the *j*th firm at the terminal date T is often considered as output at this date.

It may also happen that the initial capital of the firm does not appear explicitly in the model but is taken account of in the definition of the production set Y .... A vector y then belongs to Y if it represents the net productions of a programme that is technically feasible for the firm on the basis of its available capital (p. 237).

Three remarks appear to be in order here. The first is that, unlike Debreu, Malinvaud refers explicitly to the 'capital *of the firm*', and not simply to the capital of households which is rented by the firm, thus suggesting the idea of the firm as a (semi-) permanent institution. The second is that Malinvaud does not show that his quoted remarks suffice to justify his earlier statement that 'the null vector naturally belongs to Y ' (p. 53); can the firm not have (still future) delivery commitments contracted in the past? The final remark is that, while Malinvaud's opening sentence in the above passage is, no doubt, correct, one should not accept too easily his earlier statement (1953, p. 235, n. 4) that the 'distinction between natural resources and produced means of production is not important as far as past activity is concerned'. Since the initial time is arbitrary, the produced means of production extant at that time have, presumably, been chosen just as rationally as will be future capital stocks. Hence the initial quantities of capital goods are *not* arbitrary, by contrast with the quantities of (non-exhaustible) natural resources. For some purposes, at least, this distinction may be important.

Before turning to Section (B), we note finally that, while Malinvaud does offer some qualified defence of this type of theory as an aid to explanation (pp. 241–2), he seems to feel more comfortable in suggesting that 'the conceptual framework on which it is based is much better adapted to the examination of the normative problems raised by the organisation of economic activity over time' (p. 242).

In his Section (B) Malinvaud introduces 'a new representation of technical constraints ... which does not contradict the representation used so far. Its particular feature is that it applies directly to the production operations relating to an elementary period' (p. 248). Considering one particular firm, Malinvaud writes, 'Let us now try to represent its operations between two successive dates t and $t + 1$, this time-interval being called the "period t"' (p. 248). 'At date t, the firm puts into operation inputs a_{qt} of the various products or services; as a result of its activity, it obtains outputs $b_{q,t+1}$, which are available at date $t + 1$ ... we can describe production during period t by the pair of vectors $(a_t; b_{t+1})'$ (p. 249). Malinvaud naturally notes that

both a_t and b_{t+1} must include semi-finished products and new
and old capital goods, distinguished by their age. For the purposes
of equilibrium analysis, this 'implies that there are well-defined
prices for existing equipment and for products in course of manufacture' (p. 249). 'With this new formulation, it is natural to represent
the technical constraints which limit production during period
t by

$$g_t(a_t; b_{t+1}) \leq 0, \qquad [A1]$$

where g_t is a real-valued function ... called the "production function
for period t"'(p. 250).

Just as in Debreu's *Theory of Value*, time has a 'granular structure'
in Malinvaud's *Lectures*; yet the treatment of time is nevertheless
significantly different in the two cases. In Malinvaud's representation,
no deliveries take place *within* an elementary period (i.e. within one
of Debreu's 'dates'); they are all concentrated at the 'junctions'
between elementary periods (i.e. at Malinvaud's 'dates'). By contrast,
all productive activities − which include transportation activities −
take place (subject to an unspecified time pattern) *within* the elementary periods. Since, in Malinvaud's analysis, all payments refer to
period junctions, all prices refer to some instant in time, *not* to some
period of time as in Debreu's analysis.

The Malinvaud representation of the timing of economic activity
avoids *some* of the difficulties which arise from that used by Debreu.
In particular, in Malinvaud's analysis there can never be any doubt as
to the precise instant at which a commodity is to be delivered/received,
so that one need never be in any doubt, for example, as to whether the
'old' owner or the 'new' owner of a piece of land is entitled to receive
the corresponding rental payment for a given elementary period of
time. Nevertheless, difficulties remain. A storage activity, for
example, can *only* take place for an integral multiple of the length of
the elementary period, in Malinvaud's representation. Again, while
there can be absolutely no doubt here as to the instant t at which an
electrician must make himself available at a specified location, it
remains ambiguous, in Malinvaud's representation, just what time-
path of electrician's services he must put forth during period t. And
the time taken by a transportation activity *must*, like that for a storage
activity, be exactly an integral multiple of the length of an elementary
period. No matter how short Malinvaud's period may be, problems
can, in principle, arise. And, of course, the shorter the period is made,

the more pressing become one's doubts about the existence of sufficient markets.

Malinvaud considers a firm which, facing competitive markets, 'tries to maximise its discounted total profit subject to the technical constraints which govern it' (p. 257). He shows that it is sufficient for the firm to maximise profits for each period, *successively and independently*, taking account in each period only of the production constraint relating to that period (p. 257).Unfortunately, this result depends on highly restrictive assumptions: 'This property assumes the existence of perfect markets for all commodities including equipment in use and products in course of manufacture. In particular, it implies that no transactions cost hinders the sale or purchase of second hand material' (p. 259). He continues:

In short, the property under consideration assumes that capital is freely transferable at each date, at well-defined prices. In the real situation, a large part of capital is 'fixed'. The cost of transferring it from one use to another is often prohibitive. Thus the general theory with which this chapter is concerned ignores one aspect of reality which is important in certain cases' (pp. 259–60).

Malinvaud could certainly not be accused of gross exaggeration at this point!

Notes

1 Page references will be given to the first edition, 1972; the additions made in the revised edition, 1985, will not concern us.
2 The 'stricter limitations' referred to are the possibility that a consumer can never be a debtor and the possibility that there is quantity rationing of some individual demands (p. 24).

Bibliography

Åkerman, J., 1959. 'Shackle's System and Theories of Business Cycles', *Metroeconomica* XI: 3–11.

Arrow, K.J., 1959. 'Towards a Theory of Price Adjustment', in M. Abramovitz *et al.* (eds.) *The Allocation of Economic Resources*, Stanford, California: Stanford University Press.

—, 1974. 'General Economic Equilibrium: Purpose, Analytic Technique, Collective Choice', *American Economic Review* 64: 253-72.

Arrow, K.J. & Hahn, F.H., 1971. *General Competitive Analysis*, San Francisco: Holden Day.

Arrow, K.J. & Hurwicz, L., 1977. *Studies in Resource Allocation Processes*, Cambridge: Cambridge University Press.

Barone, E., 1896. 'Studi sulla distribuzione', *Giornale degli Economisti* 12: 107–55, 235–52.

Baumol, W.J., 1970 [1951]. *Economic Dynamics: An Introduction*, 3rd edition, London: Macmillan.

Bergson, H., 1911. *Matter and Memory*, London: George Allen & Unwin.

Blaug, M., 1978. Review of Michio Morishima's *Walras' Economics: A Pure Theory of Capital and Money*, *Economica* 45:412–13.

—, 1985. *Economic Theory in Retrospect*, 4th edition, Cambridge: Cambridge University Press.

Bliss, C.J., 1975. *Capital Theory and the Distribution of Income*, Amsterdam: North-Holland.

Burmeister, E., 1980. *Capital Theory and Dynamics*, Cambridge: Cambridge University Press.

Burrow, J.W., 1966. *Evolution and Society. A Study in Victorian Social Theory*, Cambridge: Cambridge University Press.

Coddington, A., 1982. 'Deficient Foresight: a Troublesome Theme in Keynesian Economics', *American Economic Review* 72: 480–7.

Dasgupta, P. and Heal, G., 1979. *Economic Theory and Exhaustible Resources*, Cambridge: James Nisbet & Co. and Cambridge University Press.

Davidson, P., 1980. 'Post-Keynesian Economics: Solving the Crisis in Economic Theory', *Public Interest*, special issue: 151–73.

Debreu, G., 1959. *Theory of Value*, New York: Wiley.

Edgeworth, F. Y., 1881. *Mathematical Psychics: An Essay on The Application of Mathematics to the Moral Sciences*, London: Kegan Paul.

—, 1889. Review of *Eléments d'économie politique pure* by Léon Walras, *Nature*, September: 434–6.

Fisher, F. M., 1983. *Disequilibrium Foundations of Equilibrium Economics*, Cambridge: Cambridge University Press.

Friedman, M., 1955. 'Leon Walras and His Economic System', *American Economic Review* 45: 900–9.

Frisch, R., 1936. 'On the Notion of Equilibrium and Disequilibrium', *Review of Economic Studies* 3: 100–5.

—, 1950. 'Alfred Marshall's Theory of Value', *Quarterly Journal of Economics* 64: 495–524. As reprinted in Volume III of Wood (1982).

Garegnani, P., 1960. *Il capitale nelle teorie della distribuzione*, Milan: Guiffrè.

—, 1976. 'On a Change in the Notion of Equilibrium', in M. Brown, K. Sato and P. Zarembka (eds), *Essays in Modern Capital Theory*, Amsterdam: North Holland.

Georgescu-Roegen, N., 1971. *The Entropy Law and the Economic Process*, Cambridge, Massachusetts: Harvard University Press.

Hague, D. C., 1958. 'Alfred Marshall and the Competitive Firm', *Economic Journal* 68: 678–90. As reprinted in Volume III of Wood (1982).

Hahn, F. H., 1952. 'Expectations and Equilibrium', *Economic Journal* 62: 802–19. Reprinted in Hahn (1984).

—, 1966. 'Equilibrium Dynamics with Heterogeneous Capital Goods', *Quarterly Journal of Economics*, 80: 633–46.

—, 1970 'Some Adjustment Problems', *Econometrica* 38: 1–17. Reprinted in Hahn (1984).

—, 1973. *On the Notion of Equilibrium in Economics*, Cambridge: Cambridge University Press. Reprinted in Hahn (1984).

—, 1984. *Equilibrium and Macroeconomics*, Oxford: Basil Blackwell.

—, 1987. 'Information, Dynamics and Equilibrium', *Scottish Journal of Political Economy* 34: 321–34.

Hansson, B. A., 1982. *The Stockholm School and the Development of Dynamic Method*, London: Croom Helm.

Harrod, R., 1930. 'Notes on Supply', *Economic Journal* 40: 232–41.

Hayek, F. A., 1928. 'Das intertemporale Gleichgewichtssystem der Preise und die Bewegungen des "Geldwertes" ', *Weltwirtschaftliches Archiv* 2:

33–76. Translation, as 'Intertemporal Price Equilibrium and Movements in the Value of Money', in Hayek (1984).

—, 1937. 'Economics and Knowledge', *Economica* 4: 33–54.

—, 1940. Review of Lindahl's *Studies in the Theory of Money and Capital*, *Economica* 7: 332–3.

—, 1955. *The Counter-Revolution of Science*, Glencoe: Free Press.

—, 1984. *Money, Capital and Fluctuations: Early Essays*, edited by Roy McCloughry, London: Routledge and Kegan Paul.

Hicks, J. R., 1933. 'Gleichgewicht und Konjunktur', *Zeitschrift für National-ökonomie* 4: 441–55. Translated as 'Equilibrium and the Cycle' in Hicks (1982).

—, 1934. 'Léon Walras', *Econometrica* 2: 338–48. Reprinted in Hicks (1983).

—, 1935. 'Wages and Interest: The Dynamic Problem', *Economic Journal* 45: 456–68. Reprinted in Hicks (1982).

—, 1946 [1939]. *Value and Capital*, 2nd ed., Oxford: Clarendon Press.

—, 1965. *Capital and Growth*, Oxford: Clarendon Press.

—, 1976. 'Some Questions of Time in Economics', in Tang A. M. *et al.* (eds.) *Evolution, Welfare and Time in Economics*, Lexington, Massachusetts: Heath. Reprinted in Hicks (1982).

—, 1982. *Money, Interest and Wages* (*Collected Essays on Economic Theory*, Volume 2), Oxford: Basil Blackwell.

—, 1983. *Classics and Moderns* (*Collected Essays on Economic Theory*, Volume 3), Oxford: Basil Blackwell.

Hutchison, T. W., 1953. *A Review of Economic Doctrines: 1870–1959*, Oxford: Clarendon Press.

Jaffé, W., 1967. 'Walras's Theory of *Tâtonnement*: A Critique of Recent Interpretations', *Journal of Political Economy* 75: 1–19.

—, 1980. 'Walras's Economics as Others See It', *Journal of Economic Literature* 18: 528–58.

—, 1981. 'Another Look at Léon Walras's Theory of *Tâtonnement*', *History of Political Economy* 18: 313–36.

Jacques, E., 1982. *The Form of Time*, London: Heinemann.

Jevons, W. S., 1970 [1871]. *The Theory of Political Economy*, Harmondsworth: Penguin Books.

Kierstead, B. S., 1959. 'Professor Shackle on Time in Economics'. *Metroeconomica* XI: 44–50.

Kirzner, I. M., 1976. 'On the Method of Austrian Economics', in Edwin G. Dolan (ed.) *The Foundations of Modern Austrian Economics*, Kansas City: Sheed Andrews and McMeel.

Koopmans, T. C., 1957. *Three Essays on the State of Economic Science*, New York: McGraw Hill.

Kuenne, R. E., 1963. *The Theory of General Economic Equilibrium*, Princeton: Princeton University Press.

Lachmann, L.M., 1943. 'The Role of Expectations in Economics as a Social Science', *Economica* 10: 12–23. Reprinted in Lachmann (1977).

—, 1950. 'Economics as a Social Science', *South African Journal of Economics* 18: 215–18. Reprinted in Lachmann (1977).

—, 1951. 'The Science of Human Action', *Economica* 18: 233–41. Reprinted in Lachmann (1977).

—, 1959. 'Professor Shackle on the Economic Significance of Time', *Metroeconomica* XI: 64–73. Reprinted in Lachmann (1977).

—, 1971. 'Ludwig von Mises and the Market Process', in F. A. Hayek (ed.) *Toward Liberty: Essays in Honor of Ludwig von Mises*, Institute for Humane Studies. Reprinted in Lachmann (1977).

—, 1973. 'Sir John Hicks as a Neo-Austrian', *South African Journal of Economics* 41: 319–32. Reprinted in Lachmann (1977).

—, 1976(a). 'From Mises to Shackle: An Essay on Austrian Economics and the Kaleidic Society', *Journal of Economic Literature* 14: 54–62.

—, 1976(b). 'On the Central Concept of Austrian Economics: Market Process', in Edwin G. Dolan (ed.) *The Foundations of Modern Austrian Economics*. Kansas City: Sheed Andrews and McMeel.

—, 1977. *Capital, Expectations, and the Market Process: Essays on The Theory of the Market Economy*, Kansas City: Sheed Andrews and McMeel.

—, 1978 [1956]. *Capital and Its Structure*, Kansas City: Sheed Andrews and McMeel.

—, 1986. *The Market as an Economic Process*, Oxford and New York: Basil Blackwell.

Laplace, P. S. de, 1820. 'Introduction à la Théorie Analytique des Probabilités', in *Oeuvre Complètes de Laplace*, vol. 7, Paris: Gautheirs-Villars et Fils, 1886.

Lindahl, E., 1929. 'Prisbildningproblemets uppläggning från kapitalteoretisk synpunkt', *Ekonomisk Tidskrift*. Translated as 'The Place of Capital in the Theory of Price' and reprinted as Part III of Lindahl (1939a).

—, 1939. 'The Dynamic Approach to Economic Theory', Part I of Lindahl (1939a).

—, 1939a. *Studies in the Theory of Money and Capital*, London: George Allen & Unwin.

Loasby, B. J., 1978. 'Whatever Happened to Marshall's Theory of Value?', *Scottish Journal of Political Economy* 25: 1–12. As reprinted in Volume III of Wood (1982).

Long, A. A. & Sedley, D. N., 1987. *The Hellenistic Philosophers, Volume I*, Cambridge: Cambridge University Press.

MacIntyre, A., 1985. *After Virtue: A Study in Moral Theory*, 2nd edition, London: Duckworth.

Malinvaud, E., 1953. 'Capital Accumulation and Efficient Allocation of Resources', *Econometrica*, 21: 233–68.

—, 1960–61. 'The Analogy Between Atemporal and Intertemporal Theories of Resource Allocation', *Review of Economic Studies*, 28: 143–60.

—, 1972. *Lectures on Microeconomic Theory*, Amsterdam: North-Holland.

Marget, A. W., 1935. 'Monetary Aspects of the Walrasian System', *Journal of Political Economy* 42: 170–5.

Marshall, A., 1920. *Principles of Economics*, London: Macmillan.

Meade, J. E., 1965. *The Stationary Economy*, London: Allen & Unwin.

Milgate, M., 1979. 'On the Origin of the Notion of "Intertemporal Equilibrium"', *Economica* 46: 1–10.

Mises, L. von, 1949. *Human Action*, New Haven: Yale University Press.

Morishima, M., 1977. *Walras' Economics: A Pure Theory of Capital and Money*, Cambridge: Cambridge University Press.

—, 1980. 'W. Jaffé on Léon Walras: A Comment', *Journal of Economic Literature* 18: 550–8.

Newman, P., 1960. 'The Erosion of Marshall's Theory of Value', *Quarterly Journal of Economics* 74: 587–600. As reprinted in Volume III of Wood (1982).

—, 1965. *The Theory of Exchange*, New Jersey: Prentice Hall.

Newton-Smith, W. H., 1980. *The Structure of Time*, London: Routledge & Kegan Paul.

Niehans, J., 1978. *The Theory of Money*, Baltimore and London: John Hopkins.

O'Driscoll, G. P. and Rizzo, M. J., 1985. *The Economics of Time and Ignorance*, Oxford and New York: Basil Blackwell.

Opie, R., 1931. 'Marshall's Time Analysis', *Economic Journal* 41: 199–215. As reprinted in Volume I of Wood (1982).

Pareto, V., 1971. *Manual of Political Economy*, translated from the French edition of 1927 by A. S. Schwier and edited by A. S. Schweir and A. N. Page, New York: Augustus Kelley.

Patinkin, D., 1965. *Money, Interest and Prices*, 2nd edition, New York: Harper Row.

—, 1972. *Studies in Monetary Economics*, New York: Harper Row.

Pigou, A. C., 1927. 'Laws of Diminishing and Increasing Cost', *Economic Journal* 37: 188–97.

—, 1928. 'An Analysis of Supply', *Economic Journal* 38: 238–57.

—, 1935. *The Economics of Stationary States*, London: Macmillan.

Ridolfi, M., 1970–72. 'Aspetti del sistema teorico di Alfred Marshall: Una revisione critica di interpretazioni moderne', *Annali della Facoltà di Scienze Politiche* 12: 121–204.

Russell, B., 1946. *A History of Western Philosophy*, London: George Allen & Unwin.

Samuelson, P. A., 1983 [1947]. *Foundations of Economic Analysis*, Enlarged edition, Cambridge, Massachusetts: Harvard University Press.

Scarf, H., 1960. 'Some Examples of Global Instability of the Competitive Equilibrium', *International Economic Review* 1: 157–72.

Schumpeter, J. A., 1954. *History of Economic Analysis*, London: George Allen & Unwin.

Shackle, G. L. S., 1940. Review of Lindahl's *Studies in the Theory of Money and Capital*, *Economic Journal* 50: 103–5.

—, 1958. *Time in Economics,* Amsterdam: North-Holland.

—, 1961. *Decision, Order and Time in Human Affairs*, Cambridge: Cambridge University Press.

—, 1964. *General Thought–Schemes and the Economist*, Woolwich Economic Paper No. 2. London: Woolwich Polytechnic.

—, 1965. *A Scheme of Economic Theory*, Cambridge: Cambridge University Press.

—, 1966. *The Nature of Economic Thought. Selected Papers 1955–1964*, Cambridge: Cambridge University Press.

—, 1972. *Epistemics and Economics. A Critique of Economic Doctrines*, Cambridge: Cambridge University Press.

—, 1973. *An Economic Querist*, Cambridge: Cambridge University Press.

—, 1979. *Imagination and the Nature of Choice*, Edinburgh: Edinburgh University Press.

—, 1981. Letter in Alex H. Shand, *Subjectivist Economics: The New Austrian School*, privately published.

Shove, G. F., 1942. 'The Place of Marshall's *Principles* in the Development of Economic Theory', *Economic Journal* 52: 249–329. As reprinted in Volume III of Wood (1982).

Sorokin, P. A., 1964 [1943]. *Sociocultural Causality, Space, Time: A Study of Referential Principles of Sociology and Social Science*, New York: Russell & Russell.

Stigler, G. J., 1941. *Production and Distribution Theories: The Formative Period*, New York: Macmillan.

Viner, J., 1931. 'Cost Curves and Supply Curves', *Zeitschrift für Nationalökonomie* III: 23–46.

Walker, D. A., 1987. 'Walras's Theories of Tatonnement', *Journal of Political Economy* 95: 758–74.

Walras, L., 1954. *Elements of Pure Economics or the Theory of Social Wealth*, translated by W. Jaffé, London: George Allen & Unwin.

Walsh, V. & Gram, H., 1980. *Classical and Neoclassical Theories of General Equilibrium: Historical Origins and Mathematical Structure*, Oxford: Oxford University Press.

Whitaker, J. K. (ed.), 1975. *The Early Economic Writings of Alfred Marshall, 1867–1890,* London: Macmillan.

Wicksell, K., 1893. *Über Wert, Kapital und Rente*, Jena: Gustav Fischer.

—, 1977 [1934]. *Lectures on Political Economy*, Vol. I, New Jersey: Augustus M. Kelley.

Williams, P. L., 1986. 'A Reconstruction of Marshall's Temporary Equilibrium Pricing Model', *History of Political Economy* 18: 639–53.

Winston, G. C., 1982. *The Timing of Economic Activities*, Cambridge: Cambridge University Press.

Wolfe, J. N., 1954. 'The Representative Firm', *Economic Journal* 64: 337–49. As reprinted in Volume I of Wood (1982).

Wood, J. C., (ed.), 1982. *Alfred Marshall. Critical Assessments*, London: Croom Helm.

Index